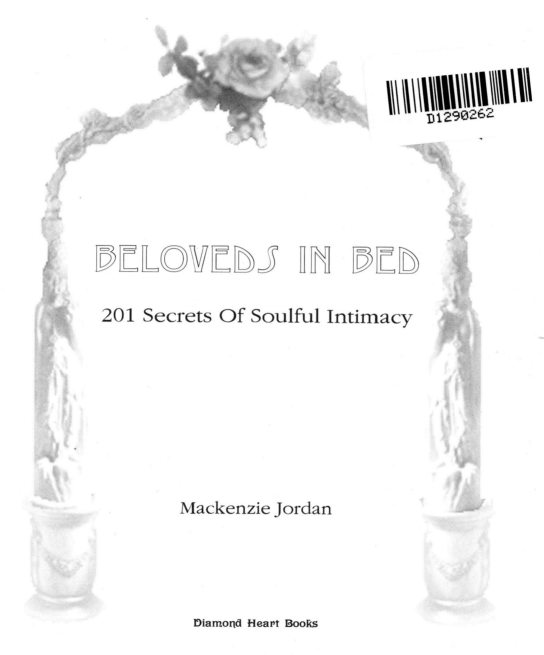

# BELOVEDS IN BED

## 201 Secrets Of Soulful Intimacy

Mackenzie Jordan

Diamond Heart Books

## Disclaimer

Beloveds in Bed is designed to inspire you. Common sense and your better judgment— including consulting your physician, should always prevail in your practice of the suggestions presented. Also, ejaculatory control is not birth control, and wishful thinking does not prevent venereal disease or AIDS. Please practice safe and conscious sex.

Grateful acknowledgement to Lew Epstein for his permission to quote his talk given on *Listening Compassionately*.

ISBN 0-9661044-0-4

May 1998
10 9 8 7 6 5 4 3 2 1

1. Sexuality     2. Relationship     3. Self Help

For information about workshops by Mackenzie Jordan, contact:

Sacred Mountain Seminars
P.O. Box 10594
Scottsdale, Az 85271
(602) 860-8470
(800) 636-6780

Photography Art Direction by Mackenzie Jordan
Photography by Scott Foust
Cover Design, Book Layout & Illustrations by Shayla Roberts
Technical support by Bob Ray

According to *WEBSTER'S*[*]:

**Be-lov-ed,** (bi luv'ed, -luvd'), *adj.*, 1. greatly loved; dear to the heart. —*n.*, 2. a person who is beloved.

**Bed,** (bed), *n.*, *v.*, bed-ded,. 6. the marital relationship. 7. any place used for sleeping or resting. 8. a. an area of ground in which plants, esp. flowering garden plants, are grown. 11. a piece or part forming a foundation or base; *tuna on a bed of lettuce.* 19. to put to bed. 21. to lay flat. 24. to have sexual intercourse with. —*v.i.* *25.* to have sleeping accommodations. *27. Archaic.* to go to bed. 28. **Bed down,** — *Idiom.* 30. **go to bed with,** to have sexual relations with. 31. **make a bed**, to fit a bed with sheets and blankets.

Non-dictionary definitions of these words as a phrase:

**Be-loveds in Bed,** 1. realizing Divine Love through sexual relationship. 2. the heart of spirit united with the complexity of physical form. 3. heaven on earth. 4. great love awakening spiritually-sleepy environments. 5. Divine Love expressed through human conditions. 6. Embracing the mystic and the mundane.

[*]Random House Webster's college dictionary — 2nd. edition.

*Beloveds in Bed* is dedicated to
the remembrance of *Loving* in all ways, in all people.
The time *is* now— in this moment.
For in the absence of this remembrance,
our fears run the world.
Our collective love heals us and heals our world.

◊

And to the memory of Princess Diana.
During these last few weeks before the first edition of Beloveds, I have
been deeply moved by our global heartbreak–heart awakening, as we have
all mourned and grappled with our loss of Diana.

For in her final gift of compassion— her own funeral— she has reached
into this fractured world to ignite the hearts of countless millions, uniting
us in a resolve for a more compassionate and authentic humanity.

It is clear to me, witnessing our collective outpouring of emotional expression and interaction, just how hungry we really are for this kind of spiritual
food. My hope is that everyday we will prepare this kind of open-hearted,
emotional food for ourselves, family and friends, and serve it often, even to
those we do not yet understand or appreciate.

Thank you, beloved Diana.
*Bless your heart*

# Acknowledgments

Special appreciation to all my family, closest friends
and intimates, past and present,
who have loved, grown and struggled with me
to find the heart in matters—
without whose exchange of stings and nectar, I would not be
who I am as a woman, a teacher, or a disciple of *Love*.

The following people have each particularly hi-lighted my journey in some wondrous way: Rainya, Jeru, Lita Fitzwater, Linda Stoltz, Bernice Barnett, Sharmen, Waj, Dharma, Patrick, ESP, Charles Muir, Caroline Muir, Doug and Guy, Sahajo, Jean Leidloff from her work— *Continuum Concept,* Joyce and Barry Vissell from their work– *The Shared Heart,* Cynthia Turner, Mom, Dad, and Justin.

Juiciest thanks to these people, my hero's, for helping me birth *Beloveds in Bed*: Shayla Roberts, Libby Call, J'lein Liese, Gloria Sandvik, Scott Foust, Gail Larsen, Linda (Angel House Lady) Lunden, Lisa Honebrink (for late night editing), Bob Ray, Barry Minoff, Beth and Jen, Leta Macdonald, Lonnie (the angel on the plane), Patricia and Raymond of Anchorage. And to every person who ever pointed out that I should be "writing this stuff down," thanks for the encouragement— I am blown away by the gift that writing has become for me.

And deepest appreciation to these three couples who so beautifully and vulnerably let us glimpse the sweetness of their love. They are Gary Bianconi and Miriam Saadi, Denise Albright and Pieter Oosthuizen, and, Star and Man. *You are exquisitely inspiring*.

I am forever deeply grateful to Osho— through his teachings and vision, but particularly through those who have loved him also. I have been touched in more ways than I could ever say. And most of all, I am grateful to *Divine Spirit* who guided each word.

Thank you

# CONTENTS

**CHAPTER THREE**

**CHAPTER SIX**

**CHAPTER SEVEN**

**Embracing Sexual Variety** _____ 129

# Preface

I remember the moment I recognized the subconscious wisdom that I had regarding sex, and the event that launched me into my lifelong exploration of sexual energy and soulful intimacy. I was a young teenager then, my parents were out for the afternoon and while their trusted baby-sitter looked after my younger siblings, I was sneaking my first wet kiss with my "boyfriend" out in the garage. I felt free to explore the thrill of my budding curiosity. Right in the middle of that delicious, scary, exciting kiss, the door slid completely open and the baby-sitter caught me in the act. She sent him home and me up to my room. As I sheepishly climbed the stairs, I knew I was in big trouble, huge trouble! Grounded for life.

Then an extraordinary thing happened. The baby-sitter *said* something that changed everything. She said, "You know, you shouldn't be doing this sort of thing because you're going to run out of things to do when you get older." Well, time stood still . . . and then, *Poof*! The anxiety I felt disappeared. The spell was broken as I somehow understood a deeper truth in that moment, and I *knew* she was seriously mistaken. There *is* an unlimited menu of sensual "things" to do when you grow-up. If you are open to it, you will never run out.

At the time, I didn't even know what those unlimited menu items could be, nor did I really care much then, since I was having so much fun simply experiencing a kiss. What seems clear now is when sex is limited to physical sensations, it can set up a fear of scarcity, boredom, or a feeling that something is missing. But when your *soulfulness* is expressed through your body, the menu of sexual union possibilities is unlimited.

Interestingly, "I will be grounded for life," has taken on a whole new meaning; sexuality expressed as part of my meditation practice has, for me, turned out to be quite "grounding." During my late teens and twenties it was becoming clear I had a penchant for sex education because of how easy it was for me to discuss the "unspeakable" with friends and clients. However, as I matured, I discovered something even more unspeakable than talking about the physical reality of genitalia, or arousal, or what "positions" you can get into. It was more intimidating to talk about the inner realm of sexual connecting— vulnerable emotional intimacy, authentic and truthful sharing, and the soul's connection to our flesh and heart. Also, back then we did not have a "language" which would give us the words to express this deeper promise of intimacy or reverent honoring. As a culture we are still desperately without a language of love.

Sometimes I think the most common hindrance to passionate, sacred sexual loving is the ability to discuss sex in emotionally healthy and conscious terms. My mother was the first person I heard say sex was a sacrament, a sacred act for marriage; that it is holy. But those talks were too brief and too rare, I imagine because we were both so painfully embarrassed.

The *vibes* then became more and more about "not having sex" rather than preparing me for when I would eventually engage in the "sacredness of sex." I understand my family dynamic is not rare, that most families just don't talk about sex. You're *vibed* to not do it *and* not talk about it, and then somehow after marriage, you're to *know* how to do it. And know how to do it "holy." Or did marriage alone make it holy? Nobody really explained that part.

The journey of self-discovery for me began after my first sexual experiences. Sometimes it seemed my education about who I was as a human being and was becoming as a spiritual being, came most during those tender, passionate and, many times, clueless, intimate embraces. This exploration led me to my first "spiritual" boyfriend when I was twenty-two. He was the first person to mutter to me the word "red-tantra" (red *energy*), and to tell me I had a lot of it— whatever that was! I only knew I enjoyed being with him.

I had not yet realized that I was looking for a tantric life at the time. However, I *was* hooked on the spiritual awakening aspect. I wanted my life to be more conscious, and headed that direction more intentionally all the time. I had a lot of questions— most of which I had no idea how to even formulate. As I began to experience some of this *tantric* life essence, there continued to be many questions, but life also seemed to be flowing differently and making a little more sense.

Since those earliest sexual experiences I have recognized the immense opportunity for self growth and realization that can come from the vulnerability and consciousness of intimate union. I have learned from wise teachers and lovers; and have engaged in experiences that nurtured my understanding about intimate loving. I have learned equally from the painful fallout of love such as betrayal, hopelessness, bitterness, and jealousy, as well as from the *sweet* fruits of love, the moments of tenderness, peace, forgiveness, rapture, and Divine Presence recognition. I can tell you what I ultimately know can be described in two ways: Love and common sense.

Love and common sense may not seem very sexy (and possibly even too practical), but there are infinite depths of love for us to explore, without which certain erotic experiences just cannot happen. Coupled with common sense, there are boundless sensations and emotions to unveil. I feel a passion to share what I've learned about sexual intimacy, especially relations which are soul*full,* to promote a well-being in our culture which is healthier, more caring, and less neurotic— one where more of us can benefit physically, spiritually and emotionally when profound love and sexual energy are united.

When receiving feedback from readers and seminar participants, I always feel extremely gratified to hear someone rejoice and express relief that they've found their feelings and desires for love spoken for them. They then feel released from their aloneness— no longer unique in their soulful desires, or embarrassed for having them. Intimacy just seems to be such a tricky subject for us, doesn't it? I feel we *all* need to be students of open hearted love, as well as *teachers* of these qualities, and learn how to bring this openness into our bedrooms.

Many of us are now making the soulful journey into the conscious exploration of wholeness. I hear very courageous people ask the really tough questions as they bounce up against the limitations to their spiritual ideals. "If sexual energy is so powerful, why can't I feel it?" "If sex is so sacred, then how come I feel so used and discarded?" or "I'm a very loving person, so why is my sex so bland, so disconnected?" or "We both love and want sex, but we're miles apart on what we each want sexually."

Few of us have it together sexually; few of us have sex integrated into our lives in all ways— consciously, emotionally, spiritually, mentally, and healthfully. It's really clear to me that we *all* have questions about sex! Whether you are highly educated or skilled, married happily for years, or married and hoping to be happy, whether you are an artist or a professional, engineer or minister, rich or "wanna" be, we all wonder how to:

- Get good sex
- Renew lost desire and romance
- Integrate sexual encounters into spiritual life
- Or integrate spiritual life into sexual relating

And so many variations of these questions!

You won't find every answer in any book. What you will find here in *Beloveds in Bed* is a travel guide that helps you to begin, or *deepen* your journey into what the mystery of sexual loving could mean for you. You'll find a "language" for intimacy which enables you to embrace your visions and experience of love. You may also find on this journey that the answers you desire can be found more easily right inside your own heart.

If you've picked up this book, I assume you are longing for, or at least curious about making sex be more than a physical phenomenon, or a ten-minute disappointment. Perhaps you desire something more along the lines of ultimate union, ecstatic nirvana— "beloved dancing with beloved."

Enjoying wondrous lovemaking and appreciating its many benefits and complexities is usually more attainable when sex is loving and its participants are *soulfully* connected. Not surprisingly, sex that is off the pleasure charts is more easily attainable when the sharing is felt heart-to-heart.

It is a great honor to invite you, through the material in this book, to embrace sexual loving *whol*istically— as sacred and attainable for any and every person who yearns for, or needs it, begs for it, dreams it, or dares for it, and for anyone who *remembers* . . . the *sweetness* of *soulful sex* from some inner, distant— *knowing*.

## Intimate Penetration

*Intercourse also means opening an inner dialogue*
*with your emotional and spiritual self*

Sex can be embraced for many reasons— just like eating. You can stuff yourself at Thanksgiving Day dinner, grab a burger on the go, relax with a glass of your favorite wine, or socialize with friends over a cappuccino. You can savor each morsel of a nine-course meal, live on three square meat-and-potatoes meals a day, or on a lean diet of 1200 calories.

Without even being aware of it, you often choose different foods and eating situations to satisfy different emotional and physical needs. Yet the choices you make can be very telling. Ask yourself now what circumstances affect your eating patterns. Why *do* you eat? Do you eat to stop the hunger pangs, or just because it's the lunch hour? Do you reach for snacks when you're bored or anxious? Perhaps you eat till you are numb, self-medicating yourself from life? Is food a friend?

You probably know which foods give you gas or indigestion, but do you recognize which ones make you feel heavy or sleepy? Can you think of certain foods that make you come alive as if you could float or sing or play? You might not have noticed it was possible that certain foods actually make you happier.

What are your tastes? What do you *long* for? What do you settle for? Do you take time to *chewww*? Do you even taste your food after the third bite?

Similarly, sex has tremendous variations, with many motivations, advantages, purposes, and outcomes. Just as with food, your sexual appetite can be affected by your mood, time constraints, energy level, stress, and other factors. Sex is also a fertile breeding ground for many areas of misunderstanding, illusion, and disappointment. Take a direct step toward the soulful lovemaking that you long for, and consciously choose who you are as a sexual participant. This is a vital step toward fabulous lovemaking.

Take a moment to reflect on what role sexuality plays in your life What role do you wish it to play? Do you hoard it? Savor it? Gorge on it? Delight in it? Just do it 'cause it's there? Grab some on the go? Use it to help you sleep? Deprive yourself of it? Relax with it? What? Consider your last three sexual experiences. Were you satisfied, happy, fulfilled? What made each one work for you? How do you feel about those three encounters? If there was anything missing for you, try to be very specific and identify what it was.

Sexual energy has more uses than people may be aware of, many of which have not yet even been considered. Perhaps you don't realize the energy you raise in lovemaking can be channeled to heal feelings of loss that a miscarriage can leave, or to lessen the symptoms of PMS. Maybe you haven't experienced yet the whole-body, multiple orgasms that a man can have or the bliss that awaits you both, rivaling any drug experience. You are probably familiar with the inevitable sleepiness after lovemaking, at least for the man, but do you know how to use sex to give you more energy than you had before you started?

## Consciously choose *what you're doing sex for*

How you make your choices is indeed a very personal process. There really isn't a wrong answer; however, when a person *specifically* asks what would be most satisfying sexually— and in all areas of one's being— today's answers may be different than those settled for yesterday.

The goal may be to produce children, or to perform a certain way such as requiring and having exactly one orgasm per sex session. You may desire an athletic workout from your sex. You may want sex to be your escape from the hustle and bustle of everyday life where you relax and go into another world, or pursue sexual orgasm for the release that sends you into sleep at night, like a tranquilizer.

Today, you may want sex to be soulful, cuddly, soft, tender, quiet, gentle, emotional, loving, nurturing, easy, playful, celebrational, energizing, rejuvenating, releasing, healing, slow, embracing, renewing, pleasing/pleasuring, spiritual, endless, enlightened, otherworldly, wordless. And on another day, you may want sex to be liberating, devouring, animal, passionate, rough, fast, powerful, hard, animated, loud, athletic, dangerous, vocal, surrendering, youthening, cleansing, spirited, merging, juicy, wet, multi-orgasmic, ecstatic, exhausting, exhilarating, all weekend.

Volumes of information are available on how to make sex better by "doing" something more: by perfecting your sexual performance, by adding this new sexual position or watching that popular sex video, or by dressing in the hottest new lingerie. Unfortunately, what is still missing when you *do* all these things (and you're still unsatisfied, unhappy or bored) is *you*. And **you** are the most important component in becoming a beloved in your relationship and having the satisfying sexual encounters that you desire.

When you are busy trying to be the best lover of the century, trying to like sex when you don't, trying to get your partner interested in sex when he is not, trying to have an orgasm, trying to get your partner to have an orgasm, trying to have simultaneous orgasms, or a host of other pressures, (whew!) . . . then you are too busy *trying* instead of being present to the delicious-ness that comes from not trying, but from *being.* This can leave well intentioned lovers feeling empty inside.

People are *hungry* to understand how sex and intimacy actually work to experience more joy and less pain in love. Clearly, sexuality and gender roles have become confusing in the bedroom, the workplace, social situations, and even inside the family system itself.

## Nourishing the hunger and longing

*Beloveds in Bed* is about rediscovering *you,* as well as revealing your own natural ability to experience passionate lovemaking and soulful intimacy. Revealing your authentic self is a main ingredient in becoming a beloved. Break free from acquired pressures, so you are available to a lovemaking which is nurturing, erotically pleasing, and beyond boredom.

Just like the act of eating, sex is a basic, natural act. But it has been made unnatural by our thinking of it as dirty and un-Godly, and by thinking of sex as purely physical, or only for reproduction, or primarily for men's pleasure, to advertise cars, or to blow off tension. Most of all, we've contributed to it being unnatural by not talking about sex in an open, and conscious way. These conditions have distanced us from our precious, soulful nature.

If you are going to have a chance at experiencing the intimacy and relationship that would be as deep and profound as your longing, you must change something in your current understanding. To unite your experience of sex with an experience of respect and sacredness, there must also be union between *you* and your lost innocence.

Sexual intimacy is a sacred mystery. *You* are a sacred mystery. Neither mystery can be actually *figured* out, and certainly not contained. Regrettably, trying to do either causes tremendous suffering from the effort. You must let go into the unknown. The sooner one surrenders the "know-it-all" part of the ego, the sooner the journey into each mystery really begins.

## Letting go of what you know

This is not about a new sexual trick to seek out and then learn. Indeed, the soulful journey of *Beloveds in Bed* is more about *un*-learning. Releasing some of the unconscious relational habits that have been hanging on you, shielding you like a big box shading a bright lamp: the light is there continuously, yet hidden, and to shine, it must be liberated from the box. Becoming a beloved in your relationship means becoming liberated from the box of limitation, confusion, sexual shame and suffering. This freedom allows the remembering, knowing, and the ability to experience that sexual energy is vital to well-being, and is as healthy, and natural, as birth.

Sometimes people complain that if they try a new way of lovemaking, then sex won't be spontaneous enough. This may be true only until the new becomes familiar, and then, *it* feels natural. Whatever you are doing right now in your sexual loving practice, it is natural to you only because you've been doing it that way for as long as you have.

Understand then, when situations are comfortable to us, we call that our natural way of being. As you try out some of the material in the following chapters, it, too, can become as familiar and eventually as comfortable. At that point, you can decide what to keep and continue doing from your current sexual practice, and what you want to embrace and explore from your new experiences.

The following pages of information are like a fun puzzle to put together. While you will need all the pieces to see the whole picture, you will also need to contemplate each point individually. Look to find the value for yourself before you easily pass over something seemingly too simple or obvious. Perhaps it is *these* very obvious and simple little jewels that are being neglected in your actual life experience and could benefit your sexual awaking tremendously. There is an order to where the puzzle pieces will appear, and *all* the pieces will play a part in laying your foundation. Savor each morsel. Explore. Venture *inwards* on an intimate adventure of sensual-spiritual awakening.

Prepare yourself for how the following material is presented. Sometimes I will be speaking directly to the woman, and at other times, the man. Women, there is a lotus flower symbol for you as a signal. Men, there is a candle stick symbol for you. It's valuable to read *everything* though, regardless to whom it is directed.

It is also my hope that those of you not presently in relationship, and those of you in same gender relationships will creatively adapt the material to suit your needs. Also, in an attempt to reduce the constant distraction of s/he, him/her, instead, "he" and "she" have been used in alternating examples throughout the text. Almost all of the examples are speaking to you too, even if the pronoun used is for the opposite sex. Also, although it can be very tempting to skip to the more sexual chapters, if you do not integrate the previous chapters you will miss the essentials that make this journey so very soulfully juicy.

The spirit of *Beloveds in Bed* is dedicated to the liberation of our soulful and natural selves, the selves who naturally love life, emotional intimacy, and healthy sexual love. Being beloveds and enjoying wondrous lovemaking is a natural outcome.

*Bon Appetite´!*

FIRST DOORWAY

# BE WILLING
# AND ALLOWING

*Preparing yourself
for the connection you desire*

## Mystical re-union

Consider that your *being*, your very soul, is longing to be ultimately reunited with the *Beloved*, that mystical thread that connects us all. We are each an aspect of *The Beloved*. In marriage, romantic relationships, and friendships, we are given the opportunity to reestablish this sacred thread of connection within ourselves, and with others. We have ample opportunities in life to experience either separation or connection. We always have a choice. To love, or to be indifferent. To fear and react, or to embrace and flower.

The sexual union between bodies is relatively easy compared with the spiritual and emotional union of intimacy between lovers. Unveiling the vulnerability of one's heart and emotions in a sexual relationship is often too unpredictable to the ego-mind and it is scary. People will often become unconsciously evasive at this point. Trust is needed, as well as compassion, honesty, and courage. But, as the willingness to unfold these qualities becomes present, routine sexual expression expands beyond the domain of the physical, and people are enabled to connect in richer, more meaningful ways.

When someone wants more sexual frequency, insists on orgasmic release, or requests *fewer* sexual encounters, understand that the truer desire is usually much deeper than these actual requests. While the cultural norm in one way has been to exploit or judge our sexual desires, it has in another way been passively naive about what potential our sexual energy has toward spiritual transformation and personal liberation—but also, surprisingly naive about the potential for bodily pleasure, as well. This naivete then shapes and limits our personal perspectives on what we can hope for regarding sexual fulfillment. However, our soul itself has never been fooled or limited, and has continued to long for a re-union with body, heart and spirit. The urgency and the longing for a soulmate, a spouse, or an affair, may have in them also the same longing for **spiritual union.**

Unable or unwilling to accept a personal relationship with God (or spirit, or creator, the force, universal consciousness, or whatever you call it or don't call it), many people will often, in a desperate, needy way, seek relationships with others to attempt to fulfill that longing. Or, they may embrace situations that mistakenly seem to prove that separation and suffering are all there is in relationship— that relational harmony is a fantasy and does not exist.

Both of those reactions are the extreme and create unnecessary suffering. Obviously when you seek to put up emotional walls around you, the resulting loneliness is painful, or maybe worse, is numb. But equally painful is the feeling of betrayal when the partner you've expected to be no less than God himself, turns out to be mortal after all.

Sexual activity has as one of its many reputations, that of "Can't get no satisfaction," along with various other flavors of emotional suffering. This is because the sexual connection to spirit has been lost to the phenomenon of fear by cultural beliefs; and sexual potential has been limited by an automatic adherence to social mores, laws, and sexual ignorance.

In the exciting and worthy transition from sexual repression to conscious expression, there is tremendous chaos and confusion. Each person may feel or experience certain things as a source of shock. These may include hot issues such as: pornography, soft porn, kiddy porn, MTV, cross-dressing, sexual harassment in the workplace, sex scandals, confusing gender roles, teenage pregnancy, topless nightclubs, prostitution, adulterous affairs, crimes of passion, child molesting clergy, incest, partner swapping, group orgies, sex addiction, co-habitating, personal sexual preference quandaries, bi-sexuality, group marriage, nudist beaches, genital/nipple piercing, homophobia, sexually transmitted diseases, and AIDS. Opportunities for judgment, fear, and reaction abound.

These issues are not only confusing, but overwhelming. Fear can take over in a heartbeat, along with worry about what all of this "chaos" means, and wondering about "what the world is coming to." While there is no excuse for violence or for any harm imposed on another human being, the controversial issues of sex (and our reactions to them), can reflect either a deep need to break out of a fear-based, repressed sexual box *or*, to sit more ferociously on the box trying to contain its "chaotic" sexual energy at any cost.

The truth is, it's not possible to keep the "lid" on the sexual "box" any longer. In fact, the chaos suggests that people tend to flirt with the potency of sexual energy, then innocently move into sexuality without much regard for the sacred knowledge it takes to channel its potent energy responsibly. Even driving a car is dangerous without knowledge and experience to operate it.

Channeling sexual encounters in a conscious way is not only beneficial for your own personal pleasure and satisfaction. When you embrace a consciousness that sexual energy is for you sacred and potentially enlightening, you give others permission to be knowledgeable and conscious about sexual power and promote honoring of sacred union.

Permission is an interesting concept to entertain because culturally it seems that sex is thought about as a free, maybe too free activity. *That kind* of sex is for the most part one-dimensional and generally unfulfilling to those desir-

ing soulful lovemaking. I believe that the culture at large, and each of us individually, can greatly benefit by accepting permission to explore the mystery of sexual expression free from unhealthy shame, guilt, and performance pressure. For example, a person may feel free to be extremely sexual, but is it okay to be prayerful before, during and after sex? Sexual and sacred at the same time? For most people, the most challenging freedom of all is to be intimate and vulnerable, free to: *come as you are!*

A certain maturity is required for soulful sexuality that surpasses simply being old enough to engage in sex, or having an official license to do it with a spouse. This maturity has to do with acquiring the wisdom of Love, loving wisely, accepting the responsibility of the sexual energy raised, and becoming multi-dimensionally conscious. How can the vital transformative power of sexual energy be tapped if it is essentially suppressed at best, or at worst, fully repressed?

Before you can attain a flow of sexual bliss, you must heal the places where you are not satisfied sexually. You must ask new questions. Consider the desperation of a woman who hasn't been able to climax. She may feel embarrassed, unsatisfied, deeply ashamed. She may be harassing herself, thinking, "How can I *learn* to orgasm?" or "What's wrong with me that I don't orgasm?" But these questions are too superficial.

Orgasm is a state of *being*, like breathing, not something you must learn to do. So the only answers you can get from questions like these are more things to try or "to-do." Since sexual energy is not about "doing," inevitably, people become disappointed and disconnected trying to learn and then "do" something. A more natural approach to climaxing is to *be* sexual, and *be* sensual. Climaxing will happen naturally. However, in order to *be*, we must be in touch with our own intuition and authority regarding matters that concern us.

Indeed, a richer question to ask would be, is it really okay (with parents, teachers, rabbis, priests, politicians, spouse, and God) that you embrace opening up to orgasmic sexual power? Sometimes there is a resistance to being sexually authentic when the sexual adult in you is willing to grow and explore, but a younger you, an *unconscious* part of you, is worrying about what the authority figures would say. These authority figures may have taught you these beliefs forty years ago, yet daily you repeat to yourself those messages of suppression, tentative intimacy, and shame. Well, it's time to reevaluate those messages that no longer serve you.

Sexual expression and orgasm are transformative energies. You can channel these energies to fuel your enlightenment, enhance your quality of life, and build a wonderful, nurturing relationship.

The question is not simply how to achieve an orgasm, even if that's all you say you want. Ask, "Are you prepared to transform your life, inside out, on all levels?" **Whooaa.**

If total transformation sounds too ominous, stay relaxed, and realize that your journey to transformation has already begun, that you are in it now, and each unfoldment of your transformation will come in a time frame that you will be able to handle. With a little mastery, you can channel this transformative sexual energy to more easily embrace its vastness— along with the kind of orgasms, soulfulness, intimacy and enlightenment that are available.

Your soul is calling you. You must know that if you are reading this book. Maybe you have been denying your soul's intuitive messages quite nicely up until now, but now your lover has subtly, or not so subtly requested that you memorize this book cover to cover. We too often don't listen to our own soul's desires, probably not for lack of listening ability so much as fearing that we do not *deserve* our true desires, or fearing the risk if our longings are denied.

Luckily, life usually brings our path to a lover who *will* voice these longings right out-loud. You might at first resist a lover's invitation into an expanded experience of sexuality. The invitation may be followed by nagging and, ultimately, intense pleading and emotional ultimatums. You may react and mistake your lover's desires as only belonging to him or her. After your initial resistance, you may find that your lover's message of longing for more intimacy or richer sexual experiences is your secret desire also. On the other hand, you could be the lover who is always voicing a desire for sexual awakening, searching for your intimate equal in relationship after relationship. Life may respond by presenting you with lovers who are tentatively intimate and emotionally wounded as a reflection of your own hidden and shadowed inner places, where you are fearful and holding back from deeper intimacy.

It is at this very place of discovery when we realize how valuable our partner really is to us. Indeed, when we awaken to a meaningful alignment for relationship, a joint purpose of relational union, this is when our sexual/spiritual partnership actually begins.

The transformational potential of sexual union has long been discussed in ancient tantric texts. The modern longings that people have for orgasm and deeper connection with a mate are longings for a similar ultimate union. When you answer the call of your heart's desires by expressing your sexual/emotional energy in conscious, soulful ways, you are exploring this ultimate union, a mystical *reunion*.

## Electric sex

Nature, like sex, has been confused with conditions that *can* be controlled. When you honor nature's rhythm you are happy with her. But if you fail to honor her way— let's say by raising a city on the man-made banks of a controlled river— nature will make you very unhappy the day the town is wiped out by its flood. Is nature's energy— the river— to blame for the disaster, or is the cause actually the "box" the river was conformed to fit into, a box which was too small and inconsistent with the needs of the river?

Just as the river is ever flowing within its banks, sexual energy is ever flowing through the body. Do you know what happens to a river that is dammed up by design? When the contained water is released, and consciously used, the force is so powerful that electricity is generated, and it can then be channeled to turn on our kitchen lights. However, when the power is unconsciously used— say the dam breaks from pent up pressure— then the whole town below can be wiped out.

Similarly, unconsciously dammed-up sexual energy in a person can be extremely painful for her, resulting in emotional bitterness, extreme negativity, and even premature aging. Just like a river that has been restrained from flowing freely, that energy must release at some point, hopefully through a conscious process; because otherwise the outcome can be destructive both emotionally and physically.

Sexual energy that is consciously raised, contained, and channeled is also electricity. You can use this kind of electricity to turn your *spiritual* lights on.

## Be open and willing

Your personal willingness will guide you toward an intimate, soulful, enlightening sex life for you and your partner. It is not primarily your partner's willingness you are seeking even though you may insist that it should be. When seeking a change, although a willing partner comes in handy, always start with yourself. Simply, because you can. Your partner may or may not be ready to grow with you each time you get interested in something new, but if you work on yourself first, your partner may become curious about what you're doing and decide to join you.

Have you ever had the experience that you already knew just about everything there was to know about something and so you closed your mind to learning anything new about it? Most people have. People do this regularly regarding the subject of sex, too. Just think about all the stereotypes you've heard over the years. Those same people, when they apply the information and techniques you'll be reading about soon, say it's as if they had previously sworn that the world was flat, but then they discovered that it is round as a baseball— and realized that they will not fall off if they venture out exploring!

There are four basic steps in willingness to describe. The first step has to do with being willing to review what you've come to know about sex and loving up until now, while also considering the concepts you'll find throughout the book.

The second part of willingness has to do with considering that humans are more than their physical bodies, and therefore are able to experience life on many different levels, including, but not limited to, the physical. This step, then, has to do with your willingness to become aware of the connection sex has to, your feelings, your partner's feelings, your spiritual self, and your partner's, and also the electric flow of energy that runs through your body, your partner's, and between the two of you. It has to do with the connection that sex has to your health and well-being. It has to do with becoming aware of how the sex-energy is connected to your heart-energy and that of your partner's.

The essential question in this step is: If great sex is more than merely rubbing two bodies together, then *what else is there?* In the curiosity of this question you build the foundation of your willingness. Another way to ask this is: What other components besides good friction are required to generate the lovemaking of soulful beloveds?

The third step has to do with your willingness to hang out temporarily in a possibly uncomfortable transition place while you're integrating your new experiences. Some hidden objections and resistance may surface out of habit and familiarity. You need the willingness to explore like a scout, to be as curious as a kitten, and to renew the innocence of being childlike.

Consider one more vital step: Being open to having and experiencing the essence of Love in your life, and realizing how Love itself will connect you with sacred sexual energy. The material and practices included in the following chapters have been presented to help you generate more love in your life. More love for yourself, your body, your human-ness, your heart and mind. More love in all ways for your beloved, and more love in numerous ways and unimaginable situations for your relationship together.

In matters of love, it's not only how much we give love but also how willing we are to receive it. No matter how much we may be currently complaining that we aren't given enough love and respect, often the miracle of feeling loved is in the receiving of it and acknowledging it. In this scenario, receiving isn't a passive thing we do while we wait for someone else to give us something. It is in actively being available to *be* loved.

This may be a new way to experience receiving and it may require practice for you to realize its powerfulness. Probably even lots of practice, because we're usually so much more experienced at— and able to control situations by— our giving. Allow yourself to discover how safe and rewarding it really is to let love in by following some of the comments and directions you'll find ahead.

If you feel excited or even fearful about stepping into this mysterious territory, this is par for the course. The thought of having more love in your life may even seem unattainable. It may possibly even feel threatening. This book, and these practices, are meant to be accessible even for those who feel love and good sex have passed them by. "Let go" into it as a process. When you are in the zone of openness, and your timing is ripe, sometimes it will be easier for you to flow with these fresh *Beloveds in Bed* concepts than it is to trust the limiting decisions you may have previously made out of past emotional wounding.

Give yourself and your relationship the gift of your willingness in each of these areas.

Try the material on. If you like it, keep it and continue your practice. Simply modify and adjust when necessary to accommodate your personal situation. Be flexible. Be courageous. Allow your inner wisdom to unfold you.

## Opportunity

All the desire in the world will not help your sexual connection if you do not make a conscious choice to make time for intimacy and lovemaking. If you will look at your daily appointment calendar, would you find all of the important appointments that keep your career successful and your kids on time to their functions? Of course. We are more and more ruled by the clock and most of us live by our appointment calendars.

Now scan your schedule for dates, appointments, engagements, rendezvous or arrangements that you have allotted for intimate time with your partner. Most people report they only have dinner engagements with friends, tennis court times, or vacations scheduled in writing. Showing up for these events is important, right? You wouldn't want to miss your vacation just because you failed to remember it was scheduled. Scheduling these things and not scheduling *couple time* is not unusual, but it points to where our actual priorities are. People often think, If we scheduled our *couple time,* things wouldn't be spontaneous anymore, *right?*

Besides, we assume that we will have time to spend with our partner, after all, *We do sleep together, don't we?* But too often, people fall into bed after their last detail is cleared up, and wake up in enough time to meet their first scheduled timeline of the day. Couple time must somehow be fit in between lights out and the alarm. Regrettably, at this point, a couple usually feels that to have quality time together, they must steal from their own sleep allotment, or from their careers, kid's activities, or some other of life's realities. They have scheduled themselves right out of the opportunity to be together in a consistent, easy way.

People say they want their sex lives to be more, better, different, sexier and intimate, but in reality, where is there time to experience it? Scheduling may not be easy, yet, to have the soulfulness that you desire, you *must* make time for it. Plan time together to just hang out. An impossible request? Realizing how important this is to your relationship in general, and to your sexual fulfillment specifically, will help increase your motivation!

A soulful connection requires spaciousness, and needs you to slow down and be present, which is hard to do when you are cramping a romantic moment in between two other tight agenda items. Hi. Bye. While stealing ten minutes here and there may contribute to relational maintenance, a few rushed moments will not bring the relationship into the depth of spirit that is possible.

You desire many things no doubt. If you aren't spending the kind of quality time with your beloved that you'd like, you may need to reevaluate your desires. To place a higher value on couple time, something else may have to take a lower priority. Not always, but be open to it. Must you really try so hard to achieve a certain lifestyle if your relationship suffers in its wake?

Schedule time to be together. At least three quality hours each week as a very minimum (more would be great). Trade child care time with another family for a few hours on Sunday afternoon or Saturday night, so that you get the house to yourselves (if possible). Be creative! There is a way to work it out, just keep looking for the way. Make the time. Then guard the time with your love life!

## The tantric heart

Tantric loving is about union. Union of spirit and flesh. Union of heart and passion. Union of mental and emotional. Union of masculine and feminine. The union of partners becoming beloveds is rooted in the art of *being*. A discipline called Tantra has been the teaching of this *art of being* for thousands of years. It becomes reborn again every so often, and it is making a strong appearance all over the world now. The vast discipline includes, but is not limited to sexuality. Tantric living and loving has to do with: leading an integrated life that is impeccable on all levels, weaving together all parts of ourselves, known and unknown, seen and unseen, the physical with energetic, heart with mind, the soul with source, our humanness with spirit, unifying our lost or disowned aspects of self and becoming *natural* again, no longer split off from our divine connection.

It has to do with living life from love rather than avoiding life because of fear. When we don't know how to do this, tantra teaches us that it's okay to learn, make "mistakes" as we go, and grow. Tantra teaches us how to be at peace even when everything else seems to be falling apart. It also teaches us to take in all the wondrous joy and beauty that is always available to us from our world . . . by simply lending our attention moment to moment.

Your mind may buck and strain trying to make sense out of these ideas, but the true understanding resides naturally and easily in your heart. In your heart is where tantric loving will make sense to you. Discover for yourself the essence of *your* tantric heart and the profound benefits gained through your own exploration of becoming beloveds.

## The big "O"

There seems to be a lot of concern among people about orgasm. Whether it's happening or not; that it might not be happening enough; or that the coming of it is just *too* fast or *too* slow. Magazines are always telling women how to achieve this seemingly elusive experience, and men are on the look out to learn new tricks to avoid coming prematurely.

This promotes the stereotype that females come too slowly, infrequently, or not at all, and that males ejaculate too prematurely or may pound away without much care or regard that a partner is even there.

It is true that orgasms feel extremely wonderful and there are many benefits of how they add to health and good well-being. However, chasing them, and shaming ourselves and others about whether or not we "achieved" orgasm creates entirely too much unnecessary fuss about a very natural process. In fact, it is the chasing after them and the application of guilt or shame about performance that inhibits orgasm.

For most couples the solution is exactly the same for each person— man or woman. *Relaaax*. Slow down. *Brreeathe*. Take your time.

Indeed, it is a very wise man who appreciates the slower speed he must harmonize with to give his woman pleasure. This slower rhythm actually helps him pace his own tendency to hyper-speed to ejaculation. For a woman to experience full orgasmic pleasure and for a man to be in conscious control of his body's ejaculatory function, both need to slow down, avoid trying to "get to all the bases in thirty minutes or less," and *relaaax*! No kidding. Soon, you'll be having new orgasmic experiences, too.

## Orgasmic release

The secret to satisfying sex is more than sexual release. Otherwise, everyone would be content with twenty-minute-or-less romps that result in climactic release for each partner in a rather frequent, consistent way.

Climax is often felt as a reward, emotional release, or even as an entitlement. However, even when lovers become skillful at "getting one another off," there can be a sense of missing something, a feeling of loss or regret. *Beloveds* want their sexual encounters bathed in a loving exchange. Heart connected climax.

## The courage it takes

It's not surprising to meet couples who mention at some point that they have not made love for one, three or even ten years— it is not a rare scenario. Folks like these have come to an intimacy course like mine in hopes of discovering a rekindled sex life complete with emotional connection and, perhaps, to find out if there is more to the sexual encounters than they had been experiencing before they completely shut it down.

It is also not unusual for a couple to forego certain expressions of the lovemaking experience, such as kissing, massaging each other, either the giving or receiving of pleasure through oral/genital contact, cuddling, sensual play, and more. At some point, the couple had encountered an uncomfortable spot or hidden iceberg and just never touched that subject again, literally.

And no wonder, because few people have been taught skills in how to deal with all the things associated with a sexual relationship: The tremendous feelings that can surface, the huge sexual energy that arises, or how it actually works. Communication skills relating to sexual activity are rarely rich, and some couples still observe a taboo of not discussing anything at all with a sexual or intimate content to it. You may relate to one of the above scenarios or you may have an example of your own.

These brave couples, previously scared out of bedroom activities for some reason, took a chance together to reopen the subject of sexual loving. Sometimes this happens after the kids have moved away and they feel they can be free in their own home again, and desire to re-engage each other intimately. For others, one partner declared he would not continue living in an essentially platonic husband/wife relationship, without a sexual connection. Some discovered, to their surprise, that the partner was willing, frightened, but able, to jump in and learn, ready to heal accumulated emotional wounds and grow together in a sexual loving relationship.

This is true courage. And if this has been your story in some way, congratulations to you for taking the risk to open again, vulnerably, stepping out there into your sexual energy in a whole new adventure. You deserve it.

Most everyone has learned to rub bodies together but, clearly, great sex is more than bodily friction. There is so much to learn from expanding your loving, living, and communicating skills. Take a deep breath . . . and let it out.

## To do or not to do

Wonderful lovemaking doesn't necessarily involve doing a variety of new things or even doing some of the old things more and better. It is doing some things completely differently: doing them *consciously.* Sometimes it means *not doing* some things you've been performing habitually, which really have nothing at all to do with intimacy or good sexual relations.

Enjoying great sexual loving is the freedom to be yourself, to have your love, your interests, your pleasure, play, and passion expressed. It is to have your boundaries respected and your requests sincerely considered, not ridiculed. It is an exchange of love in a divine dance-like movement.

## The last three sessions

Great sex and loving intimacy work best when you are relaxed. Consider your last three lovemaking sessions to determine what factors contributed to your good fortune (if your love life was going well). Become aware of any beneficial conditions and model your own successes! And review what may be out of balance (if you are in a sexual-intimacy or love slump).

Living in balance and harmony will always play a vital part in lovemaking. It can be comforting to realize that the root of dry sexual experience may be in the overwhelming stresses you and your beloved have been plagued with at work or with family, rather than an actual waning attraction for each other.

The stresses in your life can be corrected or accepted, so that you are more available for satisfying lovemaking. This should be comforting to you both. But it's also true that, if you have lost some or all of your feelings for your partner, *this* can also be corrected. It certainly can. It may not always be appropriate, as in cases of abuse. However, in situations where you've grown apart or have simply become stagnant, there's lots of hope— if you are willing, and if you do the homework.

If you are like most people, all you know is that your love life is either hot or it's not. When it's hot you simply enjoy. If it's not, you want it back! The coming chapters will outline the most common elements that can keep your love alive, as well as how to adjust when you're caught in a love slump.

## The gift of "non-doing" sex

"I'll learn to *do* you really good and you can learn to *do* me really good and we'll call that great sex." This is what I hear so often as the key to assure that sex is good. If you're even this lucky, you'll each find out somehow what you each want and are stimulated by, and then you'll try to give it and get it, if you can.

Naturally, wanting to please one another is crucial; however, this goal in itself can lead to a whole area of misunderstanding because we rarely give ourselves permission to talk openly about sex, intimacy, and loving. This lack of permission also extends to the attitudes we have about our bodies and its particular functions, as well as all things unpredictably wild associated with the sex energy.

Great sex is more than "doing each other perfectly." Actually, it is foregoing the goal-oriented nature of "doing," and instead, "allowing." More pleasure will come your way from *allowing* a natural flow of ecstasy and pleasure than from structuring a brilliant plan for more sex and then *pushing* for it to happen. Granted, flowing naturally is the domain of the feminine, while the masculine is more comfortable with a plan. But with practice, everyone makes it look easy and is thrilled by the pleasurable outcomes achieved effortlessly by *non-doing*.

## Great lovemaking and the unknown

Ask 100 people what great lovemaking is and you will get 100 different answers. Distilled, however, all the responses meet at some common denominators. People want to feel wanted and needed . . . to feel alive . . . to give love and feel loved. And people want to express themselves, to have ecstatic pleasure and to have fun.

Ask 100 people why they avoid sex and you will get 100 more answers. Distilled, there is still some commonality. People want to protect themselves from things that have hurt them in the past. Or, as a matter of conditioning, they don't believe they deserve love, intimacy, companionship. Sex may feel too vast, powerful, or mysterious. It can be just plain scary and sometimes terrifying to let go into all that unknown.

What seems to relieve the terror of the unknown is simply relaxing with the breath. Let go of the pressure to be the queen of the sex goddesses and just be your personal version of *Love Goddess* or *Sensual Queen*, created by *your* standards, rather than *Playboy's*. Let go of the pressure to be Mr. Macho performance stud according to some standard developed by *Hollywood* or commercials, and allow your natural passion for sex and love to motivate your desires and self image. Proclaim yourself a *Love God* or *Romance King*.

Soulful sex has nothing to do with all the sexual images you haven't been able to live up to. Having a fabulous sex life comes from letting those standards drop away and then reinvesting the energy you previously "spent" trying to keep up. Instead, use that energy now to be yourself. *Or,* to learn about yourself, who you really are under all those images and projections that have come from the outside world and which you've taken on. Be your most wonderful, sensual, intimate, sexy, caring, and delicious self! Look for it. Look for these qualities in your beloved as well.

By the way, this discovery is not another "doing" in disguise. If you are looking for the new *plan*, forget it, you'll miss. It is in your *allowing* that the mystery of beautiful lovemaking unfolds itself to you. Yield to Love. Let go into the feelings. Allow your special energy to flow naturally.

## Becoming conscious sexual lovers

How could we know everything there is to know about sex when the subject is so tremendously vast, and when our best childhood teachers were other little kids, embarrassed parents, and pornographic magazines? There is so much that we don't know. For the most part we don't even know that we don't know.

Yes, it's okay to learn. It's not only okay, it's natural to be curious to explore and learn. But, even more importantly, it is valuable to make conscious that which we already know and experience in sexual encounters.

This is an especially important message to many reading this book who have resisted feedback about themselves because of machismo, or because they figured they already knew all about sex. When presented with a beloved's critique or request for more sensitivity or education, they were at first afraid and then shameful to admit there was something more they could learn.

We all have something to learn regardless of how masterful we have become sexually. We all have certain areas of our sexuality that we want to focus on, to heal, awaken, explore, and ignite. Everyone does! As you continue reading, talk with each other about your desires. Reveal what you are sensitive to, fearful about, and what you sense you are learning and wanting to open up to and discover. Compliment each other often on your shared willingness to be conscious sexual lovers.

## What's in a word?

Make a list in your mind of the words you use to describe your genitals . . . and your partner's genitals. What words do you use to describe lovemaking . . . and oral sex? Where did you get these words or phrases from? Health text books? Cultural perspectives? Porno films? Don't know?

Words are very important. The words you choose to use will actually use you in return by defining your experience. The words paint a picture in your mind and can essentially set the tone for your whole sexual expression. Consider finding words or phrases that are congruent with the kind of emotional space (environment, tone, or mood) you are trying to create in your sexual loving.

Do you use clinical terms: vagina, penis, intercourse? Do you use the popular words that porno films use? Slang words?

Perhaps you avoid actually talking about the subject at all because you don't have any words or phrases that you feel comfortable with. Some people just say "down there" or "it."

When you say: cock . . . pussy . . . cunt . . . prick . . . ramrod . . . hole . . . box . . . bush, or any other slang terms . . . how does it make you *feeel* in your gut? How about in your heart? Do you feel *cocky? Nasty? Naughty? Powerful? Sexy?* What about *loving? Heartfelt? Intimate?* If you are interested in animal gusto, then some of the slang words voiced with some heat will probably give you that. How does your partner feel when you use these words? If you don't know, you can ask.

When you say or hear these kinds of words, are you soulfully inspired? Does your heart rejoice in celebration? Or do your shoulders cringe in discomfort and your belly feel a jolt, even subtly? These words have a derogatory history meant to shock and to shame, and even when they are said lovingly or sweetly, they still carry with them the historical intention and underlying offensive resonance.

When the desire is to create a sacred space, these words will work against you. In my classes when these kind of words are used to describe a woman's vagina, participants who were previously joyfully laughing, fall very silent. Everyone knows, on some level, that a woman's vagina is a very sacred place, and to voice these slang words is somehow degrading of that honor.

When you use or listen to derogatory words referring to your genitalia and you say it's okay for you, *is it really?* Is it okay for your partner? Or are you just using words you feel stuck with? If either of you are using words that bring a history with them that offends either of you . . . *notice*. Become conscious of how you are responding and how you feel. Look for new words that don't come with shameful connotations, words with which you can both grow in love.

The phrases you will see in the following chapters will help you invite into your lives caring intimacy and natural sexual loving. Try using them. See if they will work for you. They have a history of beloveds honoring each other. When you use these words, you summon *that* history, one of dignity and respect.

*Yoni* (pronounced Yo-nee), an Eastern word, means "sacred space" and refers to a woman's vagina. This is her sacred inner territory. Using a word that has such a clear, honoring meaning helps a woman begin to reclaim a respect for herself, one which is holy and sacred in her body and her genitalia. It also signals to a male partner to bring his respect and reverence whenever he approaches her *Yoni* temple.

Two words, also eastern in origin, refer to a man's penis: *Lingam* (len-gum), which means "wand of light," or *Vajra*, symbolizing power, shining clarity and truth. A man's Lingam is a sacred vector of energy; and when there is appropriate vocabulary to describe the Lingam's truer function, men finally can have the confidence of possessing such a wondrous tool for pleasure-making. This naturally makes men proud in the finest sense, beyond macho.

Holy men and women have used words like these for thousands of years to express their devotion to Love and to one another. They have honored the human body and the holy act of sexual loving.

Why not invite this powerful, positive vibration into your bedroom and into your love life?

## Trust your gut feelings

Lots of people— particularly women, but men included— have been feeling for a long time that there should be more to their sexual intimacy. Trust those feelings. All too often, people deny their feelings by questioning the validity of them. "Who am I to know something" and, "Even if I did, how could I explain it to my partner so he would understand it?" Or even more risky, "Who am I to *want* something?"

There *is* something more, you were right . . . and you deserve to experience it!

This book may very well be your opportunity to at last feel acknowledged, find words for your feelings, validate your intuition, and explore examples of how to experience the intimacy you've been desiring.

Always trust your gut feelings. You may not always know what to do with the information you are getting from your gut, but do not deny these feelings. Don't stuff them away or check-out of your body. Be curious. And if you need more clarity, you can always petition your inner knowing for clearer understanding of your feelings. Ask (quietly to yourself) to understand what a feeling means. Do this right before you fall asleep at night. The answer to your question may come in a dream or as a spontaneous insight during the day, or even come alive in a book, movie, or conversation.

When the timing is right and you are prepared for the information— when you are receptive— the understanding will come to you.

Always trust your gut feelings. Avoid judging them as frivolous, wrong, inconvenient, weak, or bad. Begin by listening to them, really paying attention and listening. Feel the lumps in your throat, the knots in your belly, the palpitation in your heart, the sweating, coughing, the little itches and scratches, sneezes, the lapses in your train of thought, and the spontaneous pictures that come up in your head. Notice the signals! Start there. Your feelings are your steering mechanism.

What are your feelings steering you toward, or away from?

## Being beloveds with yourself when you are single

Sometimes we are without a partner to become beloveds *with*, whether that is by choice, death, or divorce. There can be great loneliness for us in the loss of a partner, as well as the lost hope of the dream that was originally shared.

There may be pain or shame felt in thinking we "should" have a partner when we do not, and this in itself can prod people into choosing mates no matter how inappropriately, just to be "normal" or to "avoid" being alone. Whether you are sharing your life with a partner or not, you still have opportunities to learn about love, and to be loved and share love. Certainly, you will *miss* your opportunities if you avoid interacting with others and just watch television, or, if you spend your attention complaining that there are not enough "good men" or available women out there.

Becoming a beloved— realizing love through relationship— begins in one of three ways: connection to God (including volunteering self-less service); connection to others (mate, friends, family, including animals); and connection to self (including love of nature). When one of these doors opens to embrace you and you walk through it, you let the love you experience there "work" on you, to open your heart and heal you. In the process, you become a beloved of life.

When one of these doors seems to close, you are asked to open more fully to the other two doorways. A door may close, not for punishment, but for a kind of "spiritual remodeling." In its absence we're more prone to awaken new appreciation, sensitivity, and wisdom. So, please don't wait for a mate until you become a beloved in your own life. When a closed door reopens, who knows what or who will be standing in the doorway waiting for you, if you are available.

In spiritual terms, life as a part of a couple is not easier or better than being single, it's just different. In fact, when you *are* in relationship it seems *more* difficult. In relationship, our own ego and shadow places are so much more obvious to us. As a single person, if you have enough time to complain that you haven't found "Mr. or Mrs. Right," then you probably just have too much idle time on your hands. Find a way to celebrate who you are and what you are up to in life. Discover ways to interact with people which allow you to experience *yourself*, your ego concerns, and your true interests in life. Realize that wherever you go, *you* are still there— whether you are a mate, a parent, a widow, divorced or single. *You* are still there.

Being single can still include soulful intimacy. In some ways this intimacy is more important now than ever. Unfortunately single people will too often *not* be sexual at all, or will partake in the kind of sex that leaves them emotionally unsatisfied after the release of sexual tension. If you have not already done so, make a list of all the qualities you would enjoy in a mate. Make a list of all the things you would enjoy sharing with this person, or having him or her *do* with you. Now, go down the list, one by one, and give those things to yourself.

Romance is very high on many people's list. As an example, in the evening (turn off all the lamps), light seven or eight candles in your bedroom and bathroom before you begin your preparation for bed ritual. Light some incense. Notice how changing your environment will reflect in softening your mood. Perhaps you feel more relaxed, more sensuous, as you float across the room. People often sense more of their own beauty in the mirror by candle light. Just this much attention given to yourself, not as a treat or something special, but as a way of life, will alter how you view romance. Although romance with another person is lovely, it is not dependent on it. Romance yourself. Develop or deepen your romantic heart with the person you love, or want to love more, *you*. Make long, sweet, tender love with yourself. Don't miss out on these wondrous experiences waiting for a partner. Be beloveds with yourself when you are single. The intimacy you develop with yourself will only enrich your experience of life. There will be opportunities for you to work through the emotions that may surface— abandonment, aloneness, worthiness, and probably feelings of inadequacy also ("Can I . . . *fill in the blank*— survive, give myself sexual–emotional satisfaction, be creative enough alone to be romantic?) Help yourself through these feelings from the understanding you'll develop while reading *Beloveds in Bed*.

The intimacy you cultivate with yourself will also enrich your future relationship. Fall in love with *you*— leave little love notes for yourself to find later with a bottle of massage lotion; light those candles; draw those bubble baths; set aside the vibrator and use your hands to explore your entire body in sensual and tender ways.

## Imagine

Imagine yourself shame-*less* about your body. Imagine yourself guilt-*free* regarding your sexuality. Now imagine living in a world where everyone else was free to be the same.

Imagine a world where a sexual relationship was considered a common path to spiritual life and self-fulfillment. Wherever you looked, you found evidence and support for soulful relating. Talk shows, where instead of people exploiting negative relations, ninety-eight percent of the themes were people exploring harmonious, conscious, evolving relationships.

Ponder a world in which men were not threatened by the feminine qualities of women, but were inspired to greater mastery in themselves. A world in which a woman did not complain that she had to compete with men on male turf, but instead she led from the equal strength of her conscious feminine power.

Imagine locker room talk in which men proudly speak to each other about how important they feel because their mate opens to their full love and attention. Talk that has each man comparing notes about how to love his beloved in profound ways, how to open to her more deeply, and how to spiritually benefit from the emotional and mental differences as well as similarities they have between them as men and women.

Imagine girlfriends talking on the phone discussing what they enjoy about their mate. Women's talk about men that is respectful, where each woman embraces an empowering viewpoint of her beloved to be all that he can be. Women happy to be women, glowing because they feel safe, adored, and honored by the men in their lives.

Imagine a world where men who loved men, and women who loved women were respected for loving.

Imagine a world where teenagers had a promise of a future ahead of them. One where adults inspired them to feel that they made a difference, and were counted on to continue making a difference, and so they behaved accordingly. One where adults made teenagers feel included and special. A world where teenagers feel so loved inside themselves that they wait to have children of their own until they are older and more emotionally, mentally, and financially ready. At that time, they have children because they want to love and raise children, not because they want those children to fill a void of love in themselves.

Now, imagine someone reading this book in a few years getting to this passage and thinking to themselves, "*Huh*, why am I being asked to imagine the obvious?"

SECOND DOORWAY

# BEING PRESENT

*Soulful sex begins when you show up –
body, mind, heart and spirit*

## Soulful sex begins when you show up

Being present simply means that you are *here*, wherever you are. Your attention is in *present* time, not worrying about yesterday or tomorrow. You are present to your senses; smell, taste, sound, sight, and the touchy-feel and the *f-e-e-l* of your surroundings. You are engaged in your partner. You are sensitive to your feelings, sensitive to your body and to your thoughts.

You are aware of *this* moment. You are not back at the office working out some problem in your mind, and not worrying about how the washer is going to get fixed on a Sunday. Also, don't confuse this intimate moment with the other kind of important talk you must have with each other about family, home, and the "to-do list" of things you haven't discussed yet.

This moment is an opportunity to let go of all the busy worldly pressures and help each other relax. Relaxation is crucial for great sex as well as good health and well-being. Being fully relaxed includes having your mind be still without a zillion distractions filling it up, and especially without having expectations for yourself to do something about each one.

When you desire to have better sex, be more interested in sex, or have your partner be more interested, then you'll probably want to practice being present.

The time you share before your sleep, or on a lazy Sunday morning, or after work, whether it's ten minutes or an hour, *is just for you*— lovers enjoying the loving, practicing loving, relaxing, and being present to being beloveds. You will carve this very moment out of your busy schedule, with the intention of being free.

## Clearing the day

It's 6:30 P.M. and you just got home from work. Dinner has to be made, the kids have homework, your partner is nervous and cranky because of an important presentation tomorrow. The *last* thing you want to do is make love— or maybe the *only* thing you want to do is make love. Before anything happens, let go of all pressures! It is easier than you think, but it takes practice.

Begin by letting go of any expectations and then trust that everything that is supposed to happen this night will. Decide as a priority that you will be connected to yourself and to your family. You do this by cleaning off the business of the day to help get relaxed and present, so that you are available to do *whatever* you do tonight.

What from your family's to-do list, can't be done with more heartfelt enthusiasm or commitment than after a genuine greeting hug and a short catch-up talk?

## Be yourself

It's important that both partners are aware of their personal needs, wants, rhythms, styles, and boundaries. When you are trying to like sex just because a partner wants it for you, it is more difficult to be authentic to yourself. Instead of trying to act a certain way for another person, tune in to yourself, breathing into your body, becoming aware of how you feel, of what you might be afraid of or what you may be concerned about.

It's possible that the reason you think you don't like sex, or do not prefer it very often is because you have never really experienced it for *yourself.* This, unfortunately, is common for a lot of women and some men, too. When sex is about performance and pressure (yes, even pressure to enjoy it), sex can become like a job; something people use to barter for things they want, or an act they perform to *avoid* something, such as disharmony.

Spend time coming back into a centered place inside your own body-mind and begin to become aware of your personal rhythms, desires, distastes, and wishes. This process may seem difficult at first if you have not asked these particular questions before. You may find your answers different from your partner's and seemingly inconvenient. That's okay.

While this process of discovery is imperative in becoming beloveds, responding to the change may require compassionate understanding from both of you. For a period of time, you may actually be having less sex than previously. Don't be concerned; it is not permanent. A healing is in progress. This accounts for not doing automatic, unconscious sex anymore: the kind of sex that people settle for when they don't know there's another choice. When you begin to express your sexuality for *you,* your partner may be quite pleased at how much more of you is available for sexual sharing. And the stress that was burdening your partner, the one who was pressured trying to get more sex, will begin to relax. Sex then can become something you share together rather than something you manipulate to get from one another.

Be authentically yourself. Let go of one partner bending to the other, or one being dominant, because neither partner wins in such a situation. Both partners emotionally starve. Being beloveds is dependent on each partner genuinely accepting themselves and allowing space for their partner to do the same. Celebrate your similarities and celebrate your differences.

## Sleep

It is not unusual to have sex so that you can sleep better. Sex is a natural tranquilizer. However, it works the other way around also. Lovemaking is better if you are not sleep deprived! If overworked, sleep-deprived people would just get enough sleep, sex would naturally get better.

There is an amount of sleep that you can get by on, and there is an amount of sleep that you can thrive on. Find out what that is for you and get it!

When your body is truly rested and thriving, you are present to lovemaking in a way that you cannot be when limping by with only a part of your attention, resources, and energy.

Get enough sleep so that your lovemaking is optimal. Take naps together. Some of you sleep-deprived lovers will find taking a long afternoon nap to be the most phenomenal foreplay ritual you have in your little bag of tricks. Try it! Get some sleep.

## Harmonizing

Enjoying the best lovemaking yet is dependent on how attuned you are as a couple. Some couples will try to use the lovemaking itself to get back into harmony with one another, but with varying degrees of success.

Being out of harmony is bound to happen from time to time. Don't worry so much about how often this happens; rather, focus on returning to harmony between you as soon as you are able. The rich reward will always come from reconnecting with each other, versus winning a disagreement.

Plan on harmony, but when everything but harmony happens, practice *reconnecting*. Count on it. Commit to it. Remind each other of the importance of it. Any potential problem between you can become an issue that's in front of you, instead, if you'll simply reconnect, join forces, and deal with life issues as a team.

Practice the exercises from this section and the rest of the book regularly (particularly breathing, movement, eye contact, spooning). They will help you and your partner regain your connection.

# Goals are for executives, not lovers

*"When the Power of Love replaces the Love of Power,
then we will know the blessings of peace."*

author unknown

Love has no goal except to experience itself. To make love is to allow love to flow through you, which it does as consistently as day breaks each dawn.

If you close the blinds in a room, you'll miss the experience of day break. But blocking out the light does not stop the dawn from breaking. The same is true of Love. This is how *Love* is, always available to us unless we shut it out. There are too many ways we shut it out. Being driven by goals to perform in a certain way in lovemaking is just one of the blinds.

If achieving a certain number of orgasms or having simultaneous climax is the priority, and failure to do so brings unhappiness, frustration or disappointment, this is a clue that performance has become more important than the sexual-loving itself. And it will be the drive toward that goal that keeps you further from reaching soulful lovemaking. Other goals that motivate performance-driven sex and promote the accompanying anxiety are conditions such as:

- he's gotta always be ready to perform . . .
- or at least perform till "the job" is done
- she must always be wet . . .
- or at least not complain when she is dry and want to stop
- she must have her "one" orgasm
- he must ejaculate
- she must look like or at least act like a centerfold
- you gotta do it a certain number of times each day or week
- if we don't do it differently each time we'll get bored

These are just a few of the stereotypes. But there are many unfortunate pressures. What are the pressures you place on yourself or your partner to meet an expectation or try to avoid something like disappointment or frustration?

The good news is that when you allow your attention to focus on being present rather than on producing a goal, you will have more pleasure, more often. Your sex life has a chance of becoming boredom-proof when you are pressure-free!

Leave your strategic plans at the office along with all those ways you've become very successful in the world, because mergers in the bedroom play by another set of rules entirely. If you adapt, you will have a more rewarding, pleasurable, outrageous love life than you even dreamed possible.

## How do you know when sex is over?

For the average American couple, sex is over when "he comes." If he is a sensitive lover, his partner will also have an orgasm before he finishes or sometime soon after. If he is inexperienced or hasn't yet learned the benefits of attending to *her* needs, he may come fast and not consider this a problem. Both partners usually have their attention on *his* coming. He focuses on it so he gets his just desserts, and she focuses on it so she can know she has done well as a lover.

*Beloveds* realize that a man's orgasmic potential— even whole body climax or multiple climax— are not dependent on his ejaculation. When this realization becomes a reality, ejaculatory control for the man will add immense pleasure to their lovemaking. Ejaculation is generally not an optional step left out of a sexual encounter unless a couple understands this, or that the sexual menu is much vaster than they previously thought.

Mastering whole-body and multiple climax requires a new understanding about how our bodies operate and what needs our bodies have to operate at their peak. Until you discover the rest of the menu, as you read through *Beloveds in Bed,* it's wise to note that arriving to a lovemaking session with a goal of "getting off," or "coming," *is still a goal.* And it's a motivated goal that is registered in the psyche as an expectation. It is the *emphasis* on getting off, not the act of *coming* itself, that will limit soulful lovemaking.

How would your sex life be different if, instead of trying to see how fast or how often you both can come, you sought how close you could feel with one another? Embrace your beloved and approach each loving session with the purpose of simply loving each other. This is the most intense aphrodisiac available, if you can handle the potency.

Men, can learn to have their orgasms full-strength, separate from ejaculation. The pull to ejaculation is often what motivates a man to get off, as if he is releasing a burdensome tension. So when the needy urgency to ejaculate is removed, but the orgasms remain, a man is free to come to a lovemaking session to connect with his beloved in a close, intimate way.

## The hug

What could be more satisfying to spirit and body than the human touch? Touching helps you become present. Think of the pleasure you receive from soft caresses of the face, tossles of the hair, a *genuine* handshake, a game of toe tag under the table. And, of course, the embrace of embraces (no A-frame hugs here, please!) . . . The Hug. *Hugggging*.

Allow your body to touch your partner's, full-body to full-body, and, while breathing fully, let in the comfort, the sweetness, and the connection of the hug. A two-second hug has its place, but a warm, lingering hug can heal little rough spots, mend unkind words, and send your beloved off on his day till you welcome each other home in the evening to the safe haven of your hearts.

A hug that lingers is a hug that says, "I love you, I care for you, I trust you. I have time for you. You count. I count. Our relationship counts."

Wrapped in the comfort of each other's arms, without a goal of going elsewhere, begins to relax the inner being at a deep level. Notice how you feel when you stand up and share a hug that lasts about two minutes (sixteen-ish full breaths) or five whole minutes. If you are comfortably positioned, you may notice that your shoulders begin to relax, your tight jaw loosens, your whole face softens, your way of thinking is less tense and busy. Relaxing can be easier than imagined. One must simply make the time for it, breathe fully of course, and enjoy some juicy hugging.

## Getting into water

Water is the great healer. It will rinse off the blues of the day. Water will prepare you for soulful lovemaking.

- Soak in your bath tub.

- Rinse off in the shower (hot, cold, hot, cold wakes up your vitality). Sit in your hot tub.

- Expose your body to the outdoors in a rain storm (especially the warm rain of a summer day).

- Splash your face with water or apply a hot face cloth.

- Soak your feet.

- Run through the sprinklers.

- Swim in a pool, lake, river, or ocean.

- Stand in a waterfall.

- Squirt a water bottle on your face when that's all you have.

Get into water often. One good shower before work may be plenty to keep the body clean, but another good rinse after work will help release you from thinking like you're still *there* and help you get *here*, in your body, ready for love.

And after being hydrated in water, your skin is softer, more touchable. *Ummmmmm.*

## Exposing yourselves to nature

Nature heals us. With every step we take and with each breath, we are renewed and brought into the present moment. Venture out into nature often with your beloved, allowing enough time for your minds to unwind and your hearts to contemplate. The wind blows us clean, the ocean inspires peace, the mountains awe, the wilderness humbles, enabling us to be more vulnerable and available to learning and growing.

Wander out into nature long enough to feel your *naturalness*. Immerse yourself in the wind and wildlife so entirely, that the urge to romp and climb and talk to the birds is as natural to you as hunting for a parking space in the city.

Find places in nature where you can make love sometimes, even if it's on a blanket under the stars in your own back yard, gazing up at the moon.

## Dance into your life

Moving your body isn't just a good idea to keep the extra pounds off. Moving your body is imperative for well-being and for an exciting sex life. Moving your body helps you relax and get out of your head— complete with all its concerns and to-do's and into your present self.

Do your feet almost involuntarily tap when you hear a certain song? You can't stop those feet, then your head starts nodding to the beat? Maybe you're even humming along or singing outloud with the music? Thought goes out of your mind and you get up and dance! *That's the song!* And others just like it, that you want to have on hand to fill your dance hall . . . the one next to the sofa and stereo in your living room.

At the end of your work day, put on three or more of those irresistible songs and let your body dance. *Mooove* your body. *Shaaake* it up. Let yourself really get into the music, don't worry about looking good or being coordinated. Let the purpose be a cleansing of your work day and releasing of accumulated stresses. It's not a dance contest or a comparison to anyone else. You're simply dancing you.

Shake your hands and arms and shoulders, gyrate your hips and pelvis, pulsate every inch of your body, undulate your back and neck like a snake. Stretch every muscle. Feel the rhythm of the music. Move to it. Breathe deeply and fully. Get up and dance! Move your energy in some big way, if not dancing, shaking or gyrating, then by hopping, running, and skipping. Move enough to get your heart rate up, get your breath quickened, and your circuits turned on. Just do it! No excuses. You'll feel better. But most of all, you'll feel more connected to your own body and more able to connect with your beloved in an intimate or blissful experience.

If you're inhibited by what the neighbors will think, either get over it (consider that your spontaneity may be inspiring to them) or, close the drapes. If volume is a problem, then perhaps you could wear head phones on a long cord. Whatever the obstacle, find a way through it. Moving your body is important. Move like this every day if possible, but particularly before you meet your beloved for a lovemaking session.

As a minimum, dance wildly to three songs with a beat. Nine minutes of total let-go movement, and you can be a renewed human being on the journey toward conscious lovemaking. To be beloveds and enjoy soulful sex, you must be in your body. All your being must be present and accounted for and in touch. If you or your partner are not present for lovemaking, you may feel scattered and disconnected, or like two robots going through the motions, unfulfilled. Dance and move as if your love life depends on it. It does!

Get *up and mooove*. Dance your way into your love life.

## Breathe

When was the last time you considered how important your breath is? What happens if you stop breathing completely? Unless you are a proficient Yogi, death comes soon after absence of breath. If lack of breath is that important on one end of the spectrum, then perhaps breathing fully and completely must be extremely valuable at the other.

Some would say that the quality of your life depends on the depth of your breath, on how much oxygen you take in. Too many people, without paying much attention, breathe shallowly— not enough to fill up the lungs and cleanse them properly. Your moods, mental alertness, joy and your depth of experience are all affected by the fullness of the breath taken in. Naturally, if you want to improve the quality of your sex life, become aware of your breathing patterns.

Become aware of your breath now. Close your eyes if that helps. How far down into and below your chest are you breathing? If you're not breathing much below your neck, notice the mental activity in your mind. Just notice. Are you feeling: *Numb? In control? Scared? Judgmental? Anxious? Relaxed? Available?* Breathe a little deeper into your chest. How do you feel now? There might be some initial tension if you haven't stretched those lungs for a while, but go ahead, you won't hurt anything. Breathe fully and evenly.

Close your eyes. Now, breathe fully into your belly. Place your hands on your belly so you can feel when it's moving. It will puff out when you inhale and retract when you exhale. Just allow it— no need to force it. Practice.

It may take some time if you haven't allowed this much breath for a while. Pay attention to your moods and to your thoughts: You may notice that it's very difficult to have self-defeating thoughts when you're breathing deeply. If you are haunted by negative thoughts, judgmental nightmares, and impossible standards for yourself, consider taking a moment a few times a day to simply experience your full breathing. Place your hands on your belly,take in a breath, hold for just a second, then let it out, hold for just a second, then allow breath to fill back in, and so on. Do this for two to twelve minutes several times a day. Ear plugs can really help you tune in to your breath, especially when you're in restaurants or other noisy public places. Carry a pair for just this purpose.

## Star gazing

When you are emotionally available and open-hearted, making eye contact with the one you love is like looking into eternity. The eyes are the windows to the soul. Western-ers in general don't have much context in which to hold healthy substantial eye contact. However, to look into your beloved's eyes— to visit her divine essence, to *look* for it, to *expect* to experience it, to share with your beloved the divine essence that lives inside of you— is to invite the intimate dance of *Love* to bless your relationship and your home.

You may be uncomfortable letting someone look into your eyes this way. You may not consider yourself *that* kind of person. However, any discomfort you may have with intimate eye contact may be coming from being unfamiliar with that kind of closeness. Situations you are not familiar with always seem a bit strange.

Try open-eye contact during different situations together and become more comfort-able with doing it. For some people, looking into their own eyes in a mirror helps famil-iarize them with the process. Allow your eyes to become soft, rather than staring some-one down, which, *of course*, is uncomfortable. Soft eyes means you are offering your presence and vulnerability. Misinterpreted too often as weak or ineffective, vulnerability in soulful relating actually means being *available* to be seen, loved, and cared for more deeply. Begin with everyday situations, such as when you're having a conversation with your partner. Just allow your eyes to stay with them a little longer. You can sit quietly with your partner without talking and gently offer your eyes to one another as a wonder-ful exercise in centering. More about that later. During a kiss, try keeping your soft eyes open some of the time.

## Heart Center Meditation*

This meditation can be easier to learn in the beginning if you have music in the background with a heartbeat drum rhythm to it. A musical suggestion is *Shamanic Dream* by Anugama. Many trance-type pieces or ocean sounds will work beautifully also. And, silence can beautifully set the tone for your sacred space as well.

Sit in a comfortable position and place your hands over your heart, your right hand first, with your left hand covering your right. Fan them in such a way that the fleshy parts of your thumbs can come together and rest.

Bring your attention to your breathing by slowly allowing it to become deeper and fuller, letting go of tension on an exhale. Now bring your attention to your Heart Center, the area beneath your hands. Breathe your blessings right into your heart for all your heart does for you.

Contemplate the resources of your energetic heart: compassion, healing energy, peace and harmony, and unconditional Love. These resources are always available to you simply through your attention to them. Call on them when you need them, count on them to be there for you, and bless your willingness to receive these valuable resources.

When you begin any meditation, it is a common reaction for your mind to be busy and distracted— even telling you that you don't have time to do the meditation. Through sitting quietly, focusing on the heart and the steady flow of your inhale and exhale, you

---

* This meditation is inspired by the transformational work of Brugh Joy, MD., author of *Joy's Way* and *Avalanche*.

begin to have peace of mind. Meet yourself here at this peaceful place often. Recognizing how to access peace for yourself will deepen the quality of your lovemaking.

A Heart Center meditation can last anywhere from five to sixty minutes. You can do it at home, in your car at a stop, anywhere you feel comfortable connecting with your Heart Center.

Your heart has its own unique intelligence and you can tap this wisdom anytime simply through your request. When you have concerns and difficult situations, you can bring them to your heart. Feel yourself centered in your Heart presence, and then imagine bringing your concern into the center. Recall the energetic resources once again, and listen for your heart's wisdom. You can ask your heart specific questions also. The responses might be mental words in your thoughts, or feelings or just a *knowing*. Listen, and behold your Heart loving you in yet another miraculous way.

*Brreeeath. Relaaax.*

## Help each other home

If you and your beloved don't help each other become centered, balanced, and happy together, who will?

As beloved partners, you have a great advantage to inspire, support, remind, and bless each other's efforts. Did you ever see anybody do this? One partner comes home from a hard day at work needing some soothing, and gets mad because the partner had his own problems at work that day and didn't have any extra comfort to give? Some version of this is actually a very common problem in relationships.

What do you do?

Get real! *Tune into yourself.* Try not to blame each other. Don't expect the other to fix y*our* bad mood.

From there, the more open you become, the more your partner can help you. She can squeeze you, humor you, snuggle with you, breathe with you, make love with you. However, she can't shift your mood unless you are available to be shifted. It's a choice.

You can help each other to be centered, sometimes by doing nothing except loving them. But do trust that your partner will be sane and happy again *sometime*, and do try to avoid the blaming statements such as: "You never . . . " or "You always . . ."

To be helpful, use statements that remind your partner of who he really is in spite of the foul mood. You can make these statements to yourself inside your head, if you can't for some reason say them out loud. This will help you stay present to who he is when he is *acting* like something else. And the good–will also communicates and registers with your partner on some level.

Help each other get centered. Don't criticize the other because he is not centered. Be a team. Specialize in bringing out the best in your beloved. Allow the best to be brought out in you.

## "How I feel now is ... "

This is a talking meditation that you can do together to help you become aware in this moment, as a preparation to lovemaking or to help clear a problem area. Sit facing each other so you can begin to take turns answering the statement, *"How I feel now is..."* and then answer with just one response each: a *bodily felt sensation.*

It might go something like this:

You:        "How I feel now is too crazy in my head to do this exercise."
Partner:    "How I feel now is tense in my shoulders."
You:        "How I feel now is knots in my stomach."
Partner:    "How I feel now is sleepy."
You:        "How I feel now is tight-jawed."
Partner:    "How I feel now is happy to be home from work."
You:        "How I feel now is hungry."
Partner:    "How I feel now is thirsty."
etc. . . .

If you go back and forth about twenty times, sometimes up to forty or so, you can become so conscious about how you are feeling in your body that your answers may gradually and naturally change from those of tension to those of relaxing.

## Sacred touch

Touch your beloved's body as if you are touching a holy treasure. *You are!*

Imagine the essence of your heart delivering this message of honoring to your beloved through your hands. This touch is conscious, sensitive, probably slow, intentional– – *not distracted.*

This touch you offer to each other will help you become centered and present. It helps the touched person get into his body. It helps the person touching become aware of her Heart Presence and the healer aspect of herself.

Pay attention. Bring your whole being to the touch. Continue breathing fully. You can touch and be touched so completely that you become the touch, no longer aware of time or outer distractions. You actually *are* the touch.

Bring your awareness to the part of your body that is being touched. Feel. Sense. Relax. Let go. Become the touch. And *Relaaax* even deeper.

## Conscious spooning

Another way of harmonizing with one another is spooning together. Many of us usually fall asleep in this position, which is yummy to do. But when you spoon regularly throughout your waking day, you'll have additional benefits as well.

The spooning position is ideal for reconnecting after being apart. It's also a good habit to get into as you begin each lovemaking session. Recall how close you can feel after you make love? If you begin your loving session in this conscious spooning position you can become as connected with one another when you begin to make love as you typically were only by the time you were just finishing.

Try this in the morning before you leave your bed and then again when you see each other at the end of your work day. Lay down in a spooning position on your left sides. You'll be taking turns being on the inside position whenever you do this exercise. The person behind will be known as the giver, although there is no action to do. The person on the inside will be the receiver, although both partners receive benefit.

Giver, gently reach around and put your right hand on your partner's heart. Place your left hand on or very near the receiver's forehead. Pillows can help you with your comfort. Now you are in position and you can relax. Bring your attention to your breath individually, becoming aware of how fully you are breathing and allowing your breath to deepen and let go into a rhythmical pattern.

After you are feeling grounded with your own breathing rhythm, if it hasn't happened already, allow your two breaths to move in unison, inhaling and exhaling at the same time.

Feeling each other's breath makes it easier to master conscious spooning, so it's important that your breath is full enough for your partner to feel or hear it. You are now lying down with your breath moving in tandem. If you fall out of sync, one of you can hold the breath while the other takes one, and then you'll both let it out together and begin tandem breathing again. Don't be burdened by perfection; mastery will come with relaxation and practice.

When one of you breathes so much faster and shallower than the other that you can't keep the rhythm, try this. The slower, deeper breather will breathe at the faster rate in the beginning to establish the rapport. Once

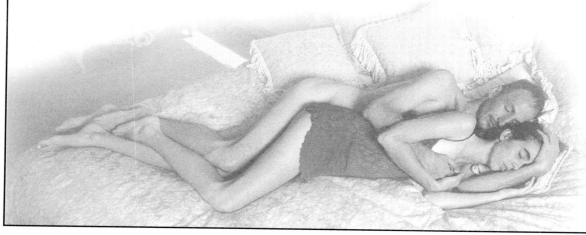

accomplished, you begin to slow your breathing and its depth, and this should help the normally faster breather to adjust to a slower pace. The more fully, deeply and slowly you breathe, the more relaxed you will become.

Stay awake, be conscious, and aware of the energy moving between you. Don't worry if you don't feel it at first (it may be subtle). You will sometime.

We are such a sleep-deprived society these days so if you keep falling asleep, you probably need the rest more than the harmonizing right now. Try conscious spooning again after you are rested. If sleep still comes too easily even when you are rested, you can try some variations or stimulations. Make sure the room is cool enough to keep you perky and that it has good ventilation. Use your mind to focus your attention on each breath as it moves in and out. Start the conscious spooning after you have moved big energy through dancing, running, yoga, etc. This fills you with vitality and perhaps enables you to be comfortably still and awake.

With your conscious attention to the breathing and the letting go, this makes a wonderful meditation. This also tunes your chakra system, the energy centers of your body, so that you feel more balanced and vital.

Try this for fifteen to twenty minutes for a full experience of what's possible. Making this a daily ritual will add soulfulness to your intimacy, but sometimes, just a few minutes will do.

Many of the exercises in this book can lead you into states of bliss, but few more easily than this one. If you are open to it and will allow the space and time, you can experience such divine bliss simply laying together gently breathing in unison.

## Drugs and alcohol

Mood-altering substances are a personal choice. Sometimes a glass of champagne adds an extra blessing or celebration to an intimate moment. However, if you find that you can't have sex if you're sober, you might want to take a closer look at it.

Giving soulful lovemaking a chance to blossom may surprise individuals who have wounded hearts. When someone is accustomed to being treated poorly or has been abandoned frequently, sometimes it may be easier to have a couple of drinks, some marijuana or something stronger to get into the mood and through the sexual encounter. Sadly, drugs and alcohol are used in this way for *self-medicating* and numbing purposes, a way of checking out of what's really happening.

In a healthy relationship, it is a shame to miss your lovemaking by being numbed. If either partner is emotionally unhealthy, it is even more important to avoid drugs and alcohol. Only by being present to what's going on, can you review the situation and make appropriate changes.

The best possible lovemaking scenario can happen only when you are happy and safe with yourself, your partner, and your relationship.

## Increasing your power of attraction
*When men are present, women notice*

The masculine energy, whether it is in the man or the woman, spends a lot of time chasing sex. Trying to get it, trying to get it more often, and strategizing how to get it better. The chase is futile, for the more you push, the more the other partner may pull away.

To increase your power of attraction by a thousand percent, become centered and present inside yourself. It is actually this simple. Spend some time attending to how you feel about yourself and actually have a little love affair . . . with yourself. Take stock of your positive qualities, and appreciate your looks, smile, body, personality, heart, spirit, contributions, temperament, dedication, etc.

There is no stronger aphrodisiac for a woman, than a man who is centered in his body and in his heart. This centeredness is true personal power, *not power over someone else*, for that kind of power makes demands on another's attentions. Instead, use a magnetic attraction.

There is space around you that is more available, not filled up. This is inviting to your beloved— she has room to move *in toward* you. This magnetic invitation comes from being authentically present. It's safe. You can trust it. Others are drawn to this authenticity because they are freer to be themselves. *You become* magnetic. By simply being available and present, you will increase your power of attraction.

## Being patient

Cultivating a temperament of patience will work wonders for becoming beloveds. Some of the concepts and exercises you will practice from each chapter might seem too difficult to master the first time you try, so it's better to spot yourself some patience ahead of time. There is no hurry. Hurrying will defeat the purpose, anyway. Becoming beloveds will flower over a lifetime. If you don't master something early in the process, try again later— which is better than not trying again just to avoid failure. Failure does not really exist anyway; it's only another opportunity to practice the art of being . . . yourself.

## Getting "here"

When you are present to wherever you are, you will be able to appreciate what is available and opening to you *here*. This is a requirement of soulful sex. The sweetest lovemaking you'll ever have is dependent on **you** being there. If sex is not good, look to see if *you* are actually showing up. Practice discerning the difference between being *here* and being distracted. It is an acquired taste, *you* authentically *showing up* instead of presenting your expectations or your armor, and trying to play it emotionally safe.

THIRD DOORWAY

# RELAXATION

*Why relaxing is so important
to soulful lovemaking*

## Why relaxing is so important to soulful lovemaking

At the heart of great lovemaking is relaxation. A tense woman will have trouble lubricating, climaxing, and enjoying. A tense man is more likely to ejaculate prematurely, or even have difficulty attaining an erection. This is when lovemaking seems more like a chore rather than an enjoyable experience; or when people say the lovemaking doesn't work any more or isn't the way it used to be.

Stress is more complex than worrying about too many things to accomplish, or the fear of not being able to make the mortgage payment— the body will experience stress whenever the mind is in conflict about anything. For instance, a man might be concerned about whether his partner will respond to his advances that night, or whether he will be able to get erect enough and last long enough. A woman might worry about whether she is wet enough, or if she smells okay. Will the birth control work? Will she be aroused enough to orgasm? Either will be concerned with whether sex is frequent enough or too much. And both may worry if their personal performance will be adequate as a lover.

Soulful intimacy and intense orgasming will happen in a flow, a letting go, and for this, one must be relaxed.

To enjoy the sacredness of being beloveds, as well as having soulful, fulfilling sex, you both need to relax, and slow down. Relax your body. Quiet your mind. Breathe fully in . . . and . . . out. *Take your time.*

*Make the time,* to take your time, if you want soulful lovemaking.

## Quickies

If the majority of your sexual sessions are a steady diet of thirty minute or less quickies, this will add to your overall tension and the dysfunction that accompanies it. A man will condition his body to come fast even when he wants to last longer and a woman's body will eventually shut down from lack of intimate contact and refuse to lubricate sufficiently. Ultimately, this may keep her from wanting frequent sex, or at all. Or it may encourage either partner to go elsewhere for sexual contact.

There is absolutely nothing wrong with a quickie, as long as there is abundant time for longer loving sessions at other times. If you are not accustomed to taking your time to make love, then you might begin with just one session a week that is an hour and a half long and other sessions at your accustomed pace. Other couples will enjoy two, three or more sessions a week that are at least this long or longer.

If you would like to end a habit of quickies so you can have more extended, blissful loving, and yet you have only thirty minutes or less for sex, use the time instead to become intimate without the rush to arousal leading to immediately blowing off the energy so quickly. Instead, cuddle, massage each other, bathe together, meditate, dance, sing, look softly into one another's eyes and hang out there (it's a magical place). These kinds of loving sessions relax you and prepare the body and mind for extended loving, free of tension and abundant in ecstatic pleasure.

## Extended loving

Generally speaking, the longer you engage in a lovemaking experience, the more opportunity you have to generate a *state of bliss*.

However, a frequently heard comment is "What would we *do* for that extra time?" Which can be interpreted to mean, "What *else is* there to do?" Don't let the question stress you. It will become more clear to you as you study and practice this material. So breathe deeply. Relax.

Sometimes it is a man's *thoughtfulness* that leads him to ejaculate quickly, thereby ending the sex session, because he does not want to be a source of burden to his partner any longer than he has to. A woman may declare that she doesn't want him to last any longer than he already does, *why should she?* Well, one possible answer is that an extremely large part of the sexual loving between you is missing. What might be absent is the part where there is satisfaction for *her,* and that's why she wants it over with so soon. It may have been this way for so long that you just always remember it as "she's not very sexual, not interested," or "she just doesn't like it very much." Not true. At least, not permanently.

Sometimes his desire to ejaculate quickly, or for her to want him to, has to do with each individual's previous experience with other sexual partners. Perhaps his past lovers related to him reluctantly, and he mistakenly developed an attitude that sex was a burden for a woman instead of a blessing. Perhaps her past lovers made her feel as if she was taking too long to attain arousal, and so she mistakenly gave up talking to her lover about her needs and then unconsciously forgot that she had any.

Women are extremely sexual beings; some say, with a capacity for more sexual power than men. But if the circuits aren't turned on, it can seem like she loses her sexual libido. Be confident that a woman's sexual power can only be covered over, but not erased. Give your beloved the satisfaction she deserves to turn on through *extended* loving sessions. With your care, your love and gentleness her sexual appetite may blossom.

*Ladies,* do allow this process to unfold long enough to find out if there are some sensual tinglings waiting for you just below the surface of non-arousal. This is not intended to create pressure to achieve some new standard— there should be no pressure at all. The extended lovemaking is not goal-driven. So both of you can relax. Some women were taught by their mothers that although sex would not be enjoyable for them, it is a wifely function they'd have to put up with. Unfortunately, there has been a shameful historical conspiracy to undermine a woman's value and your mother was most likely just passing on to you what she was taught from her mother. The million dollar question remains: Is it still true that you would be asked to offer your body without pleasure for yourself? Please give yourself permission to say no. *ALL women* deserve pleasure, including you!

Guys, offering a woman extended loving does not just mean two hours non-stop with your Lingam thrusting inside of her. Maybe you can do that or work up to it— she may like it— but it's not necessary to generate a state of bliss, so relax. What is needed is the intimate time you spend together, gradually building her arousal with her.

You can stimulate her with your hand, your mouth, your soft sensual voice, your thoughts, your massaging, and also with your Lingam. Build the energy in these ways, then lie still with her for some quiet time, talking, or giggling. Slowly, build the energy once again. Then relax, build, relax. During the relaxing intervals, it might even seem as if you are both finished because both of you have so completely let go of tension, but then, *swooosh,* out of nowhere comes the next rush of energy excitement. The more relaxation you allow inside of your sexual loving sessions, the richer they are and the deeper they go. A *state of bliss* has a good chance of visiting you.

## Everyone deserves loving

No matter who you are, you deserve to be loved. Regardless of what you have achieved today or in your whole lifetime, you deserve loving. You do not need to earn it from your beloved. Your beloved does not need to earn it from you. Nor is loving owed to you, nor do you owe loving to your beloved.

The *Love* offered in lovemaking can only be given voluntarily. If your sex life is too negotiated, wagered, manipulated, or businesslike, it's possible you have acquired unhealthy ideas about sexuality along the way.

In soulful lovemaking, no one must perform sexually just because it's a birthday, or Saturday night, or even an anniversary, or because the kids are away, or you did it for me last time, or under any other condition, unless you want to— from your desire to make love.

It's okay to want to celebrate an anniversary or a birthday with sex, or to offer your sexual appreciation because of dishes well done, but then do it because you *want* to celebrate or appreciate, not because you are "supposed" to. *Relaaax.*

When both partners are relaxed, loving energy can flow more naturally. Controlling each other's sexual responses is one way to use your precious energy. However, understand this is only one use of the energy, one that pales in comparison to a flowing sexual practice that appreciates and welcomes the releasing and awakening of vital sexual energy. You always have a choice about how you spend your energies.

Rather than manipulating your partner into having sex with you; you can always choose to help each other to relax. Imagine all the many ways you know to promote well-being. You can also learn what is irresistible to your partner. You can attract her to you rather than dominate. People will naturally gravitate toward a sexual encounter they find satisfying to their tastes. Find out what your beloved's needs are. Does she need more cuddling, emotional connection, safety, slowness, what? Find ways to bless and love your beloved just the way she is. Equally important, allow yourself to be blessed and loved just the way you are.

*Everyone deserves to be loved, no matter what.*


## Breathing

If you are stressed out, breathe deeply into your body. Stretch your arms up over your shoulders into the sky and lean over to one side, then the other. Then, back and forth. This will expand your lung's flexibility, and increase the amount of air you are able to take in. On the exhale, make "*A-h-h-h-h-h*" sounds, because this will help release tension, too. Try it right now.

*In matters of relaxing, breathing deeply is your ticket to peace.*


## Tension–releasing sex

Tension-releasing sex means coming together to ignite orgasms as fast as you can so that you can "relax," or fall asleep, or relieve uncomfortable emotions without really experiencing them.

Tension-releasing sex may sound like a good idea, but again, if it's become a steady diet, it could be contributing to premature ejaculation, impotence, lack of female orgasm, and wimpy satisfaction for you both.

Another way to describe this is "blowing off" your energy. Your sexual energy is the same thing as your creative energy. For a man, it's the energy he uses to procreate. The conscious use for this energy when not making a baby is to *build* the energy, like money in the bank, so you can circulate it throughout your whole body for rejuvenation, well-being, and spiritual awakening. The conventional way to use this creative energy is to work it up to a sexual crescendo and then, pop it off: Boom! Afterward, he usually falls asleep. Most people call that coming, but ask the woman lying awake next to him, and she will tell you it's more like *going.*

After a man ejaculates, he needs to recover his energy. This is why he usually goes to sleep afterwards, losing his connection to her, and his interest falls asleep also.

The opportunity here is for a man to learn how to channel the energy that he previously spent "popping off" to retaining the energy, thereby, actually making himself more youthful, more potent, more orgasmic. More orgasmic? Didn't you just read there is an advantage in decreasing his "coming?" Yes. But, in case you haven't yet had the experience, guys, you may want to know that ejaculation is not eternally tied to orgasm. *You can have one without the other.* No kidding. Although there are some proven tricks you can learn to make this transition more easily, for a major percent of men, just knowing it is possible will give you what you need to experience it. In fact, many of you may have already experienced the shaking and shimmering that goes along with an orgasm, but haven't yet thought to call it "orgasm" until the emission came out. So, look for the fluid-less orgasms!

In the coming chapters, there will be more on how to accomplish this. In the meantime, guys, become more aware of how you hold your tension and the possible addiction you may have to blowing it off instead of savoring it, and learn how to raise and *build* sexual energy instead. Your health, well-being, relationship, and personal sexual satisfaction can benefit!

## Are we going to have sex tonight?

Many couples report that once they get into a sexual encounter, things go fine, but the tricky part is figuring out if *tonight* is the night. Is he going to be interested? Will he be too stressed out? How do I approach her *today* to get her interested in sex? He may want to start sex as soon as dinner is over and she couldn't *possibly* feel comfortable relaxing into sex knowing that *she'd* be the one stuck with caked on dishes to wake up to. She hopes he will still be awake enough to make love after the kids are put to bed.

You have two individual people with two schedules, two styles, and two desires, perhaps with two kids to juggle as well, . . . you get the picture. It is natural that a couple navigates (over a lifetime) through this relating process of getting to know one another for the outcome of flowing together. This type of curious exploration is preferred over the expense of energy that can be dissipated by sexual expectations, disappointment, and pressure to perform.

The question *"Are we going to have sex tonight?"* can generate so much tension for a couple that the idea of having sex becomes less and less attractive the longer the tension goes unresolved. A couple stuck in this dilemma may worry that something about their sex life is broken, when perhaps what they need to correct is the tension around it.

*Soulful* lovers go with the flow. They realize the profundity of simply "being" together authentically. They understand that the energy of the life force naturally wants to move in them, and that *Love* wants to express itself *through* them. Soulful beloveds let go of their "petty" ego concerns. When problems surface, they know they can talk their concerns through lovingly. They need not coerce or worry about a sexual encounter in any way, yet simply present themselves to one another genuinely and vulnerably, thereby allowing intimate, sexual energy the opportunity to move through them.

Whining, complaining, sulking, coercing, resenting, challenging, or lamenting are not attractive foreplay behaviors or enticing "come-ons." Neither are criticisms, ultimatums, threats, moodiness, or emotional extortion. *"Don't* you want to have sex tonight?" or *"When are* we going to have sex?" or "You know, it's been a whole week since we did it last!" With mating rituals such as these, no wonder people have tension about actually getting to the sex part.

Sexual encounters that stem from wearing one another down with interactions like these have more to do with "pity sex." *Pity sex* is the kind of sex where one partner "gives in" for the other partner, but without heart or personal passion, and sex is acted out probably with either reluctance or resentment on both partner's part. Sex like this is disconnected. It's robotic. And it is usually polarizing, meaning, it creates more emotional distance, rather than sex being a unifying experience, where it would bring lovers closer together. *Pity sex* lets off the sexual pressure for the moment, but unfortunately, sets up a pattern of how to get sex the next time. Even though there are much more enjoyable mating rituals, *pity sex* becomes an unfulfilling "habit," preferable to no sex at all.

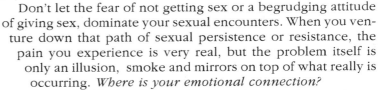

Don't let the fear of not getting sex or a begrudging attitude of giving sex, dominate your sexual encounters. When you venture down that path of sexual persistence or resistance, the pain you experience is very real, but the problem itself is only an illusion, smoke and mirrors on top of what really is occurring. *Where is your emotional connection?*

Soulful lovemaking is about making more love and generating an arena of comfort and safety, not about getting your partner in bed. Becoming beloveds is about intimate, honest, respectful, emotional, passionate, clear communication and relating. When lovers "pass" on hassling over whether sex is going to happen or not, and how often, lovers become beloveds who compassionately make love out of their union, respect, and joy.

How do you get to the compassionate part? Have a healthy respect for how your ego will mess with your soulful intentions, and acknowledge your own childish reactions and demands. Raise your consciousness in the areas where you *un*consciously deny love— reject appreciation, don't speak truthfully, resent authority, blame, abandon, go weak or dominate, rebel, react, or want to quit.

However, stay focused on your connection of loving. Find two dozen ways to return to your relational connection. Relax into this connection. Count on this connection. Cultivate a habit of relaxing with one another. A habit of flowing. Speaking truthfully. Honoring. And most of all, *relaaaxing*!

## Standing up

Men usually have more control over their ejaculatory responses when they are standing up rather than lying down trying to hold themselves up on their elbows. Standing is a great position for men to try if they are losing control of their ejaculate and strong erection before they want to. They will be more relaxed, less pulled by bodily distractions, and therefore more present to the energetic exchange with a beloved.

Try it out for yourself from this perspective, do your own research on its merits. For those who have found relief because of standing, it's been like a miracle. Your partner can be on a massage table, (*warm*) counter top, or you can also try some of the lovemaking furniture that has been coming onto the market.

## Women, control and the relaxation factor

By necessity, women have learned to control. This however, does not factor in well when it comes to a woman's pleasure. There are so many responsibilities that women handle, all day, every day.

Have you ever been a passenger with a woman driving a car during a traffic near-emergency, and out of nowhere, slam!— her arm instinctively goes into your gut as she tries to stop your 170-pound body from hitting the windshield as if you were her two year-old toddler?

You'll recover from the shock easily enough, but consider what just happened from her perspective. Her children may now all be adults, but her instinct to be protective lives on. A woman, on some level, is the mother of the whole world, and unconsciously, she has her attention on everything. While this will perhaps serve her well in running a business, and providing for her family, it will not benefit her in the bedroom. A woman needs to be relaxed, yielding control in order to let go. A women's orgasms will be elusive or nonexistent when her attention is spread all over the place and worrying about this or that, instead of on her own pleasure.

Ladies, *pleeease* relax. You deserve it. You really do.

Men, help your beloved relax by making an emotionally safe space for her to enter. How could you do that? Your care and respect for her is one sure way. Another way is in the environment. The woman has traditionally prepared the bedroom for lovemaking. She would make the bed, pull the drapes, light the candles, run the bath. Notice what she does to create this comfort and compliment her for her care in this area. *You might*, at times, create the environment in which you express your love with her. You will experience a very rewarding, unexplainable feeling when you do.

Also, become aware that your beloved might have a lot on her mind. Give her an opportunity to spill it all out, without you needing to fix it for her. Women need to talk in order to hear for themselves how they are feeling. You can help by simply listening, without fixing anything. She will get a lot of relief just in saying the "stuff." The trick is not getting hooked by the things she might say about you. Remember, she is just clearing *her* mind-stuff. It has nothing to do with you (even if it sounds like it's about you), until she says it does. At that point, it's not mind stuff anymore, it's now a request or a conversation of some kind that you will work out together. If you feel you need to respond to something, just ask her if she wants you to do anything about it, to fix it, or offer suggestions, etc. If she says "no," go back to listening. If you listen completely, she will empty her mind stuff more quickly. Sounds easier than it is but with practice it gets better.

Guys, she needs to know from you that, even if you don't agree with her, you still love her and would fight for her right to have her opinion and feelings. This action on your part communicates to her more than any "fixing" could. It heals like medicine.

Ladies, it comes down to your *willingness* to let go of control. If he sets up the room with candles, is it really so important to you that he lit the blue candles and you would have used the fragrant ones? You will always have your preferences, but do you *need* to get up right now and change something yourself, at the expense of your own pleasure and your partner's feelings? If you need a drink of water or want the room warmer, go ahead and ask that these *needs* be met. Make it part of your meditation to distinguish between asking for your needs to be met versus wanting your environment to meet your mental pictures of perfection.

Ladies, if he has offered this as an opportunity for you to clear your mind-stuff, do not engage him in a conversation, attempting to get him to agree with you, understand you, or to defend himself. *You* talk! Share your feelings from a non-blame perspective, for example: "I feel like I'm the only one who cares about buying the tickets at a discount . . . and that makes me feel alone, abandoned, angry." Speaking from the "I feel" is personally empowering for the speaker, and so much more healing for you both than, "*You* always spend our money carelessly." . . . "*You* this . . . " and, "*You* that . . . " On the other hand, incessant chatting may keep you from *feeling* your feelings. Let your beloved hold you in his arms as you begin to breathe fully and *be still*. At first you may become aware of all the things you feel you must say or burst. Thoughts will be going by your mind's eye at lightning speed, then you may begin to feel the feelings beneath the thoughts. Don't be surprised if you start to feel anger for instance, or sadness. Just feel the feeling, you don't have to do anything with it. Also feel the strong arms that are lovingly holding you in this moment. Don't push away the feelings, just allow them to be there. Appreciate yourself for doing such a good job and appreciate your partner for holding and loving you.

**Trust** is the most important quality to help a woman let go of her need to control and easily flow into pleasure. She must trust that she is emotionally and physically safe. When beloveds are aware of the importance of this trust and they work together to keep it present, the sexual loving and intimacy that flowers is truly fragrant.

## Touching the entire body

Everyone from the newest of newborn babies to the oldest of the elderly needs to be touched. Preferably, lovingly. Just because someone is being sexual is no excuse to avoid touching the non-erogenous zones. In fact, there are no non-erotic places if you awaken the senses of your entire body. Just ask someone who has lost feeling in their legs, and they'll tell you how much more feeling they have in the rest of their body. Fortunately, you do not have to lose feeling to become more sensitive and more erotic.

The disadvantage of limiting regular stimulation only to the nipples, genitalia and mouth, is that those parts can become over-charged, possibly resulting in less sensitivity to pleasure. This can lead to an unfulfilling, emotional neediness or hunger.

Integrate touching the body all over in non-sexual ways as well as in sexual ways when appropriate. Touch each other over your entire bodies to awaken sensitivity. There are too many situations in life that contribute to a *numbing* of your body, from the long sitting spells you do at your job or while driving, to the loud, incessant noises you're bombarded with. Your conscious attention is needed to counteract those effects. Touch. *Massage. Caress. Stroke. Touch. Awaken.*

## Pregnancy

Men, if your beloved is in her child-bearing years and you are interested in her ability to express herself sexually, spontaneously and naturally, then you have a very big role to play in this. When she is not expecting to become pregnant, she expends an enormous amount of attention, either consciously or unconsciously, on *not* getting pregnant.

Her attention will not be with you or with the love scene fully if she's not relaxed with her birth control (BC), or she's dealing with *your* frustration with the BC or any other related tension around it. This is a huge issue that women think and worry about, so you both need to give the subject the attention it deserves and be gentle with yourselves as you work it out between you.

What you can do to help her relax, men, and help assure her, is to be actively involved and supportive in the birth control process, never pressuring her to have unprotected sex or shaming her or begrudging her when it's time to prepare the birth control. Involving yourself doesn't mean being her boss in the matter, managing her, getting mad at her for not having it ready. It means you are partnering with her in the situation, getting/preparing the BC sometimes, caring how it is for her, being concerned if it's healthy for her body or not, these kinds of things.

Do everything possible to be a team together, rather than leaving the whole subject up to her. Include yourself in the process so that you both can have better lovemaking, but, especially get involved because you love her.

Ladies, if you have the BC handled but your guy keeps complaining that he's concerned about you getting pregnant or that he wants to be included, work with him on it. His ability to relax with you and be free (to perform well) will depend on trusting the BC process, and if he doesn't know what's going on, on some level, he'll continue to be worried about it. He's letting you know he wants to understand and participate, so please consider his feelings and include him. It really does affect both of you and the soulfulness your connection.

This can be a sensitive subject, so be very gentle with yourselves.

## Holding the Jewels

There are few things more relaxing to a man than having his Jewels (*testicles*) held. Some men already know this and hold their own as often as they can, maybe while he is just lying around the house. Many men have never thought to ask their partners to do this for them, and more still haven't yet had the pleasure at all. A man's Jewels are the center of his energetic being. When the Jewels are held, he feels safe and relaxed. A man in *this* condition is more likely to enjoy life and soulful intimacy.

The male partner can lie down on his back with his legs gently spread, while his partner sits between his legs or in any position where she is comfortable and has easy access to his Jewels. With one hand she will cup both Jewels and with the other hand, she covers them. Then she will pull them toward her just a little, not enough to hurt, just enough so that he knows she's holding him. In unison, begin breathing fully and letting go. Hold this posture for five minutes to twenty minutes, you'll know how long. Holding his Jewels lovingly, without movement, is what is healing in this situation.

The giver's eyes are best left open and directed softly, attentively toward the one receiving. For ninety-nine percent of men, this exercise will make them feel extremely safe and peacefully calm.

His eyes may be open or closed. For the rare percentage of men who may get agitated by this posture, more will be offered in Chapter seven, but in the meantime, hold him for just one minute or for whatever he can stand and then move on to something else. Come back to this periodically during your lovemaking for short one-minute or less sessions.

Before you begin Jewel holding, tell him that he doesn't have to do anything, he can just lie back. Having permission to not return the favor right away settles his mind, particularly if he is a man who has trained himself to "spring" into action and activate pressure to perform whenever "it" gets touched.

You can also imagine sending your love into his Jewels through your hands.

## Cradling the Yoni

To help a woman to relax, apply pressure with the palm of your hand to her exterior Yoni area. Offer your hand to her in such a way that your palm is firmly covering her Yoni opening and your fingers cover her pubic bone. *Or,* your palm is on the pubic bone and your fingers are covering her Yoni opening. The pressure should be firm and assuring without being tight or confining. Women, please assure your partner when he has the right pressure.

Once in position, his hand should not move or go toward stimulation. You can both go into your full breathing pattern, allowing sounds to emerge on the exhale. Men, you can imagine that your *caring* for this woman is emanating from your hand into her body through her yoni.

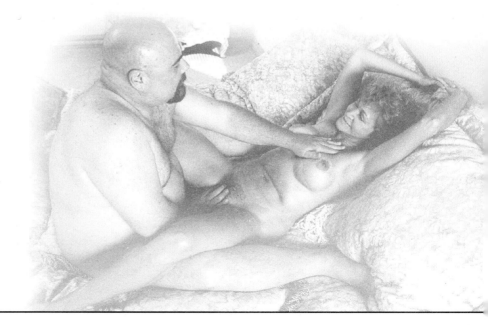

You can stay in this position for as little as five minutes or as long as an hour— you decide— but ten minutes fairly frequently is a wonderful gift to the woman in your life. At some point after complete stillness, you may begin to rock her so slowly with your palm so that you can barely see the movement, holding firmly. Sometimes she will actually purr when you hold her like this. Only you can know what it feels like to *you* when you make your beloved *purrrr.*

Women, you may already be doing the solo version of this or may want to try it. You can sit on your own hand placed underneath you and begin to rock very slowly and gently back and forth. Notice the pressure and how it makes you feel. For many women this is completely grounding.

## It's a sacred honor to love and serve

A man loves to *serve* (propelled to protect, contribute to, and make her happy) the woman in his life. Women love to *love* (her mate, her children, all those close to her, and all those she hears about, but most of all, she just loves to love). Both men and women are *completed* spiritually, emotionally, and physically, when they are allowed to express their innate qualities. The other side to the equation is the *exchange* of energy. The serving and loving are most rewarding to the couple if the other partner *receives*. In fact, *not* receiving the love offered from a mate generates another web of dissatisfaction.

Beloveds come to understand this miracle of the masculine–feminine union, and realize that if either the expression or the receiving of this exchange of energy is not happening, then *somewhere* the energy is being blocked. It must be opened, healed, and released. We do this by having compassion for ourselves and for our beloved partner for the difficulty it seems to take for us to shine outwardly our most glorious selves. Sometimes we are simply so wounded, that we actually feel unsafe to let in someone's love or care for us— no matter how much we need it or even *demand* it.

Beloveds also realize that if they or their partner are not expressing the love or caring service they expect, it is not that they are purposefully holding something back, it's simply an unconscious *reaction* to be in the safest place they know. However, beloveds don't stop there and let each other live in the pain from not knowing true love. As a team, beloveds venture forward toward healing— letting their joint compassion melt the emotional armor that would either prevent giving love or receiving love. Clearly, both aspects are required for relationship to be satisfying.

When couples realize that each person has love to give (and is actually *dying* to give it), but if it is not flowing, then they know there is something to heal. Both people are empowered by *unitedly* working it out. Blaming, shaming and nagging our partner to give us the love we want does not work. Understand that it is our sacred honor to help one another clear the way for love to express through us in all ways— emotionally, sexually, and spiritually. Surrendering to this sacred honor may not always be easy; however, *by* surrendering, we relax very deeply inside of ourselves. We relax just by realizing that we no longer need to fight to get our needs met— we just need to open up and help one another heal.

FOURTH DOORWAY

# MAKING
# MORE LOVE

*Sustaining the environment to flow
and grow through
Love's cycles and rhythms*

## Love is a renewable resource

Creating *more love* does not mean engaging in more sex (*although it could*). It means experiencing more love in general with everyone you come in contact with, displaying qualities like caring, thoughtfulness, tenderness, joy, and a sense of community. It has to do with knowing that experiencing love in your life is not an accident of fate.

In a long-term love relationship, your relating is always growing, changing, ebbing and flowing. Love, like nature, has her cycles and rhythms. Sometimes, though, it may seem that the ebbing slows to a standstill, as if it will never come out of Winter and flow into Spring again. It's times like these that challenge lovers to question if love can endure and flourish again, or if it really exists at all. Partners striving to become beloveds reflect a basic belief in the existence of *Love* — even when it has lapsed into dormancy. They assume that love can be rekindled where it has been forgotten, has retreated into apathy, or currently lacks *erotic* passion.

Sometimes *Love's* Winter may last longer than necessary because the couple does not have the relating skills to catapult themselves forward and get out of their slump. The skills a successful couple needs to master include: how to make more *Love*; engaging in real communication; and utilizing sexual energy for healing purposes, increasing intimacy and partnership, and pleasure.

A life full of love is yours whenever you are *being* loving to others and to yourself in this very moment, and when you actively receive another's loving toward you. To experience relationship or an entire life devoid of love occurs when we aren't actively being or receiving loving right now, in this moment. *Love* is one of our most renewable resources. It is available right now if you will open to it. If you send out caring thoughts and actions, you will feel love in your life, perhaps where there was none. And the receiving is just as important as the giving, both for you and your giver.

This section is an invitation to make more conscious *Love* wherever you are able to within your lifestyle. A foundation like this will support the ebb and flow of cycles in your sexual relationship, and will nurture respect and trust between you.

## See the Divine in your beloved

To bring out the best in your beloved, see the best in her! See your beloved as centered, beautiful, friendly, loving, accepting, wise, confident, joyful, sensual, etc. You may be amazed at who you find standing right in front of you. When you gaze into her eyes, *look* for the Divine soul who lives there. *Know* it is there and then *look* for it, bless it, and be bathed by it.

The one you love is more than his job or bank account, more than his *IQ* or list of accomplishments. He is a spiritual being unfolding into who he is, *and,* so are you. Accept the divinity in both your partner and yourself. "I know you're *in* there," you might say to yourself about your beloved when you are thinking of him or whenever you are looking into his eyes. "I *know* you're in there."

A wonderful way to practice seeing the Divine Presence in your beloved is while taking turns giving and receiving a foot bath massage. There is something very profound about sitting in a chair while someone you love is on his knees, bathing and massaging your feet. When you allow the practice of loving to transport you into this sacred territory beyond ordinary consciousness and distractions, you can begin to accept that you are more than your physical body, more than your flaws, your age, or your position in life. If your eyes are open, soft, and available, this meditation helps you accept your spiritual essence. As you begin to experi-

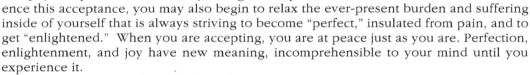

ence this acceptance, you may also begin to relax the ever-present burden and suffering inside of yourself that is always striving to become "perfect," insulated from pain, and to get "enlightened." When you are accepting, you are at peace just as you are. Perfection, enlightenment, and joy have new meaning, incomprehensible to your mind until you experience it.

As your eyes meet, imagine that what you are communicating is: *The spirit of love in me, greets the spirit of love in you.* Greet and be greeted! When the "giver's" eyes are open to the beloved he is massaging, then he is more able to enter into a deep sense of sacred service to the *Love* presence inside you both.

## What if I can't see the Divine

What if you look over at your dear beloved partner and you see only an opponent or a stranger? There is still hope. First, it would be helpful to relax your mind and your belly, and take some full, connected breaths. Get in touch with your own heart space. This may take a few minutes or longer depending on how stressed out you are. Then try looking for the divine in your partner again. Repeat the breathing process when you need to.

Sometimes your partner may act out in a way that is just too darn challenging for you, and it's hard to even imagine there is anything inside him other than a brat. He may be angry, defensive, depressed or complaining— a lot. It's important to understand that the reactions are not a personal rejection of you, necessarily. Those feelings or behaviors are an expression of something *he* is dealing with, which may involve you or not, but you did not *cause* the reaction.

Let's say your partner is putting on a lot of weight and you feel critical of it ("How could she do this to me?"). You must try not to take it personally. Most likely, an unconscious fear has surfaced for your partner and the extra weight is in place to act as a form of protection. Your criticism will just add more fear, but your compassion and openness will help your partner feel safe as she explores these feelings.

Other assistance may be needed at times, also. No one is expected to be a trained therapist to her beloved; however, there is no replacement for a compassionate friend. Hold your beloved and rock her gently. Feelings may be expressed, so be available to listen. You could say, "Tell me everything, I'll listen with my heart. I won't judge your feelings. Whatever you say is okay with me." You won't be trying to fix it, or give advice, simply listen. *Only listen.* No kidding— listening, is like medicine for a wounded heart, and food for the soul.

Your conscious listening will help you access your Heart essence and see the Divine Presence in your beloved, as well as her humanity. The experience of a person's interior world is shaped by her perspectives. If a wife allows the same negative thought to dominate her mind without re-examination such as "My husband is such a wimp, he never stands up for himself," she'll likely see every thing he is and will become through that little negative-thinking portal. She is having a temporary case of amnesia, forgetting that the reason she fell in love and married him in the first place was because of his gentleness and peaceful way. She didn't call it wimpy then. Why should she now? She can renew her appreciation for his qualities. She may also wish to ask herself if there is anything "wimpy" inside herself that she fears.

Working out inharmonious struggles in life will be easier to handle if you are in touch with what you love about one another.

## From your heart

The sweetest and dearest gift you can give your beloved is love from your heart. You can send the love straight from yours to his. But how do you do it? Sending love to your partner expresses itself as caring, gentleness, warmth, a radiating vibration of feeling and healing energy.

A great delivery system for this is to say, *meaningfully*, "I love you." Another way is to send this message directly to your beloved through your touch. Place your hands somewhere on your beloved's body, wherever he needs it or wherever you can reach. Imagine a flow of caring energy traveling up from your heart to your arms, into your hands and then into your beloved. Do this for a few minutes, or for much longer.

You may actually feel this flow of energy, visually seeing it traveling, or you can imagine it moving. Sometimes, at first, you might feel like you're making it all up. Try it anyway. Trust when your partner tells you what she has felt. Don't be discouraged. Don't give up. Energy wants to move— you are simply directing it.

Be conscious. Become aware of your heart energy waking up and moving through your body to your beloved's. If you are the recipient, be open to receiving the gift. It *is* a gift and you deserve it.

## Giving and receiving

Lovemaking continues to deepen tremendously when both partners are able to be givers *and* receivers. However, people have usually gravitated toward one role or the other. Exploring the role you are less comfortable with is a wonderful relationship skill to develop. Do this to balance and support great lovemaking.

This doesn't mean having the more passive partner become more aggressive or vice versa. The more active partner must become more open, spacious, more available. This means relaxing and allowing an opportunity for the beloved to come toward you. This is vital because, if both beloveds are in active, initiating, *doing* modes, *no one* is receiving.

By becoming more assertive, the usually more passive partner allows the usually more active partner to participate as an active receiver instead. Become very sensitive to what gets altered in your energies. These energies may be very subtle, but extremely profound. This is a rich area for personal and spiritual breakthroughs and insight. You will always gain personal insight when you explore undeveloped aspects of yourself.

## Love your body

Make a special effort to love your body. Your body needs attention and love, especially from *you*.

Perhaps it's a strange point to make, *love your body*, but for so many people, their body is simply accepted as a dense mass of flesh that never meets their standards of perfection and taste. The media knows how to benefit from this lack of self love by barraging us with a negativity about the body and then offering various, tempting ways to correct these intolerable "imperfections." With this ongoing body-bashing brainwashing, it is vital to cultivate an attitude of appreciation for all the body is and can do. Love your body.

The body is magnificent. It truly is, and *your* body is no exception. You may regret that you don't have a cover girl's beauty, or a body builder's muscles, but please do not judge yourself unworthy of love for these reasons.

Every person deserves love and every person is capable of loving no matter how they look. *Everyone* is lovable.

Even though TV commercials urge you to buy their products so that you can be beautiful "enough," smell fresh and dress "right," be assured that your self-worth is inside of you, not outside of you. Be the first in line to love yourself.

Find a way to fall in love with your own body, warts and all. If you have always hated your big nose for instance, think of some reasons to like a big nose: It makes it easier to wear glasses, as an example. Have fun looking for your assets and notice how much more love there is available to you when you pay positive attention to that particular body part. This may take some time and perhaps a little humor, but more importantly, it will take your willingness and your creativity.

Everybody has something they feel insecure about or would like to change. Everybody! Even the famous, the beautiful, and the rich. Putting yourself down and denying yourself love because you do not look the way you "should" is a harmful habit that has nothing to do with the truth. Break this habit and replace it with one that inspires you: For instance, each time you look in the mirror while combing your hair or brushing your teeth, remember that you are impeccable just the way you are. Smile at yourself in the mirror. You can be as beautiful or handsome on the outside as you allow yourself to be on the inside. Any changes that occur will come from your love of yourself rather than from your rejection.

Help yourself love your body by dancing it, stretching it, and feeding it healthy food. And by playing, breathing fully, wearing comfortable clothes, drinking plenty of water, being touched, massaged, and making love with someone you feel comfortable with, and who loves you. Let your beloved's love in.

## Love the body of your beloved

Your beloved needs to be secure that you love her body in order to feel trusting and to be an expressive lover with you. When your partner hears you say negative comments or senses unkind, unsaid remarks that you are *thinking*, she may shut down to you, or worse, she may even shut down to herself.

Fall in love with your partner's body. Open your heart and become aware of how much love you feel for this person, which includes appreciating her body. Tell your partner often how much you love her body. Express your gratitude for how your partner's body gives you pleasure or nurturing.

If your partner denigrates his own body, you can help counteract this bad habit by modeling appreciation. If you don't particularly like one of your partner's physical attributes, you may need to go through a similar process of learning to appreciate it in a new way also. If your partner complains about his thinning hair, for instance, or worrying about his attractiveness, you can inform him fairly often, how manly he is to you or how sexy he is. You may come to a place where it is *true* for you to say that balding *on him* is great because you love him so much. "Darling, I don't usually go for baldness, but for you, I'm *definitely* making an exception. You're gorgeous to me! And besides, maybe if you had a whole head of hair you would have been so busy grooming it, you wouldn't have had the time to develop that good nature. And it's my favorite quality of yours."

*Look* for and find the value in often-criticized attributes.

**A *word of caution here*.** It's ideal to appreciate more than just one or two isolated body parts over and over again. For instance, when a man continually says he loves his partner's breasts and her Yoni and that's all that he mentions, a woman may begin to wonder if he likes the rest of her. He may also adore the rest of her body and appreciate her mind, but unless he voices his feelings, she must guess. And she is likely to guess that he only likes her sexual parts because that's all he's "talking" about. If you like the small of her back, tell her. If you like the lines of her shoulders as they flow down from her sweet neck, let her know.

If your beloved's arms always make you feel nurtured, say so. If touching the smooth skin of your beloved makes you feel that the world still has some softness in it, share that lovely sentiment. Your partner will not receive the *full* benefit of your appreciation unless you express it. Not everyone is psychic, but even if your partner is, it's always good to hear in words that you are special, that you make someone feel good, and that you are cared about.

Touch your beloved with a sacred touch. Massage him. Massage her. Whisper sweet somethings. Celebrate what this wonderful body can do. Explore these possibilities together. A well-loved body is more able to explore the mysteries of sexual loving.

## Making a love nest

Look around the room where you usually make love. Does this atmosphere inspire the soulful lovemaking you're longing for? Look around. *Feeel* the space.

Are there a week's worth of clothes strewn everywhere, so that you can barely find a place to lie down? Or, is this room so orderly and dignified that you'd have to be wearing white gloves just to think about making love here?

Your lovemaking room should be the most comfortable room possible. This is a room in which you can be yourself, let yourself be wild and totally *let go*. When you walk into this kind of room, you feel you've entered a very special place, one where your love is shared and expressed. If you have that fundamental feeling, the following will just be nice props to consider.

What colors do you have in your lovemaking room? Did *you* choose them? Are they colors you *both* like? Color is important to your moods and to your sense of well-being. You can redo your color scheme to match your love *style*.

Do the windows have privacy shades so you can feel free to "express" without worrying about onlookers?

Do you have five to ten candles in your *love nest* room ready to light at any moment, and three more for the bathroom? Have you considered lighting the whole house with candles? There are not many things more calming or more inviting than having your home environment bathed by candle light. Some pink or blue painted-glass, seven-day pillar candles can give the room a warm glow without being too bright.

Do you have ten or so pillows around the room in varying shapes, sizes, and firmness? These are cushy friends that help your body get into positions you couldn't possibly manage without them. And they help you both to be comfortable.

What about those darn phones? Are you able to hear the phone ring from the other room if you need to? If so, can you turn off the ringer on the bedroom phone? When a call comes, you can still decide if you want to answer it, but it won't be so intrusively demanding. Sometimes you'll want to turn off all the phones for privacy; however, for everyday living, why not avoid the shock of the ringer or the automatic reflex to pick up the bedside phone, by turning off the ringer in your love room?

Do you have, on both sides of the bed (and in various places around the house), a supply of massage oil, lubricant and essential oils? Why go looking for it when you need it? Have it easily accessible. Are there plenty of towels within reach, as well as washcloths that can be warmed up when you need them?

Do you *both* love your bed? How about the blankets? The sheets? Are they comfortable, beautiful and suitable for your needs? These things may be more important to the quality of your lovemaking than you realize. Treat yourself to what works for you both.

Are there several throw blankets nearby? Soft cotton or silk feels very nice against bare skin. Use these to put around exposed legs or shoulders when the temperature is nippy, and regular blankets don't cover you both when you're each spreading out at different ends of the bed.

## Flower scents

Make floral arrangements that include scents that will fill your home and your love space with *legal* mood-altering substances.

Gardenia    Roses    Tuberose    Freesia    Star Lilies    Star Jasmine

If your local florist does not carry them, request a special order. You'll be happy you did.

## Sacred space

Perhaps you would like to have a room just for lovemaking, a sacred space separate from your sleeping room, an attic room with a view that's remodeled just for this purpose, for instance. *Sacred space* can certainly be created anywhere you turn your attention, and is highly recommended for your bedroom also.

Sacred space is a conscious environment arranged soulfully to inspire you, but it's purpose is also to provide a safe space for you to explore— emotionally, physically, and spiritually. This is a ritual space that you can both step into and know that you will love and honor one another. A space where your body is free to express totally, your spiritual ideals are embraced and practiced. Your emotional, physical and sexual secrets will go no further than the ritual walls.

Do you have a special place in this room that is like a shrine to your love? Ideally, this should be a place that both of you contribute to, where you can display inspiring momentos of your life together. Tokens from a past experience or a shared desire for the future can be wonderful acknowledgments and declarations of who you are as a couple.

For instance, gather tokens that represent plans for children, a Fortune 500 business, growing old as best friends, and display them on your *love altar*.

Honor the history of your relationship, with stubs from your first theater date, or a remembrance of your twenty-fifth anniversary celebration. You may also want to represent tough times you've come through together. These are all experiences that have woven the fabric of your relationship "quilt."

Be creative. Display flowers and plants, jewelry, crystals, books and poems, artwork, chimes, incense, perhaps a gently bubbling water fountain. Include anything significant to you and your beloved, that expresses what you are committing to as a couple today.

Throw the television away, or at least cover it with a colorful silk scarf, and never turn it on again except for romantic videos. Bad news and sitcoms can wait till tomorrow on the family room TV. Instead, have a sound system available to match your mood with music— soft and relaxing, to vibrant or erotic.

When you live in a *sacred space*, your experience of what you do there changes. You are inspired to be more aware, a little more grateful and a little less inclined toward taking things for granted.

## Music

Music is such a powerful medium that it can put you in the mood (or rip you from a mood) and take you back to the past with a single beat.

To bring the soulfulness of music into your sacred space, the radio is okay in a pinch, but not the ideal because of those darn commercials. Put your favorite CDs on repeat and the cassettes on auto loop.

You can select music to invoke a particular feeling tone into your loving session, tune it up or tone it down, all by the rhythm of the music. Play with it. Notice what different songs, instruments, and beats make you feel like doing. Where do you *feel* the drum beat vibrate in your body? Where do you *feel* the tinkle of piano keys in your body? Where do you *feel* the lilting strings of an orchestra in your body? In your heart? In your loins? Your gut? Or, perhaps in your imagination? *Where?*

Listen for songs on the radio that are uplifting and for those that speak about love in an emotionally healthy, inspiring way. Collect them for a music library and add to it often. Surprise each other with a song or CD when you discover a good one, and present it in your own original way— put it on for your beloved while you massage her feet, or bathe him. Lip-sync it, dance to it . . . whatever gives you both pleasure.

These are some favorite albums and singles for touching the heart, awakening sensuality, celebration, meditation, movement, and ritual.

Music is healing. It's sensual. Expose your senses to music and take flight.

## ALBUMS / CDs

| | |
|---|---|
| Songs for the Inner Child | Shaina Noll |
| Bread for the Journey | Shaina Noll |
| The Eyes of God | Scott Kalechstein & Friends |
| Shamanic Dream | Anugama |
| Tantra | Anugama |
| Atlantis Angelis | Patrick Bernhardt |
| Solaris Universalis | Patrick Bernhardt |
| Don Juan DeMarco | The Movie Soundtrack |
| Phenomenon | The Movie Soundtrack |
| Moon Dance | Van Morrison |
| House of Love | Amy Grant |
| I Ain't Moving | Des'ree |
| Stronger than Pride | Sade |
| Earth Tribe Rhythms | Brent Lewis Productions |
| Enigma | Enigma |
| Journey into Love | Sophia |
| The Eternal Om | Slap |
| Mender of Hearts | Singh Kaur & Kim Roberton |
| Chronicles | Steve Winwood |
| Of Thee I Sing | Sophia |
| Totem | Gabrielle Roth & The Mirrors |
| Initiation | Gabrielle Roth & The Mirrors |
| Ritual | Gabrielle Roth & The Mirrors |
| Bones | Gabrielle Roth & The Mirrors |
| Body and Soul | Rick Braun |
| Nadabrahma / Nataraj | Osho Meditation |

## SINGLES

| | |
|---|---|
| The Power Of Love | Jennifer Rush |
| Love Is A Wonderful Thing | Michael Bolton |
| In Your Eyes | Peter Gabriel |
| You Got It | Bonnie Raitt |
| Willow | Joan Armatrading |
| Love And Affection | Joan Armatrading |
| Have You Ever Really Loved A Woman | Bryan Adams |
| Return To Innocence | Enigma |
| Come Unglued (From The Tube) | Sophia |
| Let The Spirit | Sophia |
| Takes My Breath Away | Tuck And Patti |

## Children:  A child's story

Do your children have a healthy attitude of curiosity and reverence toward sex? Are they comfortable talking to you about all aspects of sexual expression, their personal timing, pregnancy, sexually-transmitted diseases, and just discussing "things?" Few kids are, just as we were ill-prepared for our sexual journey. All parents ask themselves what their part should be in teaching their kids about sex, and how to prepare them. Some parents do what they imagine their role is, and the remainder just hope that life handles it. It's not easy, but it could be easier.

Talking appropriately to your kids during all stages of their life about all aspects of life is no doubt important, and just like everything else, what you model with your own behavior speaks even louder than your words.

Your kids have keen eyes and ears when it comes to how mom and dad treat each other. Will they have modeled for them the affection of their parents. Will they witness the respect, loving, and truthfulness you share with each other? Do they see you work out disagreements? Hug and be cuddly with each other? Kisses in public? Do they hear your love sounds behind closed doors?

One couple just setting out on a conscious loving path together decided it was important to include their little ones in the *make more love* experiment. Their children were between three and seven at the time, and not each old enough for *detailed* human sexuality discourses, so the parents revealed only what they thought was age-appropriate. And then they added, "Mommy and daddy go in our bedroom to *make more love*, and when we come out, there will be more love for you, too."

Kids, being the emotional barometers that they are, will actively demonstrate any hostility their parents are feeling toward each other, even if the parents believe they have swept it under the rug or have worked it out themselves. The kids will get cranky or unruly. Since *this* couple's children had learned that their parents were responsible for their own emotional housekeeping, instead of playing out the adults negativity, the kids often said, "Mommy and daddy, you guys go in your room and be nice to each other and *make more love* grow." Because the parents comply, the whole family is living together *as happily ever after as they can.*

Children don't have to know all the physical mechanics of sex right away; that will come in time. What they need is a healthy context for sex and for the sounds that you make. If sex isn't bad, why have parents traditionally hidden it from their kids? Or, as my mother used to tell me when I was a teenager, "sex is for married people to share the love that God meant them to experience." But the fact that sex was happening in the house was still hidden, and that was, unfortunately, communicated louder than the statement about married people and God.

As long as this powerful energy is kept secret from children (even talking about it), sadly, our kids will learn *that's* how they should be dealing with it, too: *in secret.* But their teenage pregnancies, compromised futures and AIDS-related deaths will be impossible to conceal. The consequences of their sexual activity will continue to be our heartaches, too. The message conveyed by our whole society that *mum's-the-word* is emphatically *outdated*, unhealthy, and a catastrophe that can be thwarted by consciousness and truthful communication.

Whatever works for you, please find a way to educate your children about healthy, sexual love more consciously than you were likely taught. The things you are practicing and learning from this book may enable you to talk more openly to your children and be less embarrassed yourselves because you are feeling more comfortable. Remember that sex is a very natural human act, but it is our consciousness regarding the sexual loving that makes us experience it as natural rather than something to hide or of which to be ashamed.

## Gifts

The most delicious gift you can offer your beloved is the complete presence of your being— your willing heart open to life and loving, and undivided attention . . . in *this* very moment. This is a gift worthy of sending, offering and delivering over and over again, day or night.

Although I don't advise giving gifts as a substitute for *you* or your participation, I do recommend giving gifts, from large and small, to exotic and simple, that communicate from your hearts the love that's between you.

There is an art to giving and receiving gifts, just as there is to making love. It is a sacred exchange of energy. When choosing the gift, always have your beloved in mind. Be thoughtful, heartfelt, timely, affordable (and sometimes not), respectful, not always practical, sometimes silly, usually romantic, and rarely predictable. Stay on the lookout for hints about what kinds of things he would enjoy having, doing, or becoming and then gifting accordingly.

The other side of gift-giving is receiving. Receiving can be developed into an art form. Energetically, you are receiving the gift as much for the giver as you are for yourself, so let your beloved *really* feel that you've accepted not only the gift, but also the intention behind it.

Sometimes a gift seems to come out of nowhere, or frankly, it doesn't seem to make much sense to you. If you don't know how to appreciate it . . . how about asking your beloved, respectfully, to tell you the story of how he came to think about this gift and what prompted the decision to bestow it. You may then feel the specialness of the gift and feel more included in the gifting process.

This practice of asking to hear the story of the gift can be very helpful in situations when people receive presents they don't prefer or don't understand. And, it can be a healing experience for both giver and receiver in cases where either has felt wounded in the past by attempts at gifting. For instance, a man may have a great idea for a gift, but by the time he actually gives it, he's already thinking of something else and so his presentation of the gift is distracted. She may respond to the distraction and feel like he doesn't care. He in turn, may feel wounded as if she doesn't appreciate him.

Through talking about the ritual of gift-giving, you can teach each other about your separate, personal histories regarding it. Share with one another the expectations you have about gift–giving and receiving— holiday presents, previous gift disappointments, and your gifting preferences.

When you are giving something of your heart, share your feelings, thoughts and hopes behind this gift. The gift itself is just part of the ritual. Why did *you* pick it? Share that part, too. Putting yourself into the gifting makes it very personal.

Gifts come in many forms. Washing the car can be a gift. So can a pearl necklace. A back rub. A remodeled kitchen. A wink. Triple-decker sandwiches at half time. Compliments.

Acknowledging gifts can also take many forms:

"I love that you understand me so well that you knew to . . ."

"When you gift me like this, it encourages me to love myself unconditionally."

"I feel so cared about that you have . . ."

"I feel *s-o-o-o* beautiful when you say . . ."

"My body melts when you touch me like . . ."

"Bless your heart for . . ."

"I am the luckiest man/woman in the world that you . . ."

"Thank you for loving me so dearly . . . thoughtfully . . . sweetly . . . adoringly . . . deeply . . . sensually . . . slowly . . . passionately . . . unconditionally . . . compassionately ..."

"Thank you!"

## Compliments

Love grows by watering and tending the garden often. When you pay attention to your beloved, when you *notice* and compliment how she looks, acts or is, you are tending and watering your relationship. You can have a little one-plant tomato garden or you can grow a garden the size of an extravagant plantation, depending on the abundance of your attention and your appreciation. Complimenting is a natural outcome of appreciating your beloved and not taking her for granted.

Beloveds understand the relevancy of exchanging appreciation for one another. There is no advantage to the relationship when someone expresses themselves as "unworthy" and "irrelevant." When a compliment is coming your way, let it in. Believe it. Be energized by it. Let the compliment connect with your deepest needs to be seen, appreciated and loved. Don't slough it off. When you rebuff a compliment and don't take it in, you're saying "no thank you" to a vital energy. You won't get to *f-e-e-l* it, and the compliment giver won't really get to *g-i-v-e* it. The energy exchange of Love doesn't happen when a compliment lands in the sand trap. You *deserve* love. Everyone does. Practice accepting love in the form of compliments. Accepting compliments is a skill which everyone can master, and one that contributes to your relationship in a very meaningful way.

## Acknowledgments

When you appreciate some aspect of your beloved, acknowledge to yourself what benefit you will receive. Notice how it makes you feel to move your energy through appreciation rather than suppressing your appreciation or putting your attention on complaints.

Compliments can be received deeply enough in the psyche to bypass the mental dynamic in place that helps us deny positive feedback. The idea is, if the compliment is more about you as the speaker (the compliment giver) and *your* experience of her beauty, then how could she argue with your experience. Therefore, the compliment has more of a chance to make it through the "denial guard gate."

For example, when you offer: "honey, your eyes are so beautiful." This is a perfectly wonderful compliment, but to get past the "denial guard gate," accompany the compliment with: "When you kept your eyes open to me tonight while we were making love, I felt so loved by you, and I felt truly worthy. I love your love." You include your feelings and how her beauty enhances you.

An acknowledgment is letting someone know how you are affected by them, communicating what you are learning, feeling, growing, or experiencing in the relationship. You become more of a participant when you put a little of yourself into your acknowledgments.

## Gratefulness

And what are you grateful for today?* This is a wonderful question to get into the routine of asking each other at night before you fall asleep. Take turns asking this question, giving just one example each, then going back and forth ten to fifteen times.

In this hectic, pressure-cooker world, if we didn't get an "A" on the exam, or the boss didn't accept the proposal, and we didn't have simultaneous orgasms, we think it was a bad day. Yes, those things surely may have happened, *a-n-d . . . What do you have to be grateful for today?*

Close your eyes and recall some of the events of the day from the time you got up this morning. Look for moments that touched your heart, or made you smile, lifted your spirits, gave you hope, taught you something, reminded you of a friend, relieved your conscience, piqued your curiosity, made you happy, saved you time, rekindled an old friendship. They could be big things, little things, profound or simple things. Sometimes you will even notice a benefit from the example that originally made it seem like a bad day.

When your partner asks the question, "And what do you have to be grateful for today?" answer with just one example of gratitude, and go back and forth until you get on

---

* Inspired by the work of Jeru

a roll. If any examples relate to your partner, say those also. You can end the exercise by saying what you're grateful for about your beloved if you haven't already. You will sleep well.

The garden of your relationship grows in the direction of your attention: You will grow *weeds* or *flowers* depending on where you place your attention— on the negative or the positive. Develop a skill of actively looking for the positive in any situation and becoming appreciative for even the smallest of miracles and gestures.

## Is there really a beginning, middle and an end?

In a traditional lovemaking scenario, there is the foreplay, intercourse, and "coming"— beginning, middle, and end. Also, intercourse is the main-course. In *making more love*, lovemaking is ongoing, not ever ending, not really ever beginning. Intercourse is just one of the activities that you share and probably not every time you make love. *Love* becomes your main-course— every act of touch, every thought, glance, or sensual act becomes the *main* way to share that love.

With this lovemaking concept, instead of intercourse being your main sexual activity, it becomes one from a whole menu of possibilities with which you experiment. Now, the intercourse that you enjoy at a lunch break becomes the foreplay for the kissing that you enjoy later on, which acts as the foreplay for an intimate walk in the park this evening,

inspires a hot race to the car, which leads to the tackle on the grass and the rolling and fondling before the drive home, which leads to the . . .

With romance such as this, foreplay takes on a whole new definition. *Everything is foreplay and it is ongoing.* There must only be an end to a lovemaking session when you decide his ejaculation is the end to it. Otherwise, if he is able to orgasm without releasing the emissions, he can stay around (awake, and still interested) longer to share as much loving as you both would like. Then, each conversation, stimulation, kiss or touch becomes the foreplay for the next word, stimulation, kiss, or touch. Loving becomes a continuous flowing circle rather than start. Go. Stop.

Always a beginning, all expressions of care, thoughtfulness, and loving lead to more loving. Not necessarily hard-on-active passion twenty four hours a day, although that may happen at times also, but a connected feeling of intimacy without the *start, go, stop.*

People don't often recognize how much of their energy goes into the chase and recovery of the "start-stop-start" routine until they experience the benefits that come with *making more love* all the time instead.

## Another way to recognize when sex is complete

Some couples might be concerned they wouldn't know how to *end* sex if he doesn't ejaculate in the old way which would ordinarily conclude it. When you *flow* with the sexual energies, because there is not a predetermined ending, you can close the lovemaking session for any reason that is true and appropriate for you. How do you know when your walk is finished or that dinner is complete? How do you know when you are done reading for the evening?

When you are relating to each other in a continuous flow, it's bordering on the mystical. The mystical energies move you to dance with one other, and then, when the energies have dissipated, you simply feel ordinary again, and it's time to go to the bathroom, the fridge or to sleep. You will feel the change, *you won't be doing* anything to stop it, the mystic energies will simply *do* you. You will feel complete with moving your energy in this way and then you'll feel attracted to channel your energy in another way like work, play, or sustenance.

In a scenario like this, you can gently separate physically while remaining emotionally connected to one another, rather than surrendering your keenly won intimacy in the "stop" mode of the "start-go-stop" custom. *Making more love* in all ways, will satisfy you sexually, emotionally, and spiritually.

FIFTH DOORWAY

# COMMUNICATION

*Mastering communication*
*(with self and others)*
*is an artform and we are all artists*

## Mastering communication

Whether you are opening your mouth to speak or folding your arms in front of your chest, you are always communicating. Through your body language, preferences, choice of attire, the neighborhood you live in, selection of words, lack of words, voice intonation and more, you are always communicating. Communication is a vast area in itself, and to be artful at it requires skill. Lovers need these skills to feel like beloveds. Many wonderful books have been devoted entirely to this critical skill of communication, so in this chapter a few fundamental points are highlighted to inspire your soulful loving.

*Beloveds* tend to speak to one another from the tenderness, vulnerability, and truthfulness of their hearts. Even when problem areas arise, beloveds would rather find the common ground between them or discover the spiritual lesson being learned, rather than insist that one is "right," while the other is the loser. Beloveds are willing to discuss emotionally charged topics, and understand the importance of maintaining and valuing an ongoing openness between them.

## Start from wherever you are

Perhaps you and your beloved have frequent, deep, intimate sharing. Maybe you chatter with each other, or even nag one another all the time. Even if you have simply resigned from talking at all, you *are* currently communicating. You may not like the way it is right now; you may say it doesn't work. However, because you are communicating *something*, start from wherever you are. Since you are continually communicating on some level anyway, the questions to ask yourself might be: "What would I *prefer* to be communicating to my partner right now?" "What can I say that will create a bond strong enough so that we can tell each other what we want and need?"

## Intention

Communication between beloveds is respectful, honoring, appreciative, honest, and spacious. It's also flowing, emotionally inclusive, supportive, timely and frequent. When the inevitable unresolved childhood baggage emerges from time to time, beloveds can each rely on their *intention* to communicate as impeccably as possible to identify, heal, and release areas of blockage.

What is your intention for your relationship? What is the intention of your beloved? Do you *intend* to communicate lovingly, emotionally, respectfully? Have you declared this to one another? When blockages surface, do you intend to work it out or do you hope it will go away? You might expect your partner to fix it, or just decide to put it on the shelf until . . .

Examine the communication style you learned from your family. Consider if that style worked for everyone in your family, including yourself. Think about it now. If you would like a different, more effective communicating arrangement, consider discussing with your beloved a style that could work between you and for the family you may be raising. Without consciously making this shift, unfortunately, your communication patterns will often regress to simulate your childhood dramas when relationship challenges come up.

Discuss your intention for good, clear, loving communication. Once established, your declared intention is your steering mechanism, even in stormy weather.

## Commitment

Also key is committing your energy to actualize the communication style that works for you. Honestly assess your commitment to communicating clearly. How willing are you to work to nurture and maintain clarity and open channels between you? Will you go the extra mile to communicate your love and your truth, your fears, appreciation and desires— as well as the things that might be embarrassing? Ask yourself if you are willing to receive this level of commitment and honesty in return from your beloved.

*Beloveds* have a deep level of trust with one another. Becoming committed to clear, open communication involves building that trust one moment and one experience at a time. Intimacy in your relationship is cultivated by how much trust you have in your own truthful communication. If you haven't yet done so, consider committing to an intention to communicate truthfully in your relationship, then talk about it and decide how you will help each other honor this intention as a commitment of your relationship.

Practicing good communication skills during calm relational weather strengthens your ability to speak honestly and openly even during turbulent times.

Your commitment is like the motor to your boat. Without the power of the motor, you *may* just float around out there, drifting with the winds.

## Respect

Men and women operate on different communication frequencies, and these differences need to be recognized and respected on both sides. The masculine, or *Yang*, will appear to be factual, efficient, goal-oriented, fast, hot, competitive, literal, logical, future-oriented, spirit-based, and analytical. The feminine, or *Yin*, will appear to be receptive, intuitive, cool, slow, spatial, emotional, earthly-based, nurturing, relational, and flowing. When you are communicating, be aware of whether you are coming from a *Yang* or a *Yin* focus; because it can fluctuate. A woman can be speaking from her masculine point of view and a man can be speaking from his feminine point of view at any one time, or even as a primary style, and that's okay.

For instance, it may be that a woman embodies a more *Yang* tendency to her life, being more analytical and competitive, while her male partner tends to display more of the *Yin* qualities of intuition and nurturing. As a *Yin*-style man, he may be described as easygoing, emotional, and not very assertive. As a *Yang* style woman, she could be characterized as career-driven, sharp and emotionally detached. Because of this fluctuation, partners sometimes even blame one another for not being the man or woman that they say they signed up for when they married. Balance is the key here, and in time, everything seeks balance. The ocean tide does, just as dominance seeks submission and "driven" seeks peacefulness, *Yin* and *Yang* seek one another. The vast, flowing feminine will long for a container of structure and focus which the masculine provides, and the goal-focused masculine desires to be calmed by a soft, receptive, nurturing energy from the feminine.

This polarity context is an interesting frame of reference to have when you begin to identify conversational styles. When one of you shares something from the feminine frame of reference, and the other listens from the masculine perspective without regard for the difference, that's when people say they don't connect with each other (or worse, accuse one another of not caring). Let's say the woman is talking about troubles at work, citing the details, and explaining what she's worrying about. Her partner, wanting to help but being in his masculine listening mode, responds to her by offering advice, as he lays out how she should fix the problem. She complains that he is not listening and doesn't care about her; then he feels hurt she doesn't appreciate him or his help. Has something like this ever happened to you?

You wouldn't be alone if you said "Yes," because this is such a common conversational scenario. The masculine instinctively wants to have a plan and move into problem-solving, and the feminine nature is process-oriented, learning how it thinks and feels by talking it through. The feminine does not want to be "fixed," given the answers, hurried, or belittled. Further, the fact that the feminine personality wants to talk things through does not imply that anything is "broken." This is simply the feminine process, whether acted out by a man or a woman.

To begin a healing process, a woman can appreciate the masculine-style's attempt to care for her, *acknowledge* its concern, and at the same time encourage it to listen attentively rather than offering advice. To reciprocate, a man can *honor* the feminine style and rhythm. This creates an atmosphere of respect. And, because his way is not more right than hers, nor hers more right than his, the battle over who is the winner can end.

The masculine qualities are more useful in certain situations, and likewise, times when the feminine attributes are more practical. Learn how to harmonize your differences and access the many resources in yourself to your advantage. In situations where details and factual data are needed, use your masculine skills. To empathize with a co-worker's difficulties or your child's fear of the dark, you might want to access your feminine resources, whether you are a man or a woman.

In their most conscious elements, the masculine holds the big picture of the relationship while the feminine is concerned with relating day-to-day and moment-to-moment. Both aspects are needed, or your relationship is like one hand clapping. Although each partner will gravitate to one of the aspects more easily because that is his or her strength, both partners need to participate and support the leadership— not the *law* — of the other. This is an example of respect. Honest, ongoing respect will lead to more trust.

## Engineering a sacred bond

When you are building a bridge and engineering it for strength and longevity, the *Yang* qualities of planning and logistics are very advantageous. When you are building a soulful relationship becoming beloveds, you need a *Yin* language and a spaciousness that can take you into deep intimate territory. Without the feminine attributes abundantly present in the relationship, it may feel soul-less, empty, flat. *It is the feminine qualities in you that make the relating feel alive, passionate and nurturing . . .* whether the feminine qualities originate in the male or the female partner.

Invite, welcome and express your emotional nature. Both men and women have been locked inside the masculine structure for too long. The success of our relationships, families, and communities now depends on our ability to live from more soulful values, a more *Yin* model in which to live and relate to one another.

Clearly, this does not mean that *males,* or the masculine traits, are irrelevant— not at all. Balancing these energies actually allow for the liberation of men (at last), from the robot-like expectations forever projected onto them, to be slaves to money and time, and to deny their own feelings, personal passions, and potential for pleasure. It has served neither men nor women, or their union, to live in a relationship void of the soulful *Yin* qualities. Indeed, being beloveds is not even possible without *Yin* at the core of the relationship.

Let the *Yin* qualities teach you more deeply about love, intimacy, and soulful sexual expression. Allow your loving to be more flowing and less boxed-in, more intuitive and less by-the-book, more nurturing and less goal-oriented. And if you think a feminine approach to sex won't be passion-filled or wild enough for you, then perhaps you have not witnessed or experienced for yourself the primitive *roar* of a woman giving birth. A *feminine* approach to sex is not small or less than man's. It's earthy. It's primal. It's vital. It's relational. *And,* it will have *heart.*

## Multi-dimensional communication

Multi-dimensional communication means relating on many different levels: mentally, spiritually, energetically, emotionally, and physically. Becoming familiar with and, over time, mastering the art of communicating on all these levels is a major factor in becoming beloveds.

**Communicating mentally** doesn't mean agreeing with one another or even understanding one another (although it could). It does mean respecting your beloved's point of view, being curious about it and being willing to stretch to explore or understand it. It means speaking honorably with one another, holding the other in the highest regard and clearing issues of blockage as they surface.

**Communicating spiritually** relates not only to your choice of religious affiliation, but also to your commitment to develop a sacred love life and personal life. It includes family or global spiritual consciousness as well— to grow, transform, meditate, serve others, and raise your children. It means being able to support one another in a joint spiritual practice *and* in your solo disciplines.

**Communicating energetically** occurs when your channels are open to the subtle energies that run through your body. Have you ever had goose bumps when something you experienced was synchronistic or coincidental? Think of the butterflies you felt in your belly before a first kiss. Were there *really* butterflies down there? Where did that sensation actually come from? That's energy! Have you ever felt a rush of excitement zip through your body or flush your skin? When energy bolts from your lower spine to the top of your head, people call that *Kundalini* rising. Maybe it has happened to you. Some have experienced this at some point, but to have *Kundalini* move through your centers regularly, one needs her energy centers open and tuned. Commit as a couple to help one another open and tune these centers, as well as delight in the pleasure that comes from an energetic exchange.

**Emotional communication** is the regard for your feelings, the home base of your *personal power*. It means including in your conversations how you feel, how you want to feel, and questioning what may be in the way. Our emotional nature includes all things sensitive and sensual, even mushy. Truly, communication is more than mere words. It's how you hold one another in an embrace; it's the time you've allotted for togetherness; it's the quality you allow once you're together; and it's how you take care of your body. Emotional communication is an openness to understand how one another feels without understanding how you know. It's listening with compassion and *sensing* beyond or without the *facts*. It's tuning inward and sharing from your inner truth and wisdom.

**Communicating physically** with your body is to trust the natural intelligence of your body, giving it the touching, nurturing, grooming, activity, diet, care, and love that it needs and deserves. It means supporting one another to allow these basic expressions to be natural. To physically connect with your beloved is to give pleasure as naturally as possible and to receive it in return, to honor all the senses, awaken them, stimulate them, and be sensitive to them. Your body will signal to you its needs, wishes, and concerns. Therefore, physical communication includes listening to these signals without denial, rejection, or disbelief. It means balancing the need your body has for self-care discipline, with the need to relax, and then let go into pleasurable abandon.

Communication is the sending and receiving of information between two people. It can be an emotional or spiritual exchange or an encounter of one energy center to another. Hopefully, understanding the true power you have to energize, heal, and ignite yourself and your beloved will inspire you to practice. We take for granted that we will get music and news when we plug in a radio. We may not understand how electricity works, but we count on it. Literally, the body is an electrical system as well, capable of transmitting energy (as an *EKG* machine demonstrates so vividly).

How and what you communicate matters. The openness you have in communication is a direct link to your success in relating to yourself and to others. When you declare your love through any one of the communication dimensions, and your beloved receives that transmission, your relationship builds power in the form of trust and intimacy. When you clear blockages in your belly/emotional center so that information can travel through the inner flute from your genitals to your heart center, you begin to feel like sex is blissfully intimate and soulful.

## Listening

A large part of listening is being present, purposefully becoming focused and undistracted so that you can pay attention. Listening may not be as difficult as you think, once you understand how the relentless thinking in your head gets in your way when you want to listen. The tricky obstacle to listening is the temptation to rebuke, give advice, and try to "fix" it for the beloved. Practice the act of doing one thing at a time, like putting down the newspaper or turning off the television so you can pay attention to the speaker (which is entirely different than repeating back what she has said verbatim).

Soulful listening is also listening with your *heart*, as if it had little puffy ears. When you listen to your beloved with your heart instead of your head, you have access to the resources of *Heart,* like compassion, healing energy, peace and harmony, and unconditional love. This becomes an inviting place for the speaker to share herself.

Unfortunately, in ordinary conversations it's common for the listener to be preparing his rebuttal instead of really listening. Regrettably, another common trait which stunts good communication is the habit of *judging* the speaker or the content of her message, or *fearing* how the content might be interpreted by the listener. It's hard to be a good listener when you are worrying, judging, and preparing a rebuttal. *Welcome to your next argument!*

Becoming a good listener is a primary beloved communication skill. Breathing fully and regularly into your belly will help you to be centered, and open to receiving communication from another. As a dear friend and beloved teacher to many, Lew Epstein, says, "Trust that you are loved." When you know in your heart of hearts that your beloved cares for you even if she is not acting like it at the moment, you will build the trust it takes to work through whatever challenge is before you. Remain centered and loving and always know that you are lovable, no matter what.

Breathe. Listen attentively. Listen with the soft ears of your compassionate Heart. Practice being centered. Breathe so your belly will soften. And *remember* always, that you are loved.

# "Compassionate Listening"
From a talk given in London, 1993
By Lew Epstein
Author of *Trusting You Are Loved: Practices for Partnership*

*We so often listen and then deny the other person's reality. We do not know how to listen. We listen watching our inner agreement or disagreement with the speaker. We listen waiting for the other person to finish speaking so we can speak, all the while, preparing what we are going to say next. We listen to help or fix. We judge and we evaluate what is said.*

*Usually, the way we listen, or speak, beneath the communication, is an expectation that the other person should act differently, respond differently, or just be different. We are dead in the water when we come from that point of view, because our expectations are never met, and we are immediately, once again, left disappointed. We then make a judgment out of that and are resentful and angry, withdrawing ourselves— which is finally what happens when people with the best of intentions, from the goodness of their hearts who are trying to communicate, say: "Well, it's no sense in communicating. He is not going to listen anyhow."*

*Also, we often listen that we are accused of something. We listen that we are judged. We listen that we are patronized. It's always about how we react, how **we** feel, how angry **we** are, how judged **we** are. We do not look over there, and listen to their feelings, their despair, their frustration, their anger, their pain, their loneliness, their pettiness, etc. We do not know how to listen over there!*

*My definition of "listening with compassion" is: a very, **very**, deep appreciation of another human being's feelings and experience. Listening with compassion means listening without judgment, without evaluation, with no desire to help or fix or change, without agreement **or** disagreement, and without urgency for the other person to finish speaking so that you can.*

*When one person is really listening to another with compassion, this is a most glorious and transformational experience for both the listener and the speaker. You are home. You are safe. You are without fear. You both are one. When a person is actually heard, he/she is healed. We are here to heal each other, to love each other, to honor each other. It is time that we recognize that the person in front of us is always our teacher.*

*The person in front of you is always your teacher! They are giving you an opportunity to go through obstacles that you yourself have which prevent you from experiencing and trusting that you are loved— if, you are able to listen with compassion.*

*As we learn to listen with compassion to those in front of us, we become the beneficiaries because the gift of compassion returns to us. We begin to have compassion for ourselves also. The gift we create for others becomes our very own.*

*I want you to know . . . We must express our feelings, and we don't normally tell the truth when we speak to each other. When a child is hungry, she says, "I'm hungry. **You*** *turn* to the person next to you and you say: "Are you hungry?" So simple. And yet this is how we live. Another absurdity is: "Are you upset?" Are you upset!!! If you had a feeling that they were upset, why didn't you just say "I had a feeling that you were upset."

We may not be responsible for the thoughts that we have. But we are responsible for the thoughts we give meaning to, give power to, and seek evidence for. As human beings, shamefully, we have to be right, Right! Right! Right! Dead Right!

Notice how you listen. Notice if you listen with expectation. Notice if you listen for a certain kind of response. Notice that if someone is speaking, you are also waiting for them to finish so that you can speak. If you are, you are not listening with compassion.

It is our judgment of ourselves that determines our relationships with other human beings, whether at home, at work, or at play. We do to ourselves in ten seconds of self-talk, what we wouldn't allow others to do to us in ten years.

We must heal ourselves. We must learn to love and forgive ourselves. The way through this is having compassion for ourselves. The path to compassion for ourselves is to practice having compassion for others.

We are at a crossroads. What we will do determines the future of what it means to be a human being living on planet Earth. The evidence for the destructive effects of human isolation and alienation is overwhelming. The necessity to provide an alternative to this painful scenario is real.

Our purpose is to love each other, to forgive each other and to have compassion for each other so that we can create a universe where we, and our children are safe.

## Honesty with yourself

Becoming beloveds *together* depends on each of you being honest with yourselves. If you didn't have to live up to the impossible standards that you've set, would you be more willing to be honest with yourself about your personal needs for comfort, joy, togetherness, space, pleasure, boundaries, vulnerability, support, intimacy, and spirit? Would you be more authentically *you?* Would you play more? Would you give yourself some slack to be human? Could you be less guarded and more vulnerable to love? "But, what would people *think,*" if you lived your life as if it were your last one to live?

What matters much more is what you think and feel about how you think and feel. Honesty is a core ingredient in a love relationship and certainly in becoming beloveds, but, how can we be honest with another if we are *not* with ourselves? You do not have to aggrandize yourself in order to "*be enough.*" Trust that you are plenty just as you are! Trust there are people in this world who will find *your* true flavor the best there is, because *that* is true, probably even with the people closest to you. Too many people are spiritually dying trying to be acceptable to other people. There is no better time than now to be yourself fully and completely. If not now, when?

*You* are the beloved you seek. The lover that you hope for over *there*, is actually inside of *you*. Recognizing, honoring and loving the you that *you* are, magically brings the love that you crave into your life.

Usually what trips people up is their own fear. Everyone has fears, and even terror (*no matter how masterful someone is at insulating himself from feeling fear*). Everyone. Sometimes the biggest fear is that other people will find out how afraid we are, so we hide behind logic, sarcasm, negativity, and busy schedules. But why? It's sad, really. Not that people have feelings of fear, because that is a natural survival response, but that they feel shame about it. No matter what feeling is being denied, each time it's brushed aside, it's like putting another coat of varnish on your authenticity trying to be someone other than who you are.

Some people have so many coats of paint and patches on them, they're afraid they don't know who is underneath it all anymore and, worse, don't know how to find out. For some people the feeling is rage, and the fear is that, if even a little taste of the rage surfaces, it would never stop and it would hurt someone. *Of course*, it will stop at some point but you have to get into it first. Allow it. You can't end it till you start.

*Suppressed* rage can be much more hurtful to loved ones than *expressed* rage released in a conscious and complete manner, and this is because the upset is never about the real problem. There are *phantom* problems everywhere. An example of suppressed rage: *forgetting* to rake the leaves from the lawn and porch that you *promised* to clean up before the guests arrived for the baby shower your wife is hosting for a friend. You *know* how important it is for her; but you have not admitted how upset you are that the party is on Super Bowl Sunday and you wanted to have your own party. However you didn't say so when the plans were made last month.

When you are afraid, have the courage to actually listen to those emotions and be held in the embrace of your own heart. Allow your beloved to hold you. Honor the feelings first; there will be plenty of time to figure out what it all means afterward. Or you can choose to handle it the way so many do, by covering up the feelings, stuffing them down somewhere and dealing with them later. Maybe.

Cultivating this familiarity with your emotional side will help if you feel like you don't know yourself very well, or you and your partner are out of touch. Your life comes alive. It's like the lights going on. Trusting and honoring your feelings teaches you to trust and be honest with yourself. This is true self love. From here, you offer this precious gift of you to your beloved.

## Prayer

Prayer has been mentioned often in this material for the purpose of deepening the sacredness of your lovemaking, and also to increase the satisfaction of your sexual loving. One way of thinking about prayer is to consider it a positive thought. Prayer is taking the time to put your attention on something that you need or want. Our thoughts are so powerful, that the reality of how we experience our lives is created by our thoughts.

The opposite of prayer is worry and judgment: *negative* prayer. Every time you tell yourself that you are not good enough or attractive enough to get or keep a partner, *that* is a negative prayer. That thought unfortunately has the power to convince you that it might be true, or to allow experiences into your life that will convince you. It is, indeed a law of the universe that the consequences of your thoughts will come back to you.

Positive prayer is a conscious thought that communicates what you are asking for to come into your life. What do you want? What are you seeking? What do you need? Prayer can be done anywhere and at any time. This is especially beneficial when you have just caught yourself in a negative prayer. Remove the negative thought from your mind by saying the word cancel, and then say what it is that you want instead.

Prayer is also appropriate in ritual situations, on your knees, for instance, or at your relationship altar with your beloved. Pray for improved relating skills and understanding. Make up prayers asking for more pleasure, connection, and mastery. Remember that you can pray for whatever you need or want.

Who are you praying to? Well, that's up to you. Pray to God if that is appropriate for you. Pray to *Spirit*. Speak to the universe or connect with the Divine. Prayers spring from your soul, your heart and/or mind regardless of your religious affiliation or lack thereof. Do what is comfortable for you. Prayers need not have a religious affiliation. And it's fine if they do. Simply holding the thoughts in your mind can open up the possibility of your prayers being answered. In fact, you can change the word prayer if you prefer, for example: "positive thought," or affirmation.

## Dedications

Looking into one another's eyes, dedicate the fruits of your sharing to something you both want together as you move into lovemaking. Sexual energy is as vital as electricity, and when you learn how to tap it, it can enliven your dreams and visions.

"Beloved. Bless us for the love we are about to share. I dedicate the energy from this loving session to . . . " The blessing can be anything from a common desire, like more pleasure, to something practical, like a promotion at work, to something necessary, like healing for an injury.

"We dedicate the fruits of the sexual energy we are about to raise to:
. . . twenty more years happily together."
. . . the release of the pain in your back."
. . . multi-orgasms for us both."
. . . getting an answer to a really hard situation."
. . . the courage to make a change."
. . . the willingness to let something go."
. . . the patience to weather a storm."
. . . the endurance to bear a burden."
. . . the wisdom to understand a chaotic situation."
. . . the clarity to stand for truth in a matter."

. . . a healthy prostate."
. . . healthy breasts."
. . . a speedy recovery."
. . . more passion."
. . . a heart passion and sexual passion that are always connected."
. . . more playfulness."
. . . getting the weeks we've asked for to take our vacation."
. . . winning the lottery."
. . . healing the *un-heal-able*."
. . . receiving the willingness to forgive the unforgivable."
. . . all lovers everywhere, all men and women on this little planet, that they would know compassionate, sweet, juicy, sexy, conscious sexual loving."
. . . peace on earth."
. . . children everywhere being safe."
. . . food and shelter for everyone."
. . . bring us closer to *God*, our mission in life, *Spirit*."
. . . having more abundance."
. . . whatever your needs.
. . . whatever your prayers.

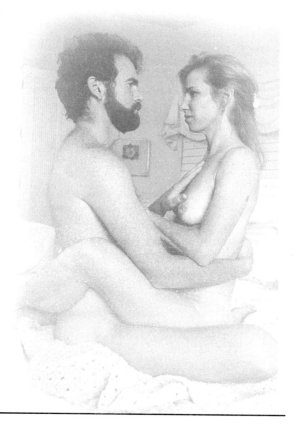

## What anger communicates

For most people, anger is not an easy emotion to deal with; they will commonly avoid dealing with it because it just seems too frightening and confusing. And for good reason: unresolved anger and inappropriate rage can fracture an otherwise wonderful relationship. Yet, just as often, it's the *unexpressed* anger that puts a relationship at risk. The key is to discern the anger which is *unresolved*. This anger, which can be chronic or unconscious, unpredictable or unreasonable, is energy that is stuck and needs to be moved. Learning to handle the emotion of anger is a skill anyone can master, and beloveds are willing to take on this task because of the benefit to the relationship.

We can have many reactions to anger, depending on what we learned about it growing up. At one extreme, you can control all situations so that everything is kept "nice" and then stuff any possible signs of anger from anyone, because it might mean the end of the relationship or that they won't like you any more. At the other extreme, there may be so much rage and violence expressed that you think it's "normal" and that you deserve it. Most of us are somewhere in between, but relatively, few have been raised with a healthy respect for the emotion of anger itself.

The interesting thing about anger or any other emotional expression is what it can teach you about yourself and your partner whenever it surfaces. Anger is an energy, like any other, and it must move. It's just backed up energy. *Moooove* the energy. Hit pillows or punching bags, but never, ever another person! You can also get the energy moving by running, lifting weights, hammering, drumming, hitting baseballs, swatting tennis balls—doing something physical before you attempt communicating.

Anger will often show up when you are not getting what you were expecting or wanting, like loyalty, respect, kindness, understanding, or . . . frequent and fabulous sex. It also shows up when you get something that you didn't want, like impositions on your time or energy, rained-out picnics, and expectations to be other than who you are. Anger can be a signal to back off, that you need some breathing room to figure out what you're feeling. Of course, anger can also be an invitation to come closer and hold you, to love you through the pain you're feeling.

Anger may seem less confusing if you will practice listening to what is being expressed by the anger on an energetic level. There may actually be a request hidden in an angry outburst, and if you listen for it, you may hear it. If your beloved is really angry, you can ask quietly (to yourself), "What does she need right now?" "How could I be here for her in a way that would work for *both* of us?" Then intuitively listen for a response.

Can you sense the value of a question such as this and the response it invites, rather than the typical reaction to an angry outburst? "You're crazy!" "How could you possibly say/think such a thing?" "How *could* you?" Resist trying to get your partner to be reasonable during an outburst because it won't happen. *Emotions aren't reasonable.* Instead, help her to move the stuck energy (mostly by simply allowing the outburst, not trying to stop it), and afterwards you can encourage talking about what's going on.

Sometimes it may be that you will offer to listen to whatever your beloved is upset about. On other occasions, you may need to let him work it through alone for a while. You may feel led to just get down on your knees and genuinely ask for forgiveness from the bottom of your heart. Or, it can be healing to simply take your beloved into your arms and hold her.

It is never okay to hurt any other person with an angry, violent outburst. Nor is it advisable to dump a bunch of anger "baggage" on your beloved. Your beloved is your help mate, not your dumping ground. It is marvelous to move the energy expressively by yourself: raise your voice gloriously! Shout everything that comes to mind to get it off your chest. Do this in a safe way so you don't frighten your family or neighbors. For instance, use a basement room, muffle the noise with pillows, or roll up the windows in your car and shout at full volume.

In these private settings, you can scream the kind of awful, terrible things that you would never, ever want to actually say to anyone (nevertheless, the kind of things you need to say so that you can "*mooove* the energy"). Blame, retort, condemn, accuse, negate, vilify, swear, yell, rationalize, shout— *really go for it!* After a session like this, you might even laugh at the ridiculousness of your trouble, because, after the charge of the anger is lifted, you are actually freed back into your own wisdom and good judgment.

What does anger teach you about what you need, or what you don't want? Think about anger as your way of establishing safe boundaries for yourself. Your anger will tell you where you are letting yourself down by not honoring your own standards and boundaries. Have you declared your needs, wants and boundaries to yourself and have you shared these with your beloved? Have you discussed clear ground rules and consequences for infractions and deviations?

For instance, are you always upset because your partner is never on time— which makes you late in return? Once you determine your standards in this situation, decide whether you are willing to be late, not go at all, go on your own, *or,* if you would rather wait and then get really angry at your partner? Clearly convey that you will leave at the agreed upon time, with or without him? Make sure your partner understands that you still love him but you choose to be on time because that's important to you. It is a matter of consciously exploring your options.

If you are always the late one, become aware of what your boundaries are. Are you agreeing to attend events that really don't interest you? Is being late your passive way of getting back at your partner for "making" you do something that you don't want to do? A below-ground way of communicating what you are not willing to say in words up front?

What can your anger teach you about your standards and boundaries? It almost seems easier to go into a rage and complain about what your partner is doing, rather than declare the consequences: which might include the end of the relationship in some cases. As difficult as it may be at one end of the spectrum, accept that the beloved you are trying to bend to fit your image will never fit *perfectly;* at the other end of the spectrum, discover how exhilarating it is to be honest about what anger is teaching you while you stay *in* the relationship.

Identifying what you are angry about will tell you exactly where you are in terms of your needs, expectations, and boundaries. The anger you display may also teach you about the needs, expectations, and boundaries of your parents which you are habitually imitating, but that are not realities personal to you.

Is your anger telling you what you are not listening to otherwise? Is your anger teaching you what you can accept and not accept? It may reveal what you are hoping to avoid. The answers simply put that information on the table, out into the open, enabling you and your partner to begin a dialogue. Even the biggest of obstacles may be more surmountable when the issue is no longer hidden in the shadows of unpredictable rage. Your anger is simply the messenger, not the message. If you judge and try to avoid contact with the messenger (anger), you will miss the message (which are your boundaries and needs). Listen to the messenger so you can retrieve the message.

## What communicates loving to you ?

Sometimes the simplest things bring us happiness, if we would only notice them. How wonderful to have a sense of what gives pleasure to your beloved, also. Make a list of the things that communicate loving to you, and add to it at any time. Keep this list in a place that can be easily viewed by your beloved— hanging on a bathroom wall or inside a closet door is ideal if it feels private enough from other onlookers.

Aim high for the best, and appreciate even the simplest, for example:

ANGELA'S LIST . . .
WHAT COMMUNICATES LOVING TO ME IS :

A GARDENIA IN WATER ON THE NIGHT STAND
TICKETS TO MY FAVORITE MUSICAL GROUP'S SOLD OUT CONCERT
THE DISHES DONE AND ALL THE COUNTERS WIPED DOWN AFTER DINNER
SPACE TO BE WITH MYSELF
THAI FOOD IN BED
A WALK IN NATURE
A FAMILY OUTING
THE BED MADE IN THE MORNING
A FOOT RUB WHILE I TELL YOU ABOUT MY DAY
THE WHOLE ROOM LIT IN CANDLE LIGHT
CUDDLING UP AND WATCHING A ROMANTIC OR EMOTIONAL MOVIE TOGETHER
SLEEPING IN TOGETHER
PLAYING GAMES TOGETHER
LISTENING TO MUSIC
READING TOGETHER
WHEN YOU LET ME IN AND TELL ME ABOUT YOUR FEELINGS
WHEN YOU TREAT ME LIKE A GODDESS, EVEN IN PUBLIC

WHEN YOU REALLY LISTEN TO MY OPINION AND TRY TO UNDERSTAND IT EVEN IF YOU DISAGREE
WHEN YOU TAKE TIME TO PLAY WITH ME AND BE SILLY
JUST BEING HELD
SPOONING ALL NIGHT
WHEN YOU TAKE THE TIME
WHEN YOU LAUGH
WHEN YOU SING
WATCHING YOU HUG OUR CHILDREN
FLOWERS YOU PICK OUT ESPECIALLY FOR ME
END-OF-THE-EVENING HOT TUBS
WHEN YOU BRUSH AND BRAID MY HAIR
WHEN YOU READ TO ME AND LET ME READ TO YOU
BEING COMMITTED TO IMPECCABLE, HONEST COMMUNICATION
WHEN YOU LISTEN FIRST, ASK QUESTIONS LATER
TRACKING MY MENSTRUAL CYCLE
WHEN YOU HELP PLAN AN INTIMATE GET-A-WAY WEEKEND
LAUGHING TOGETHER
MAKING LOVE ALL DAY
THINKING **PMS** MEANS A WOMAN'S PERFECT MENTAL STATE
DRAWING ME A WARM BATH BY CANDLE LIGHT
BRINGING HOME BANANA SPLIT SUNDAES

## What I love about your loving is ...

Find a comfortable place to sit facing each other for about ten minutes. Begin the exercise by bringing your attention to your breath and to your belly. Look softly into one another's eyes. Take turns saying the following statement and responding to it with something that you feel. You each say one thing and go back and forth. You might enjoy inspirational music in the background.

The statement is: *"What I really love about you is . . ."*

Some variations on the statement:
*What I love about your loving is . . .*
*What I like about you is . . .*
*What I learn from you is . . .*
*What I love about your body is . . .*
*What I've learned about myself in your presence is . . .*
*How I hope our connection will grow is . . .*

*What I appreciate about you is . . .*
*What I love about our sex life is . . .*
*What I first loved about you is . . .*
And more . . .
What questions do *you* have?

## Love notes

Leaving a little note for your beloved to find in a day calender, lunch sack or after work is a wonderful way of saying that "there is more of that where this came from, and you're worth it and our relationship is enlivened by it."

The kind of love note to write is as varied as there are people to write them, and there are no wrong answers. You can be as creative, wise, thoughtful, sexy, sincere, or mushy as you like. If you are sincere and your heart is in it, you'll have a winner.

Sometimes a love note is the only way you know to share something about yourself or about your feelings that you are not able to say out loud. You can express how much you appreciate your beloved, how much you learn from your relationship with her, and how you feel secure and cared about.

There may be times when you are very upset, yet you feel if you explained the situation to your partner she would dismiss you or become too defensive. Perhaps you want to protect her from rage you feel inside, that if expressed, you predict might be overpowering to her. Write a love note, that begins and ends by expressing your experience of loving her and your commitment for partnership in the relationship. In between, explain in a non-blaming way what you are upset about, afraid of, want, or need. Ask your partner in the note to please just hear what you are saying so you can move the energy and get it off your chest. Don't try to place blame; just say, for example, "I am so bummed that you accepted that

job on our anniversary day. I wanted to be alone with you, and I thought you would want that to. I feel hurt that you didn't. I feel abandoned."

You can write love notes on expensive stationary, greeting cards, balloons, color Xerox copies, napkins from restaurants, his tee shirts or under shorts, whatever you can find. Variety is fun. You can sky write it, write it on ice cream cakes, mail it, e-mail it, fax it, put it on notes inside a balloon, use shaving cream or lip stick on the bathroom mirror, or trace it on the steamed-up mirror. You can write your message in the dust on your beloved's car, or better yet, have the car washed and leave your note on the steering wheel.

Of course, roses and a card always communicate. If your beloved is away on business, you could have a card or love message placed in his letter box or have flowers waiting in the room. Leave your notes around the house and put your love into them. Feel free to use someone else's words from your favorite poems, songs or movies, as long as the sentiments reflect *your* thoughts and wishes.

## More on breathing

There is a rhythm of breathing that makes running a marathon easier, which is different than the breathing pattern you use to sprint. The same is true in lovemaking. In cultivating intimacy, there is a breathing pattern to fit each activity and level of involvement. Breathing is an automatic function of the body, and when we were babies, our breathing was as natural as anything gets. As young children however, we began to harmonize our breath to our parents and those around us. They mostly breathed short and shallow, so we did too. To correct this situation, until your breathing pattern becomes natural again, you need to pay attention to the quality.

How you choose to breathe communicates messages throughout your body to relax or to become aroused. And, also how to relax during arousal so you can stay right on the edge.

The breath, as mentioned earlier, is so powerful that it holds life. The potency grows when two people synchronize their breath. Most likely you are probably unconsciously doing this whenever you are with someone you like. But especially with your beloved, when you give a little attention to synchronization, your intimate connection will deepen that much more.

## Apologizing

The fine art of apologizing is a mighty tool to have in your intimacy treasure chest. Naturally, you probably already apologize for the human mistakes that you make. But beloveds, as well as friends, can apologize from the core of their heart for emotional wounds done to them by someone else long ago that you had nothing to do with. You can let go of the responsibility for creating the wound, while you can take the place of another by apologizing for the offense, assault, misunderstanding or wrongful action.

A lover will often inadvertently step into the emotional land mines buried in the psyche of the other. When these land mines get triggered, the best thing you can do is simply to apologize (and *Breeeathe* of course). This is not the time to use your logic to convince the triggered person that it is not your fault that she is upset or unhappy. The compassion of your willing, non-reactive apology will communicate to your beloved that she is loved and is heard. Enveloped in this security of your love, a triggered beloved is likely to return sooner from the despair of the emotional land mine.

This compassionate approach to apologizing is very different from the apology you make when you feel responsible for your beloved's unhappiness. You are not responsible for another person's experience of life, not even your beloved's.

## Forgiveness

Forgiveness is the magic wand that can clear your slate of whatever may be in the way of your true happiness. Honestly search your heart and name the individuals— and the offenses— you need to forgive. The list may include your mother and father, other grown-ups from childhood, siblings, childhood itself, first loves, previous spouses, bosses and co-workers, God. Anyone else? Now, what about yourself? As specifically as possible, name the things you could forgive yourself for?

- Forgive yourself for the times when you let yourself down because you didn't appreciate that you were enough.
- Forgive yourself for times you may have been unkind or unjust in relating to others.
- Forgive yourself for times you may have *forced* your will onto another person so you could get your own needs met.
- Forgive yourself for letting someone walk all over you because you did not have your own boundaries intact.
- Forgive yourself for any unfortunate discernment in assessing or choosing appropriate, loving partners for yourself.
- Forgive yourself for judging your own body so harshly.
- Forgive yourself for over-stuffing, over-working, under-resting, under-enjoying, and under-appreciating your body for all it does for you.
- Forgive yourself for any times when you may have struck out to defend yourself, and hurt terribly someone you loved in the process.
- Forgive those who may have struck out to defend themselves but hurt you terribly in the process.

You might say something such as: "I forgive myself my own trespasses, '*i-g-n-o-r-e-*

ance,' inexperience, and learning process. I forgive those who have hurt me or have betrayed my friendship, and I appreciate the opportunity to test my compassion."

### *Forgiveness is compassion turned inward.*

When your jaw tightens, your belly knots, and your mind recites gossip or hate toward another person, it may be time to invite compassion in for yourself and to practice forgiveness. Forgiving someone does not mean he will now be your *best friend*, particularly if it's clear this is not an appropriate friend for you. What it can mean, is that *you* can finally be freed of that situation in *your* heart (because you have let go your negative bond to them) *and* mind, so that you may have peace— otherwise, as long as you continue to hold onto your anger or your criticism, the connection, no matter how uncomfortable, will continue. Your forgiveness will release you from your suffering. It's *you* who will appreciate being released so that you can return to love in a richer way.

## Talking during lovemaking is okay

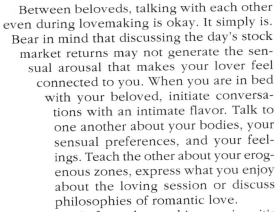

Between beloveds, talking with each other even during lovemaking is okay. It simply is. Bear in mind that discussing the day's stock market returns may not generate the sensual arousal that makes your lover feel connected to you. When you are in bed with your beloved, initiate conversations with an intimate flavor. Talk to one another about your bodies, your sensual preferences, and your feelings. Teach the other about your erogenous zones, express what you enjoy about the loving session or discuss philosophies of romantic love.

Before a lovemaking session, it's okay to discuss your needs, desires, preferences on birth control, information about sexually transmitted diseases, what you would do if the children walked in, agreements, concerns, fantasies, requests, philosophy, chemistry, and anything else you want to discuss or share.

It's okay to discuss things right in

the middle of a lovemaking session. At any time that you wish, you can slow or stop whatever activity is happening, and suggest a moment of stillness, or sharing. *Tantric* beloveds give themselves a lot of freedom to be natural, and since there is no goal to achieve, if someone wants to stop and ask for something or make a suggestion or just be still to feel the energy or to get centered, that's allowed. Actually, it's encouraged. Not that you fill up a loving session with talk, but it's important that you both feel absolutely free to express yourselves however you need to, anytime you want to, including when you're in the bedroom.

It's okay to talk to each other after sex about the sex. This is an especially tender time to share how you feel in your heart and in your body, where you can say anything to your partner about anything. If you have a correction to request, please always begin with a "I feel . . ." "I want . . ." or "I need . . ." statement, instead of blaming, nagging or shaming, like "*You* always . . ." "*You* never . . ." or "How come *you* . . ."

At first, it may take some time to become accustomed to expressing yourself out loud, openly and honestly. You may feel awkward for a while. That's okay, too.

## There are no rules

As you continue your journey into the erotic, intimate and relational realms of soulful loving, you may become even more aware of the *constraints* you have in these areas. When you are feeling constrained, it's tempting to think you are having more problems than when you started. What is actually happening, though, is that you are becoming *aware* of the limitations that have been holding you back. These are the hidden rules and agendas you have unconsciously adopted from your past. Everyone has a personal history that dictates what he thinks and feels about sex and intimacy. Your history may have proven beneficial for you, but more commonly, you may have a past chock full of inhibiting rules and taxing obligations to a moral code that no longer serves you today.

It's advantageous for you to realize that you can choose to rethink your attitudes about sex, erotica, intimacy, and relationships. You can experience them in any way you would like them to be now. It will take some conscious attention on your part, but the results are worth it. This transformation begins with recognizing your current thought patterns, and next, considering what you would prefer to be experiencing. This is the re-thinking process. Continue to become aware of your new thought preferences and then share with your beloved if you like. Align your thoughts and behavior to reflect your new preferences. Living your preferences will eventually feel more comfortable to you, so don't be concerned if you feel awkward at first.

### Sensual play

Sensual play is the language of the Goddess of Love. Men and women who make time to delight each other sensually will not only give pleasure but will build a wonderful trust foundation as well. Sensual play communicates an invitation to the body to become more alive and to awaken. Men and women who are awakened to their sensuality *feel* more intensely and are more sensitive. More on this later . . .

## Singing

Singing is nurturing for the soul. Listening to music is, of course, wonderful, but making the sounds yourself adds another dimension. Singing vibrates your whole body and awakens your self-expression center.

You may have been told as a youngster that you couldn't sing well. Quite possibly, you were specifically singled out and insulted, or had some other negative experience associated with singing, so that to this day you shy away from singing opportunities—even to yourself. Any number of reasons could keep you from singing on a regular basis and sadly, you will miss the outstanding benefits you receive when you sing from your gut, whether you ever reach a note on key or not.

Keep on singing if you already are. If you are not singing, please begin. It will make your day, and open your heart. You may even be surprised to learn that other people could be encouraged to sing if you do. Sing in the shower, sing to your pets, sing in the car and sing along with the radio. Sing to, and with, your children. Make up your own verses to songs if you don't know the words. Sing to hear your own voice. Notice how vibrant your lungs feel when you fill them with songs. Notice how your throat tingles and your belly pulsates, all from singing. Sing in the choir, sing solo, join the Christmas carolers, sing on key or off key, JUST SING! It will open your expression center, and it will prepare you to make love more fully.

Serenade your beloved while accompanying a well-known romantic song or one you've written for the occasion— or create a melody on the spot. You may be even more surprised to realize how well you sing when you are not self-conscious, thereby, able to simply focus on sending a love message to your beloved. Sing together. Sing at the top of your lungs, and coo *sweet somethings*.

And if full-on, top-of-your-lungs singing is too much of a stretch, that's okay. Begin with humming instead. Hum along with the songs, or hum by yourself. Express any kind of sounding and let your own tones resonate from your soul, your heart, your lungs and your belly. Experiment with it.

## Humming

Humming, especially on an empty stomach, is a wonderful toner for your whole internal system. It's a beautiful centering meditation as well. Take a full breath, put your lips together, then vibrate . . . *hummmmmm.*

When you sit closely and hum audibly together, as a preparation for lovemaking, you will set a tone of sacredness and you will have a vibration of aliveness and peace resonating in your being.

Put on some music with a trance-like quality to it (*Nadabrahma,** for instance). Take a full breath through your nose, filling your belly, then begin to make the humming sound. When all the breath has been released while making the hum, allow your breath to fill once again and then to release with your humming.

How long should you do the humming exercise? Twenty minutes when you are able, and at other times try it for five minutes. You'll actually feel your lungs being expanded, challenged to take in more air, and that feels extremely liberating. The vibrancy you'll feel in your body after an extended humming session is tremendous. Your body will tingle and become less **dense**. Your spirit will soar as clarity is activated, and wisdom becomes you.

## Gibberish

Have you ever had a conversation with your partner when neither one of you could understand the other because you were each so concerned with broadcasting your personal point of view? Sometimes tempers and egos get so hot that you can't expect to resolve anything till you cool down.

At times like these, try speaking to each other using *only* gibberish. Refrain from using any recognizable words. Use voice intonations with your passion and use your body language, but no actual words. You haven't been communicating anyway— neither of you is listening, and it's as if you're speaking a foreign language to the other— so why not complete the picture? Speaking gibberish won't be appropriate in all situations, but when it is, it's bound to eventually get you both laughing at yourselves.

At the very minimum, gibberish will help you move some energy, and that may create some space for harmony to embrace you once again.

## Lingering embraces communicate

When you live from one agenda item to the next with little space in between, you create a black and white world without *living* color. You can increase the quality of your love life twofold if you stay around a little longer for those intimate embraces. After making love, hold each other for an extended time *before* falling asleep or before you get

---

* A humming meditation by Osho. On cassette: *Nadabrahma / Nataraj*

up. Lie *together* when you're watching videos. Hold one another during talks, sharing feelings or when you have nothing at all to say. Embrace in the line outside the theater. Find a zillion ways to stay in touch with touching.

Embraces, touching, holding, cuddling, spooning, even holding hands, anchors into your energy system a form of ultimate comfort with one another that is filled with trust. So many students have reported to me how remarkably *this* has changed their experience of sex. They hadn't previously been aware of how much distrust they had stored in the body. The more time they spent in relaxing, non-sexual touching situations, the more freedom of expression and desire they felt during sexual experiences.

The quality of the embrace is significant. Quality is recognized by your presence, but the actual amount of time that goes into lingering embraces is also valuable. Although every couple will discover what works best for them, here is a starting point suggestion for you to experiment with: *for every half hour of a sexual activity, have two hours of some kind of close encounter without a sexual content* (include massage, star gazing, hugging, sharing feelings, reading together, conscious spooning, meditating together, dancing, feeding each other— anything up close and personal). This is beneficial for *both* men and women. The quality of your sexual loving will directly result in heightened pleasure and enjoyment.

## Staying in touch

Keeping the lines of communication open to yourself, primarily, and also to your beloved keeps the feeling of connection present. If you stop listening to the still, small voice inside yourself or stop listening to your partner, you may begin to feel out of touch. So check in. Listen, and listen, and listen some more. Communicate. And remember that staying in touch is more than just having your body show up. **You must** be present inside your body and in touch with your thoughts and feelings.

SIXTH DOORWAY

# JUICY-NESS

*Juicy is the sweetness,*
*the play and the joy in life*

## Juicy is the sweetness, the play and the joy in life

What is *juicy-ness*? Juicy is the feeling you get when things are flowing effortlessly. Juicy is delighting in being *you*. Juicy is the excitement you feel when you see, feel, hear, sense, and touch your beloved. Juicy is one way to describe *you* when your heart is open and vulnerable. Juicy is when you are vibrating with aliveness and passion. Juicy is not controlled or remote. Juicy is wet, deliciously free, pulsating.

Sharing your feelings is juicy. Being spontaneous is juicy. Taking the day off to do something fun is a juicy thing to do. Having a heart-to-heart talk is being juicy. Being yourself, expressing your gifts, and sharing the truth of your heart moment to moment is juicy. The opposite of being juicy is denying your joy, blaming the world, and hating your body.

Sex is juicy when it is *loving*, when it is natural and passionate, generous and wild, soft and gentle, when it is wonderful and inspiring, alive! and vibrant! — intimate and blissful. *J-u-i-c-y*.

Becoming beloveds is all about becoming more juicy. This chapter explores some of those possibilities. *What is juicy to you?* In what ways would you like to cultivate more *juicy-ness?*

## Without feelings, a woman doesn't get juicy

Love it or hate it, what moves a woman is the freedom she has to express her feelings. A woman needs to know and *f-e-e-l* that her emotions are valid, which, of course, they are. She prefers her emotions be embraced, and at a minimum, not be denied. And, she prefers her beloved partner share his feelings as well. Expressing her emotional nature is like breathing air. Without emotions, a woman cannot feel *juicy*.

It *is* possible for a woman to have sex, even great sex, without love or feeling in it. But in her heart, something vital is missing. She may have been having sexual love without feeling emotionally connected for so long that it has become normal to express her sexual energy without regard to her feelings. She may no longer expect a heart connection with her sexual partner, nor think it is even possible. Only she can choose if she would like to integrate her precious heart into her sexual life once again.

The soulfulness of a sexual experience is in *feeling*. Without the emotional component in a sexual sharing, the soul of sex is actually missing. Expressing *feeling* does not mean sobbing necessarily, although it *could*. It does not mean emotional outbursts and passion will dominate a quiet home. Realize that emotions are transient as they pass through your consciousness. They are innocent if you will flow with them. The more masculine-based partner, for instance, may enjoy having his beloved on top during Lingam/Yoni because it allows him to be nurtured, to let go of control and stop *doing* for awhile. When a lover simply shares that he would like to make love, but prefers to be the passive one and asks for this from his feelings, the honesty and vulnerability of the request can add to the couple's intimacy. In contrast, if he were to complain that she is never on top, rather than express his desire for her to be on top, you can sense that such a discussion could likely lead to defensiveness on her part. Leading with the vulnerability of your emotions is a skill that can be practiced to empower your relationship.

Tremendous value is added when beloveds integrate the emotional connection rather than compartmentalize and separate from feelings. When you are both able to share how you are feeling and what your dreams are as you cuddle together on a cozy Sunday morning, that sharing adds a definable intimacy, something that fills your being with joy. When you are able to express your feeling nature during the chaos of life between the soccer carpool and the PTA potluck, you add a substantial depth of intimacy that will be its own reward, plus a fabulous preparation to soulful lovemaking.

It may not seem like it sometimes, but if you both can allow more of your emotional perspectives to be present in your conversations, being-ness and loving, there will be more trust and more passion in your home. Keep in mind that having feelings does *not* mean being infantile and bratty. It means having and sharing feelings that might even seem petty or infantile. However, **you**, the adult, are still present, holding the space for the feelings to move through you.

Emotions are energy. Energy wants to move. So let your emotions run through you, not *run* you. You are not your emotions. But if you do not let your emotions run through you, if you stuff them, they will collect in you like garbage and begin to stink, eventually finding some crevice to escape from somehow— in the form of sarcasm, passive-aggressive behavior, unexplainable rage, etc.

You vent in a more healthy and successful manner by giving recognition and often times a voice to the emotion without being attached to the outcome. You are saying "yes" to feeling the emotion, while at the same time you don't have to agree with it, act on it, like it, or anything else. Feelings just want to be felt. Your natural intelligence will always be available to know what's next. When you move the feelings in a current way as they surface, when they are fresh and innocent, this is freeing to you and saves time cleaning up "big garbage" messes in the future.

Both men and women are *juicier* when emotional exchange is integrated into everyday living and it is natural. It is particularly beautiful to be around a man who is intimate and at ease with his own emotions.

## You are not the object

Your beloved is not an *object* to "turn on" at your whim, although some of our conditioning would have us believe otherwise. Your beloved is not a sex machine or a moneymaking machine, nor an *object* of beauty or grace. She is not to be put on a pedestal *or* left lying in the dirt. Your beloved is not stud service or whore service to be bartered for or used, and neither are you.

Your beloved is a human person with a soulful core, awakened to his spiritual potential in part by your loving tending. Sift through whatever negative or limited conditioning you notice you might be acting out, meanwhile relating more and more to this unique beloved standing before you, one unto himself. Rather than pursuing your expectations of her by objectifying her, look for her *"okayness,"* her inner light and life's purpose. When you do this, you are one step closer to connecting as two real people in the dearest of ways.

## State of bliss

The more able you are to drop into relaxed states of being, the more capable you will be to ride the waves of *bliss.* There is no need to go somewhere else and nothing to achieve. You need only to "let go" of where you are not, and be where you are now. Be here in your body and feelings. Practice relaxing *even in high states of arousal.*

This is not easy for go-getter types; however, armed with a *purpose* for relaxing, and with practice *being* relaxed, those same people wonder how they ever enjoyed sex without the relaxed states.

## The kiss

When sex has a goal or an outcome, for too many couples the fine art of kissing becomes one step they go through on the way to the "good stuff." When connecting with each other is the primary objective, kissing becomes liberated. Your kisses become a lot more than just a stepping stone to somewhere else.

Would you like to rediscover or deepen your kisses? A kiss *is* only a kiss if you don't show up for the *kiss.* All the material covered in the previous chapters will inspire you to give and receive your kisses from this flowing, blissful space.

Be present. Breathe fully. First bring your attention to your heart, then spread your attention to include your lips, tongue and mouth. Let go of any pressure to head this kiss toward any particular direction except for sensing the kiss.

Although it's wonderful having your eyes closed so you can more deeply feel the sensations of a kiss, allowing your eyes to stay open is also a *very* rich experience, one not to be missed.

Make your lips very soft and kiss tenderly with your beloved from your heart presence, as if *this* were the only way to make love with your beloved and as if this were the only kiss. Explore her mouth. Sometimes soft and gentle, sometimes deep and fast. Sometimes completely still, only feeling each other's breath. Invite passion. Invite tenderness.

You will not be thinking about what comes next. You are sensitive and sensual, awake to the wetness, sensations, feelings, and touch of your lips and theirs. Become so enraptured with the kiss that you no longer are the kiss-er. You are *The Kiss.* Some would call this enlightenment, and it is available to you when you are present, here and now.

## Massage and body work

Most people would agree that having a massage is heavenly. Massage is either soothing to you or energizing, depending on what kind you get. Massage will melt away the accumulated stress in your body with each stroke of the hands. Receiving a professional massage often (once a week or twice a month) will do more for your ability to be a good lover than you might expect.

Remember that a relaxed body and mind are more capable of operating at peak function and more available for true intimacy. When there are blocks in the way, preventing your body's ability to relax, you may feel disconnected from your partner or yourself, dissatisfied with your sex life *or* life in general, or you may feel unwilling to try again. A man may have trouble achieving or keeping an erection, or he may ejaculate too soon. A woman may be unable to orgasm, get lubricated or enjoy herself.

Massage goes a long way toward relieving the superficial stress of a hectic day and the accumulated stresses in an overwhelming work week. But what about the stress that has become chronic from burning the candle at both ends for years at a time? What about the armor people have donned as protection from all the "bad" things that can happen to them: bad people, bad feelings, bad consequences, threats, abuses, abandonment, rejections?

We've been armoring ourselves for so long that it seems natural to be defensive, aloof, or offensive. However, chronic stress and emotional armor keep you separate from the genuine lover that you are and the kind of loving that you need.

Body work will help you tremendously with this. Accupressure, Trager, Rolfing, Cranial-Sacral, Polarity, and Watsu are body work modalities that will work on you in a deep way to help release the blocks in your energy system. The quality of the practitioner is important, and your comfort level with him or her is imperative. Find someone you can relate to as a person. Extreme feelings may come up during deep body work and you will want to feel safe with the practitioner.

By the way, it's good to let even the *big* feelings surface— the ones that might seem overwhelming or impossible to deal with at the time. These feelings may be released now with the help of the body work if you will *mooove* them. These are not new feelings, most likely. They existed inside you as armor before, sitting idle, stagnant, unexpressed. They were the best self-protection you knew at the time when they were put into place. If big feelings are coming up during or after body work, trust that you are ready to let them go. As you learn about the power you have to live in the present, your need for the old kind of self-protecting blocks used as armor will be replaced. So just let them go. Poof!

Try body work at some point even if you think you don't need it, because you may be surprised. There are always layers to the armoring. Remember, the best loving you will ever have isn't in learning a new trick, but in dropping the blockages to your natural self expressing itself.

## The scent of a woman

The aroma of a woman is intoxicating to a man. She is built this way to attract him. Each day of her cycle she will offer a variation of her scent. Some days her scent will say "come to me," but there are a few days of the month when her scent may be saying "no-thank-you." Honor it. This must not be a problem. Visit again another day. No one, the giver or the receiver, should be made to feel bad when the "no-thank-you" scent is airing.

Unfortunately, many people have painful memories caused by the reactions surrounding how the woman's Yoni smells. All it takes is one person, saying one time, "you smell bad," and that's it! She can forever lose her desire or simply be terribly uncomfortable having her lover between her legs, kissing her Yoni again. A man could be equally shocked by pressure to perform lovemaking with his mouth when he is not ready, or during a "no-thank-you day." Pressure of any kind is always a pity. A loss for her and a loss for him.

Ladies, when he is honoring your Yoni with his mouth, he is in bliss. He has come to worship at *the temple gate of the Goddess.* This honoring, when offered consciously, is healing and nurturing for him. It balances him and opens his heart. This is how it is with a conscious lover. If your past has given you opposite evidence, then you may need to notice what is changing now. A conscious lover has permission to *really* appreciate and honor you. In the past, a man may have pushed these feelings of respect away because he wasn't ready to feel them, and in the process also pushed you away. Or, at least that's what the rejection felt like, a rejection of *you.* Be aware of how communication, consciousness, and honesty are so vital to the loving process. Without these components, new, bad memories may be made at any time.

Sometimes, if it's been a while since bathing there might be an *un*fresh aroma. This is not a problem either. Simply say, "Let's freshen up" in a light way. Either one of you can make the invitation to freshen up without any blame or embarrassment because you are free to talk about these things naturally. Have the freshening up *be part of* the lovemaking. The man can gently take his beloved by the hand into the bathroom and guide her into a warm bath or gentle shower, or offer to tenderly apply a warm wash cloth on her Yoni. He looks into her eyes lovingly to help her feel cared about and comfortable.

Freshening up is one thing. Wiping out your intoxicating fragrance is another. Ladies, *your favorite soap* just does not have the same appeal to your man as your own very special intoxicating fragrance. So, go ahead and reveal more of yourself to him. If you and your partner are open with each other, why not enjoy yourself and trust that he will let you know in a loving way if some freshening is needed. And feel at ease to hear how simply out-of-this-world your scent is to him, whenever he is honoring you in this way.

Men, if you've been telling her this all along, just keep telling her. She may understand what you've been saying now that she's read this chapter. She needs to hear in words from you though, what you love so much about being "down there." Sometimes women just don't understand why you guys always want to touch, kiss, and be in her Yoni so much. So tell her. Tell her how it makes *you* feel. She will feel included and honored at the doorway of her inner essence.

Perhaps she doesn't yet understand the sacredness of her own Yoni. How you honor her in this way will help her learn to appreciate her own femininity. So express your appreciation to her. Often and in many ways! A woman must also trust that her partner is not going to martyr himself and suffer— that he will communicate lovingly, honestly and naturally.

Some men have admitted that they are not tempted to go to the garden gate of a woman and that is fine also. These men are not ready, for whatever reason, and it is important not to pressure them. Again, there is no blame here. If one or both of you want to remedy this, then begin by focusing on the honoring nature of conscious loving rather than on your performance. This will be most helpful. He may try again when he is ready, and when he does, it will be from a new positive, conscious perspective which will delight you both.

Your senses will take you into bliss if you will allow them to move you. Allow the woman's fragrance to fill the room. Be bathed by her. And later, be filled by the fruitful aroma of you both.

## Honoring the lotus flower

When you are honoring the Yoni of the woman, always bring your love to her. It's as if your caring and your heartfulness are right inside your lips and tongue, transmitting your love to her. She will feel this and it will open her and bring her pleasure.

If you begin to clear this common block to honoring a woman's lotus flower, the fear of not being fresh enough, then there is just one other major block on which to focus. The masculine partner must always come in *under* her energy. This means that the woman's energy, not the man's, is dictating the pace. He aspires to be in rapport with her energy and paces his touch and kisses just a little slower and softer than hers.

Coming in under her energy is important because when you start going too hard, too fast, too much, she will get over-amped and possibly have to stop you before she has climaxed, resulting in mutual disappointment. "Come in under her energy and allow her to come to you" is the motto.

What does this mean? First, remember there is no goal of performance for either of you. The man does not have to *make* a woman come, and she is not *required* to come (or pretend to come) so that he feels victorious. It means he will kiss her Yoni softer and slower than he has ever done before, barely moving at all.

Guys, while this is a hot place to be, it won't be good for her if she becomes over-amped with *your* speed rather than hers. So, slow down and *breeeathe*. Begin to circulate your own energy to your whole body so that it isn't localized only in your Lingam, where it might get too built up for you to control. Breathe, and circulate your energy so that your attention can be on what your mouth is enjoying.

You can place your mouth just barely on her and begin to breathe. Let her feel only this sensation at first. Your breath alone can make her feel warm and sensual. Slowly begin to move a little more as she seems to move. Follow her breath, gyrations, and sounds. They will tell you a lot— *if* you have both agreed to be honest with each other. No more enhancing or pretending! If you haven't consented to be honest with each other about your *true* responses to pleasure, perhaps you can have that talk now. You may go faster, deeper, harder, only as a response to her, rather than as a response to your own increased arousal.

Ladies, you have probably asked him to slow down and go softer a zillion times. He may slow down for a while, but then pretty soon it's too fast or too hard again. Perhaps you've stopped giving him the chance at all. Just know that it's nothing personal about you, as if he doesn't listen to *you* or doesn't care about *you*, when in fact he does. The situation is merely that he is getting too hot. You can help him cool down by reminding him to circulate his energy and breathe. If the arousal is still too much for you to handle, that's okay, but ask that you lay together and relax for awhile before trying it again. This will help you recover from over-amping, instead of just resigning all together, and will help him to balance his own arousal with his own commitment to arouse you.

Honoring the lotus flower, no matter what end you're on, is a real joy. If there have been snags in getting to this place gracefully up until now, perhaps you can talk about it together and find out if it's time to try it again now that there might be some new information or new insight. Listen to each other. This can be a very emotional, sensitively-charged area for either one of you. Listen, and keep breathing. Share from your heart what you want to experience. Continue to dust off any mental cobwebs and allow your love to express itself in this way as you open to it more and more.

The Yoni is the temple of love. Leave your egos at the door as you surrender to your heart; he, by loving her, and she, by being loved by him.

## Planning spontaneity

Plan time to be spontaneous. *Yes!* Plan time to be together and then, with the time you've allotted for yourselves, make up the rest! You could plan to have a date every Friday night, or every fifteenth and thirtieth, and decide what to do then. You could take turns being the *date director*.

## The beloved's private space

Do you have a special place in your home that is or has become your personal, private rendezvous spot?

Your bedroom certainly can count, although, usually for the special place, the only thing that happens there is you two hanging out.

For some couples, it's the hour they spend in their hot tub outside in nature, or on the deck. They meet there in the morning before leaving for work, then again after the work day or before bed. It's a place and time to come together to share your intimate moments or feelings. Sometime it's a place to get to know each other again if you've been away from each other for a while— like a date.

Where else could your private space be? One couple reports that every night before bed they get into their bathroom tub for a soak while talking about their day, planning family life, and enjoying each other's company.

Other places that might work for you could be a porch swing, gazebo, or canopy bed out in the yard under the willow tree, a hammock or swing on the porch, in the yard, or even in the house! It could be a special sofa, a special room, your guest house, or a tree house. What about on the upstairs landing between your office and his? Just bring some pillows for comfort.

Indoors, outdoors, the attic or back room . . . if there were a special little place in your house to meet with your beloved to simply cuddle together, giggle or share feelings, where would it be?

## Go with the rhythms

Sometimes lovemaking is hot. Sometimes it is tender. Sometimes lovemaking:
- is animalistic
- moves slowly
- seems ordinary
- is extraordinary
- seems like cosmic gods and goddesses unifying
- is just best friends— like an old pair of comfy shoes going for a walk.

Many times, lovemaking will bring you closer together and, at other times will land you right into a lonely funk. Let the energy of the dance of lovemaking move you around the dance floor. You may have your preferences for certain experiences and not for others, but if you will be open to the dance of movement, your sexual encounters will be varied enough to keep you present, interested, and excited.

For instance, let's say you prefer passionate pounding, loud excitations, and mind-blowing orgasms every time, and you are disappointed when that doesn't happen. Even if that *could* happen every single time, with the way our bodies actually operate, you likely would become insensitive to the mind-blowing effects if there were not also more gentler experiences to provide some variety.

When you are busy complaining about the experiences that didn't happen and are not appreciating the experiences that *are* happening, you miss the opportunity to go with the *rhythms*. Here's an example. You've been apart all week because of a business trip. You've talked on the phone frequently and have even pleasured yourselves on the phone. You've built up a lot of sexual tension and are both excited to tear each other's clothes off when you see one another next. But for whatever reason— the stars, the tides, the World Series, whatever, the sex you have turns out to not be racy at all. Instead, it's slow and tender, erotic, sensually heightened, *sooo* sweet and completely satisfying.

What happened to all that testosterone? Who knows? Who cares? If you understand that there are rhythms that can move you and dance you with rare grace . . . *if* you will surrender— then *every rhythm* will be wondrous. Each one will delight you if you are not expecting a different one. And you'll find that each rhythm has something to teach you about yourself.

## Boredom

If you are bored, it's because *you* are not showing up. Your partner is not boring and sex is not boring. *You* are *being* boring. When you are bored, you have brought only *some* of your attention to the party. Maybe your head showed up, but where was your body? Where was your heart? Where were your feelings? When you are in touch with your body, connected to your heart space and aware of *this* very moment of exquisite ordinary-ness, it is rare to impossible to experience boredom.

Boredom is often just emotional laziness in disguise. It is also an unconscious defense from experiencing the love, intimacy and great sex you desire. When you are bored, you are never *here*. You are mentally over *there!* Of course you will be unhappy with what is happening here, because you are not even present. "Yes, but . . ." you may complain, "My partner doesn't do this and doesn't do that" . . . "If I don't fantasize I won't have any fun at all." It may be true your partner doesn't do the things you say will turn you on, but why are you giving your partner such a small stage on which to entertain you?

If *you* become present in more of your being than just the mental thoughts parading in your head, your beloved will either begin to surprise you with how interesting she has become or, begin to sexually express herself more fully now that the burden of meeting your expectations has been lifted.

If you are feeling responsible for entertaining your partner's boredom or short attention span, *please r-e-l-a-x.* You are not the reason for the boredom. It is not your fault. Instead, let go any pressure you may have experienced feeling responsible for your partner's entertainment. As you begin to feel more released and free, then you can lend your partner assistance through genuine engagement, helping him to get into his body to become centered, relaxed and available to real loving. (For help becoming centered, review chapters two and three.)

## One Hour Breast Massage

The breasts of women are in critical need of conscious loving. Rare is the woman who likes her breasts such as they are, and always has. The high rate of breast cancer is alarming and too little *loving* attention is offered to the breasts of women. Instead, there is plenty of negativity being expressed about breasts— enough so that many women feel they must surgically alter their breast size or shape, and risk health or life to do it, just to feel confident.

This is not an additional criticism against women who choose such a procedure, only concern about the messages women receive regarding their sacred bosoms. This next exercise is intended to foster emotional healing. It is fun for both of you and possibly promotes better breast health as well.

If you don't have a massage table, find a comfortable position in which the female partner can receive a one-hour breast massage. You, as the giver, must also be comfortable, and must be able to change positions when needed.

**This massage is not intended for erotic stimulation**. So, although it will be pleasurable and she may even become aroused, the main value in this massage is to send loving energy to the breasts without any other agenda in progress. You'll need a bottle of sweet smelling massage oil (Rose, Lavender, Orange, or Neroli). Begin to massage both breasts in a deep, full, slow, comforting, circular motion. This is not foreplay to another activity. Actually, it might be lovely to lie quietly together after the massage in a quiet embrace. She may be very emotionally vulnerable afterwards and you will want to comfort her.

Focus on the fleshy parts* of the breasts, not the nipple itself. Don't avoid the nipples but do not apply direct stimulation to them in any way. Send her love from your heart through your hands into her breasts. From time to time say out loud to her what you love about her breasts. Talk to her about what you love about her love of you, her caring of you, and her mothering skills. Think to yourself often how beautiful these breasts are to look at and what an honor it is to massage them. She will intuitively feel your sweet thoughts and this is very healing to her.

Women, to receive a one hour breast massage, begin to breathe fully into your belly and then let out sounds from time to time during your exhale. Your partner is going to have such a good time loving your breasts so just lie back and relax. It's okay to give him feedback. (Positive, non-blame feedback.)

You may feel emotional at times and tears may come. It would be *beneficial* to let them come, since tears are very healing. You don't have to figure out why you're crying and you don't have to fix anything. But do allow your love to be present and allow the love of your partner to come into you.

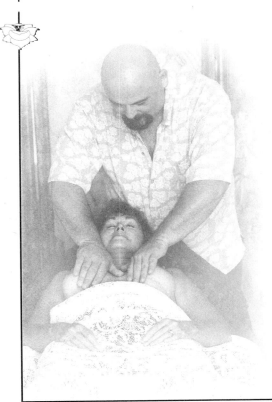

---

* When a woman's breasts have been removed, massage the breast area with as much loving attention as if they were there.

This exercise is very good for generating a trusting feeling between beloveds. It's also a wonderful, gentle way to melt accumulated emotional armoring.

In terms of frequency, doing one to two hours per month would be very beneficial and appreciated. If she has a history of rejecting her breasts or doesn't find them very sensitive to arousal, or she has breast cancer or a family history of breast cancer, you may want to offer these massages more often. One hour a week or twice a week or more.

## PC conditioning

Muscle tone is important for good sexual well-being. The PC muscle (short for Pubococcygeus), in addition to controlling urinary flow, is the muscle most contributing to orgasm— so keep it strong. Another worthy benefit of conditioning the muscle is that you may very well avoid needing adult diapers in your senior years. Ladies, keep these muscles toned and then, by taking full connected breaths while making a squeeze of this muscle, you can send waves of orgasm up your spine. Generate these orgasms all by yourself while day-dreaming in the grocery line, or while in bed together with your beloved. A toned Yoni muscle feels good on a man's Lingam also.

Keeping your PC muscles conditioned primes your body for whole body, multiple orgasms for men and women. Sadly, people are conditioned to think that a man's Lingam wilts as he gets older. Yet, Lingams are built to maintain erections as long as there is good muscle tone. A man's emotional nature may soften as he matures, and his drive to succeed and to perform great, brave feats in the world may switch to, or include, inner feats of emotional bravery, but his Lingam does not have to let him down if he knows how to keep its muscles toned for love.

Locate the PC muscle. Then, squeeze. Then, relax. Squeeze. Relax. This is a sexercise. *Squeeeze* for several seconds. *A-h-h-h-h*, relax! The relaxing phase is equally as important as the squeeze. Get into the habit of automatically doing your squeezes every time you sit down, or by stopping the flow of urine a few times before the stream is over.

Guys, you could also take a tie, washcloth, or towel, and place this on your erect Lingam while you are standing, and then squeeze. The item should be light enough that your Lingam bounces up toward your belly when you squeeze, but weighty enough to make you work for it. You can add weight to a wash cloth by getting it wet first. Spend a couple of minutes a day doing these squeezes and strengthen your erection more and more everyday.

These toned muscles will delight you both orgasmically.

## Holding the Jewels all the way home

You can find many opportunities outside the bedroom to hold his jewels. What about when you are in a movie theater? Reach over and rest your hand in his lap to hold his jewels during the show. Just rest your hand there; don't move at all, nor try to stimulate him.

Another wonderful time to try this is during long drives or floating in a hot tub. Or while he reads the paper. Where else? When? How can you fit this essential practice into your lifestyle?

Remember, the more relaxed he is in his body the more able he is to get his body to follow his directions. The less attention he spends trying to resist the tension in his body to ejaculate, the more attention he has available to share in the loving session with you. He will be less aggressive and more sensitive. Transforming sex into lovemaking will make a lot more sense to him. He will understand how being centered in the fire of passion becomes easier. He will be less likely to rush toward the ejaculation and more able to control when he releases it. And of course, this relaxation lays the sound foundation for him to be able to have wonderful orgasms for himself without losing his vital fluid.

## Soft-ons

Soft-ons are the opposite of hard-ons. The Lingam is in a relaxed mode. However, this does not mean non-sensual. Rather, the pleasure that a man is capable of having when he is soft feels exquisite to him. This goes for orgasm, too. He can orgasm and ejaculate when he is soft.

When the soft-on can be held and handled without the pressure from either of you to push toward a specific outcome, he begins to relax very deeply, even concurrently during intense arousal. The circuitry in his body gets rewired for more orgasmic capability. This means she has many more possible ways to share intimately with him and this is extremely interesting to her. For example, with a man able to orgasm while soft, a woman who may have had trouble opening her throat to accommodate his erect size, will now be able to orally accommodate his Lingam deliciously for him and her.

Hold and handle soft-ons, but also allow his soft Lingam to be put into her Yoni, and lie still. Lie together and breathe. Send loving, orgasmic energy up from the Lingam, into her Yoni, toward her heart, by using your imagination. Allow this energy to pass between you and feel the sensations. Even in this seemingly passive situation, you both can experience tremendous waves of bliss. Let go. Breathe.

If it slips out, just slip it back in. There is no performance pressure. There are no old standards to keep up with of staying hard. So experiment. This gives men the option to still enjoy a love connection even at times when he feels beat and unable to "get it up." This is the perfect solution to the problem of the man being too tired to have sex. All he needs to do is show up and present his "wand of light" for her to embrace. She can put him inside her and ride his energetic energy, which raises her own energy. Or, she can be still and energetic along with him. As she allows universal energy to run through her by the breath, she can renew and revitalize both her beloved and herself.

This is also a solution to times when the Lingam becomes soft while it's in the Yoni. There is no legitimate reason why the Lingam must be hard at all times to be orgasmic or satisfying— unless you don't believe it's possible. The Lingam transmits orgasmic energy whether it is hard or soft. If the Lingam becomes soft right in the middle of the action, let it. Relax. Hang out and look into each other's eyes. Share some sweet somethings. Share feelings or thoughts. The erection will return, sometime. There's no need to push it.

This is an excellent time to practice transmitting orgasmic energy starting through your imagination with your Lingam. With practice, you'll actually feel the energy kinesthetically. Have fun. Enjoy. Celebrate the miracle of this amazing portion of flesh.

## Loving the Vajra

The word *Vajra* rolls off your tongue when you say it. Vajra is another word for Lingam. *Vaj...ra*. Speaking of tongues, Vajras love them. Offering your tongue is a wonderful way of showing appreciation for all the pleasure that the Vajra in your life gives you. Find as many creative ways as you can to adore, honor, and delight the Vajra of your beloved. Vajras love just about anything, especially attention.

Get to know his Vajra. Play with it when it's hard as well as when it's soft. Learn how to turn up the volume to his passion as well as how to slow him down, so that he can *stay* around for awhile. Resist the temptation to "just do him," taking him straight to excitement and then right off the edge. When this happens, the habit to ejaculate as a goal is validated and the consequences of this will lead you away from your longing for sensual, soulful loving. Play him like a flute. Bite...softly. Nibble him (only lightly– no discomfort), like you're eating a corn on-the-cob, running up and down his stalk. Breathe on him. Suckle him. Take his Jewels into your mouth and gently fondle. Experiment. *Enjoyyy.*

Ladies, another way you can delight him is after you've said your good-nights. You then slip down under the covers, and take his Vajra into your mouth without heading toward stimulation. Just hold him without movement and relax your jaw so that you are just gently embracing him. When the Vajra is feeling plenty attended to, eventually it will be able to relax and appreciate the caress without fidgeting (this could take a few weeks or months of intentional Vajra-holding before he begins to actually relax with it, so be patient on the timing). He won't feel teased that he is supposed to jump to action or "go all the way." He will be able to relax and enjoy, and will look forward to this very nurturing embrace. You can wrap your arms around him; attend to your breath. And in this embrace, you both fall into sleep. You may each find this very, *very* yummy. It's a very special goodnight kiss!

Men, allow her the opportunity to find new ways to charm you. If you insist on the same motion, speed, and outcome every time, you will miss out on the pleasure of other motions, speeds, and outcomes.

Ladies, find a million and one ways to love his Vajra. Use your creativity. Use your hands, mouth, Yoni, breasts, and whole body. Use wash cloths, lubricant, honey. Use oil, strawberries, fingernails (*softly*). And tell him in words what you love about his Vajra. Tell him what you like about how it looks. Tell him what it feels like when it is deep inside you. Tell him how wonderfully he uses it with you. How conscious it is. Tell him how loving it is and how special. What else could you share with him about his Vajra? Yes! *Tell him that.*

## Men's whole body and multiple orgasms,
*"Coming" without the "come"*

Orgasm. The big "O." How successful we feel when climax shakes us to our very core! If orgasm feels that great just localized in your genital area, imagine the same feeling rushing through your whole body— rippling up your back, belly, chest, and neck, into your arms, down into your hands, dancing into your fingertips, and all the way down to your toes. Your whole body shaking, shimmering, exploding all the way up to your face, ears, the top of your head, and above with vibration. Electricity like this is hard to ignore and would naturally be missed if orgasm were returned to being specifically genitally-based once again.

The multiple orgasm is orgasm flowing into orgasm after orgasm without the need to recuperate in between. Common knowledge, until recently, was that only women could have this experience. A man in the presence of a woman multi-orgasmically exploding might think two things: "Man, I'm good!" and "I wish I could do that!" However, men have mostly settled for their single orgasm at some point during a sexual encounter, and some are seen as exceptional if they can accomplish a second or third orgasm with ejaculation in a relatively short period of time.

The potential of multiple orgasms for men means that each orgasm itself can last longer than the accepted six to ten seconds which results in stopping lovemaking. Instead, men's orgasms become ongoing waves for minutes at a time. Waves of orgasm could essentially continue for as long as your interest or stamina lasts.

Based on what or whose authority claims that multiple, whole body orgasm is an actual possibility for men? *Yours*, if you will permit it. You do not need an authority source to tell you. *Your* own experience is all that you need to substantiate it to yourself. Don't wait for traditional sources of knowledge to catch up before you try it, when you could be discovering for yourself right at home in your own bedroom laboratory!

*Here are the steps to assist you:*

1) The first step of this discovery is knowing or even hoping that it's possible. Both knowledge and curiosity are power. Your *"reality"* will be reflected by your knowledge. If you have believed the current standard of knowledge, which is a man only gets a single shot at climax at a time, and this is your reality, then in order to have a chance at multiple orgasm, you must now realize that *this* is possible. If you do, this knowledge will reflect your "new reality;" that you too can have the experience of whole body, multiple orgasms.

I discovered the power of this first step most profoundly when I was giving introductory talks on my seminars. Men who had heard me suggest that variable orgasms for men were possible, but were given none or little detail on how to achieve them, reported later that they had gone home and achieved these kind of climaxes just by knowing it was possible.

Some of the modern tantra information being offered now will suggest it takes a man years of practice to even get to this point. My experience shows that it may take a man years to master all that he's capable of, but clearly, beneficial results can be available much sooner. Many of the men who attend my seminar, with the help of their beloveds, are able to enjoy these variable orgasms during their first soulful healing sessions.

There are a few other steps that help set up the hospitable environment which encourage variable climaxes:

2) Fundamentally, he must be free of sexual pressure, relaxed and available.
3) Engaging in full connected breathing, which opens the entire body, is reliably instrumental also.
4) Exercise the sex muscles (PC) regularly to keep them toned and fit.
5) To help distribute the arousal in the genitals, use your arms to sweep the arousal energy up your belly, up to your heart and throat and shoulders.

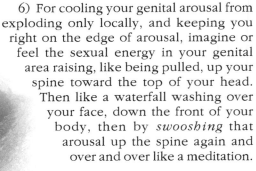

6) For cooling your genital arousal from exploding only locally, and keeping you right on the edge of arousal, imagine or feel the sexual energy in your genital area raising, like being pulled, up your spine toward the top of your head. Then like a waterfall washing over your face, down the front of your body, then by *swooshing* that arousal up the spine again and over and over like a meditation.

Under these conditions of relaxation, expanded breathing, toned PC and anal muscles, and without pressure to perform, you are more easily able to shake, shimmy and orgasmically explode all over your entire body.

There are advanced techniques of breathing, visualization, and energy locks which you can study, but start with these *basics*. Even as an advanced practitioner, you will still practice the basics.

Many men have experienced the vibrating feeling of orgasm throughout their whole body or in some parts of the body, but even those men with this personal evidence have doubted it enough to miss that they were actually climaxing simply because no ejaculate fluid came out. It's a kind of bio-brainwashing. *There is a sexual myth that climax only comes with an emissions of fluid at the same time, and this information is outdated.*

If orgasm can take place without ejaculation then why would a man choose to do it that way if it pulls him into sleep, away from lovemaking and away from his beloved emotionally? Habit! It's true. Old habits may not go quietly. Even men who are proficient at ejaculatory control and who are enjoying multi-minute-long orgasms are tempted into ejaculating half-heartedly. But that's okay. The big news is that a man can realize that he has a *choice* between a wet orgasm (*one with emissions*), and a wet–less orgasm (*one without emissions*). Choice!

Will you ever ejaculate again? Of course! If you want to. A point of reference for the beginning practitioner might be to have a wet orgasm, one out of five sessions where he is aroused, but not more than ten arousal times without a wet orgasm, even for the advanced practitioner. On the other hand, strict Taoists say "never ejaculating" is a worthy goal. Each man should seek out his own comfort zone, intimate ideals, and needs.

In light of an emerging desire for men and women to merge deeply into soulful lovemaking, men who are familiar with this information really appreciate the choice they can make of not being pulled away from their beloved by the distraction of ejaculation, so that he is more able to "stick around" for more penetrating levels of connecting.

No man is expected to give up a *wet* orgasm if he can not experience wet–*less* ones. Preferring wet–*less* climaxes over *wet* ones is not about punishment, it's about a man's liberation. It's about a man having a choice to master his own body. The conditions that make this a conscious choice of his own, rather than being at the mercy of an old habit, are the same that help him have multi-whole body climaxes. He must have the knowledge that wet–*less* climax is possible. He must understand that orgasm is not dependent on the "come" coming out. He must commit to being relaxed, being free of performance pressures, and he must breath fully.

In addition, this sweeping of the energy up his body using his hands, in a symbolic gesture to show the orgasmic energy which direction to go, will also help. This sweeping also eases the pressure that comes right before the point of no return. When you sweep, what was felt as pressure to *"Come right now!"* actually becomes the orgasmic waves that travel to the rest of your body.

## Sealing in the juices

Cradling the Yoni of your beloved is probably a daily, or nearly daily activity to share with her. It's very calming to her. She feels nurtured when she is held in this way. Place your hand over the exterior of her Yoni. Your hand is either placed with fingers at the opening and palm over the pubic bone, or the other way around depending on which position suits you better in the moment. Embrace her often. Hold her like this after lovemaking.

Some women feel varying degrees of scatteredness when they go out into the world after a lovemaking session, as if they are *leaking* their precious vitality. For some women, the harshness of the sights, sounds, and tension of the outside world is overwhelming to her in her expanded openness. Applying the Yoni cradle before she leaves the bed, seals in the juices of her vital essence. She then feels more centered and whole as she ventures out into the world.

## The erotic cradle

In chapter three we began to discuss cradling the Yoni, and that when you add movement to the Yoni cradle it becomes erotic. If you begin with sufficient stillness and then go into the soft rocking movement, combined with your breath, it can be a most delicious sensual, erotic experience. Women can do this on their own to assist awakening their pleasure zones, or do this to arouse themselves in preparation for lovemaking, and can certainly do it just for the pleasure itself.

Use your legs to cradle the arm of an over-stuffed sofa, a horse, or the thigh of your lover— anything soft, firm, and a bit thick. Bring your attention to the fullness of your breath and begin to breathe into your Yoni as if you could. Pulse your PC muscles, the ones you use to turn off your urination stream. Tighten them briefly, and then relax them. Next tighten for ten seconds, then relax for ten seconds.

Your attention should now be Yoni directed. After a period of stillness, begin to gradually move with the beat of your heart, or to some great rhythmic music you have playing in the background. Begin rocking slowly back and forth and around in a circular motion. You can gyrate your hips as you do this. You can sway and swivel your back. Since there is nowhere to get to fast, you can enjoy the sensual feelings that may begin to bring you pleasure. Hang out in this pleasure zone.

There may be waves of bliss that accompany this gentle rocking. Flow with the waves. Breathe fully and let go of any desires to figure out what you're doing, just let it happen.

Merely feeling the pressure of the thing you are straddling is pleasure enough for many women because it feels s-o-o-o good. Enjoy.

## Making sounds

The sounds that you make during loving sessions are like medicine for your body and soul. Your sounds and those of your beloved are like food, air, and water. You also need your sounds for high states of arousal and ecstasy. Never hold back your sounds, or your howls, laughter, yelps, squeals, giggles, moaning, intense breathing, *o-o-o-o-ing*, *a-h-h-h-h-ing,* or *"Oh, my G-o-d-ing."*

Too many people are perfectly silent even while climaxing, staying true to how they were conditioned to behave as good little children. Is it still true that being a good person is dependent on how little noise you make? I hope not.

Too many parents are quiet during their lovemaking sessions because they do not want the children to know what they are doing. How come your kids shouldn't know what you're doing in there? Who made up *that* rule? Is that way of thinking *still* true? "A word of advice:" One thing you might want to address with your children is to clarify that the sounds that you make are sounds of *love,* rather than pain. Children can often imagine the worst and become frightened when these sounds are misinterpreted. Tell them that they might hear "squeals of delight" and that mommy and daddy make these sounds because they are having fun and *making more love.*

Some people say they don't make noises because they're embarrassed they might seem dorky or unattractive. If you knew just how much pleasure your beloved really receives when your face lights up with ecstatic *bliss* and the room is filled with your squeals, would you still be afraid to express yourself and your excited sounds? I hope you will try, for your own enjoyment.

When you are concerned with the neighbors hearing you or your visiting in-laws sleeping in the next room, just use pillows to muffle your sounds. However, don't silence your sounds; they are important. Make your *soouuunds.*

Those who are not very vocal, say that's just how they are, that they would feel very unnatural making sounds. If you would consider that silencing your sounds is just what you are familiar with and *not who you are*, would you take a chance to explore something out of your comfort zone to see if you like it?

If you believed that making more sounds from your gut during sexual encounters would increase your pleasure two-fold *or more*, would you be interested in doing some vocal research on your own to check it out? Because, doubling your pleasure is what you might just find.

Making sounds will release any tension you've stored up. Sounding will connect you with your body. Hearing each other's sounds teaches you about one another in ways that talking never could. Like the dolphins, it is an entire system of sonic communication and a way to transmit your love energy. Hearing each other's sounds is a turn–on. Making sounds awakens your energetic system and tunes it. Your sounds balance your emotional and mental fields. Sounding just feels good!

Help each other be comfortable with vocalizing. Invite each other to make some sounds even if they are only little whimpers at first.

## Laughter

Laugh with abandon. Giggle till your belly muscles ache because they're stretching so much. Sex is not always so serious. Sexual loving offers plenty of opportunities that are entertaining and sometimes down-right hilarious. Bless your lovemaking with your laughter. Laughing *at* your beloved is of course discouraged, but finding the humor in things together adds to your intimacy.

Laughing, like making any other sounds, is good for the soul. Laughing heals and releases tensions. It reminds you to take yourself less seriously and to lighten up! Encourage humor. Giggle and play. Encourage laughing.

## Ear blessing

Recognize the sensitivity of the ears and the connection the ears have to opening the heart. Bring your lips very close to the ear and ever so lightly, *gently breeathe* into it. Some ears are *s-o-o-o* sensitive that you must not breathe into them, but simply let the ear feel and hear you breathing very nearby. Encounter the ear as if you are touching the Heart, with tenderness and awareness.

At certain times of the month or during the cycles of lovemaking, ear blessing can be the true secret of opening to feelings or raising a giggle. It is a treasured and ancient secret of tantric love. *Juicy Love!*

## Playing with your food

Think about the most sensual food you've ever eaten? And the most sensual eating session? Sharing a meal and eating food together is a wonderful way to make *more* love. Make soft eye contact often. Breathe fully. Bless your foods. You can eat quietly, talk about feelings, or laugh and play. When was the last time you ate a whole meal just with your fingers? Don't miss out on this delicious way to really get in touch with your senses.

What are sensual foods? Foods that are luscious, juicy, wet, soft, delicate, long & hard, spongy, creamy, tender, warm, thick, sweet, sticky. Then there's warm mushy foods like baked yams and squash with butter and maple syrup, baked onions and garlic. And of course, there's creamy foods like mashed potatoes and gravy, buttery pastries, cream of broccoli soup, quiche, decadent desserts like tiramisu, cheese cake, ice cream . . .

Which foods are sensual to you? You didn't think whipping cream was the only erotic food, did you? What about mangos? If you like them, they will tune you into your senses more delightfully than a pair of candied panties any day. If you can find a vine-ripened mango, it will be oozing its nectar through its skin and when its in your home it will fill every room with an intoxicating aroma. The mango is oval and smooth to handle, and rich in color to look at.

Perhaps during an extended lovemaking session, you can enjoy the mangos as part of your breakfast in bed. To prepare the fruit, section it into four parts, slicing along the longest sides of the oval. Gently pull the sections off and arrange on your plate. You can now slice off most of the mango meat, bite into it, or offer the luscious bite to your beloved. Leave about a quarter inch of the fruit on the skin because this will come in quite handy.

Separated, each of the four mango sections is almond shaped. Take a section, skin-side, into the palm of your hand with the fleshy part of the fruit exposed— Now you're ready for the Mango Massage. Caress the whole body with this aromatic, juicy mango. The mango skin will soften and mold to fit your hand. To release more fresh juiciness from the flesh, scratch it with your fingernails, a knife, or the points of your teeth. Rubbing this on the fleshy parts of the body feels delicious— especially to the breasts, tushy, anus, Yoni, and particularly to the Lingam. A section of mango in your palm is more sensual than regular lubricant for making long strokes on his Lingam. He will most likely love the way it feels.

Mangos are just an example. Many fruits are juicy and sensual, particularly when they are vine/tree ripened in season. Whether it's strawberries, peaches, Kiwi, bananas, oranges or papaya, you can eat them erotically— rub them on your body, and then apply them to your beloved's.

Meal times can be transformed into a sensual feast whenever you want one. You won't need any utensils, although a washable blanket beneath you will protect your carpet or bed sheets. With tender care, wash and gently dry each other's hands. Fill your table with tasty foods you can easily eat using only your fingers. Bless the food, and each other. Offer the food to each other as if you were not allowed to feed yourself. Give your beloved enough but not *too* much for each bite. *Receive* each bite as a wondrous gift from the Divine.

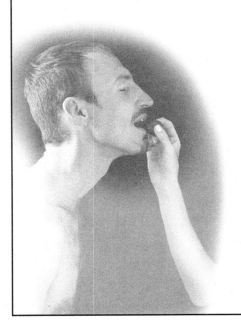

Taste the food. Smell it. Chew it slowly. Be aware. Experience the food. Be mindful. Breathe fully. Be aware of your beloved's presence, her body, his being, her eyes, fingers, smile, mouth. Be very aware of *your* presence.

As a refreshing, meditative change to mealtime chatting, make yummy vowel sounds. Laugh, make sounds without using actual words. When you are not using words, it frees up more of your awareness to tune into your other senses. Go slow, and relax.

Each ritual will be different. One may have a more playful atmosphere to it with huge belly laughs, while another may be very quiet, sacred and meditative. You decide. Actually, more accurately, it will be you *allowing*. If you are allowing and available, the sensual energies will *move you*.

## Dressing up

When you are in your tux and evening gown, you both look beautiful. You can dress up for each other like this and not have an occasion to attend other than tonight's date, at home with one another.

What is so interesting about getting dressed up? If it's not part of your job, dressing up is fun; it can inspire joy! Additionally, could it be that it brings you into a heightened sense of awareness? The newness gets your attention and you are awakened. Wake up to this moment right now!

But what about when you want to lounge in more comfortable clothes while at home in intimate situations? Wear fabrics that feel good against your skin, like velvet, velour, silk, silky rayon and soft cotton— fabrics you can wrap around you like an island sarong.

Go to a fabric store together and pick out two or three yards of different attractive fabric pieces. Get some that are thin and drapey to wrap around your waist. Lay the thicker velour-y fabrics over the bed sheets or on the floor in front of the fireplace. Find deep, rich colors or varied colored patterns that you like. Smaller pieces of fabric placed over your lamps will soften the lighting.

Filmy, sexy lingerie has its place, but just be aware of where your attention goes when you wear it. Wearing lingerie, or being with someone who is, pulls your focus into your head, fantasizing about who-knows-what and becoming *distant* from the actual sensual loving experience you are engaging in. If this is true for you and your beloved, *why do you want to do it?* If fantasizing is what you want during a particular sex session, that's okay; but don't be surprised or disappointed when titillation raised from wearing the lingerie doesn't meet your expectations for sacredness.

***Men, please dress up, too.*** No, it won't send out mixed signals about your sexual identity, I promise. It tells your woman you are participating in the love dance and are genuinely vulnerable, not only expecting her to be entertaining for you. Instead of wearing nothing at all, or just your boxer shorts, how about surprising your beloved as you make your entrance into the lovemaking room? Imagine wearing a royal purple flowing silk piece wrapped at your waist and draped to your ankles, so she can see the movement of your Lingam (soft *or* erect, both are a turn-on), swaying underneath the silk. She'll be able to see and eventually touch— your wonderful chest.

This is a wonderful opportunity, guys. If you are usually the assertive partner, dress for fun, alluding to, "I'm available, come and get me if you find me worthy." If you really are offering yourself to her and not making a covert demand for her to respond according to your plan, she will at some point become the assertive one and begin to make advances toward you, but this will be *her* timing and not yours. Be patient. A truly emotionally-available man can be very, very attractive.

Men, if you are the more passive partner, dressing up can be a useful tool for you. Consider dressing yourself for an intimate experience. When you make your entrance, carry a warmed bottle of massage oil to offer your beloved– placing your loving hands on all the parts she would like touched and caressed. This will help relax her, calming any aggressiveness, and allowing her passion and love to be left intact to share with you.

Dressing up signifies something special is about to happen: a love nest ritual, playing, or, "I'm ready if you are." You can plan before hand or make it all up as you go along. There are no rules. Oh, Boy!

## Play

Sexual loving is a dance, a flow, and is not meant to be goal-oriented. When you start to get upset or disappointed, that's a good signal that you are being too serious and it's time to lighten up! Introduce play into your sharing. Any communicating that you need to have will be better if you are more relaxed from "playing." Do whatever is playful to you: Whistling, wrestling, singing silly songs, joking, acting like your pets, mooing like cows, imitating chimpanzees, using your belly as a platter for your beloved's dinner, dressing in each other's clothes. She, putting make-up on him. He, painting her toe nails. Pretending, fantasizing, writing a sexy movie and being the stars; gambling for sexual favors. Dress each other in the morning, piece by piece as seductively as you might undress each other in the evening. What is *playful* to you?

Here's another thing you might try sometime: A sensual glamour shot of you together. Women have make-overs and get glamour shots taken for their sweethearts all the time. It's a really fun thing to do. How about a make over and photo session taken of the two of you all made up and posed for the camera in a sensual, playful, or loving way with one another? Your connection will be captured for all eternity on film. This would also be a wonderful momento for your relationship altar.

*Play* . . . It will keep you young at heart and healthy in spirit.

## Cultivating openness

As with any other area of life, your attitude is everything. If you close down because you get hurt for some reason, everything that you think about will be clouded. You might blame your beloved or judge yourself, your relationship or sex itself because you feel shut down.

Until you learn and practice appropriate skills consciously, debilitating shut-downs are bound to happen occasionally, but your willingness to re-open is your ticket back to the Garden of Eden. Develop an attitude that lets you do this sooner rather than later. An attitude that brings more love into your heart rather than keeping score or holding blame. Everybody loses when someone stays closed down, particularly the one who is closed.

Whatever is happening right now, no matter if it's joyful or sorrowful, *this is life*. You are in the garden when your mind and heart are open to the feeling and you are cast out of the garden when your mind and heart are closed. *Where would you like your lawn chair to be?*

## Lubricant

Go ahead and use a sexual lubricant. It's not a sign of failed lovemaking, it's the gold for lovers in a flow, not in a hurry. And it's juicy!

You have a large selection of personal lubricants on the market from which to choose. Genital tissue can be sensitive, so experiment with lubricants until you find those that are in harmony with you. Some have ingredients in it to discourage disease, and some are flavored for taste. Some work better externally, and are better for stimulating the men's genitalia. Some are better used internally, and are better for a woman's genitalia.

Here is a good trick about lubricants to know about also: With certain lubricants, if you apply a first light layer to the Lingam and let it dry, then apply a second layer— the slipperiness lasts much longer.

Even if you lubricate copiously, ladies, having a favorite lubricant available will come in handy at times. (More on this in the next chapter on soulful healing.)

## Learn from the loving masters

What better place for beloveds to be inspired, than in the company of a couple who are living examples of respect, honor, passion and commitment? Sometimes things may feel overwhelming in your own relationship and you can forget *relationship does really work!* During challenging times, these "mentor" couples can be inspirational and wonderful resources to you. They've "been there," and are still loving one another through it all.

What would happen if everyone was in the habit of asking others about their secret to a fulfilling marriage? We all might become accustomed to look for what works in relationship, rather than noticing the things that often don't.

What is *your* secret to a fulfilling marriage, partnership, and relationship?

## A woman's monthly moon

The menstrual blood of a woman during her monthly emptying period is a natural part of the reproduction cycle of life. Unfortunately, it is also the cause for much embarrassment and misinformation, confusion and pain, both emotional and physical.

Regrettably, because of the history either of you has concerning the blood itself, or the sexual sharing during these times can be more than a nightmare for some. If this is the case, you may be carrying buried concerns and viewpoints that are getting in the way of your intimacy. Share how you feel about your thoughts on blood: blood during sex, healthy versus dirty, messy or arousing, turn-on or turn-off, playful or serious. It's okay to talk about it and explore all your thoughts and feelings.

Naturally, if penetration is painful for the woman, you won't be engaging *actively* until she's free of pain. However, remember that there is more to your sexual loving than penetration, so explore other ways to share your intimacy with one another during these times.

For many women there is a day before or during their *moon time* that is more sensitive than any other day of the month. This is a day where she can feel so psychically attuned to everything around her that it can be too intense to engage. She may feel the need to retreat into a quiet place to read, meditate and be still. This does not mean she does not like sex or her beloved, it means she is honoring her personal flow.

If either of you deny this time to honor her femininity, try to ignore her discomfort, or fill the time chatting or engaging in some meaningless way, you may receive a visit from the goddess of ego-destruction, *Kali*. As an archetypal figure, *Kali* has much to teach in ways of surrender and obedience to sacred life. Surely you have met *Kali* at some time. She will rip, rage and roar as she struggles to cut away the clutter in you when it is denying the authentic in you. *Kali* may seem cruel and uncomfortable when she makes her appearance in you or your beloved, but she is your spiritual friend. *Kali* will relieve you of the blocks to your joy by introducing you to them. She will cut away your ego consciousness that would lead you to show a false face, engage in win/lose attitudes or keep you separate from your divine nature. When the energy of *Kali* visits you, it is a spiritual opportunity to grow.

Some women find their bleeding time to be their most arousing sexual time of the month and they just can't get enough. They feel freed, as if the energy that had been building in their womb has been released, cleansing them.

As beloveds, allow for the natural rhythm of the woman to be expressed. But when concerns arise, talk to each other about what is happening and how you are feeling.

## Tears

Tears are cleansing physically and emotionally. Tears can be for joy or sorrow, pleasure or pain. Sometimes they are a signal to you to notice that you have feelings about something. Embrace your tears and those of your beloved. Let your tears flow when they appear, both his and hers. You don't have to understand where the tears come from or assign any particular meaning to them. Simply allow them. It usually feels good to cry while it's happening, but nearly always afterwards you're glad you did. You feel more clear, light, open, and happy.

Some people were told when they were little that they were manipulating others when they cried and were made to feel as if crying were bad or wrong. This is not true. Crying is healing. Allow your tears. Embrace them. Embrace your beloved when he is crying and allow yourself to be held when you are crying. Let your tears bring you more joy and intimacy. Let your tears heal you, starting with any shame you have about crying. Allow your tears to bring you closer together.

## Amrita

*Amrita* is a name to describe the female ejaculate. This ejaculate is not vaginal fluid or urine. It flows from small tear-duct-like openings near the urethra. It is a *perfectly natural response* to a woman's arousal. Also referred to as the *Tide of Yin*, this mystery of the female can flow like little droplets of tears, or spray a fine mist, or be surprisingly copious. Each woman is unique. Although *Amrita* dries rather quickly, if the ejaculate is plentiful, use towels to cover your sheets to avoid sleeping on the "wet" spots.

A wondrous sense of well-being usually accompanies the flow of *Amrita*. These orgasms are particularly releasing. Men often report how much they like the sensation of *Amrita* spraying their face while he is honoring her Yoni with his mouth.

Some women actually have unidentifiable grieving feelings when they are able to easily climax, and know that something is not quite releasing as it could, but don't know what that is. They feel the pressure, but can't release it or move it. Other women have been ejaculating as naturally as anything else since girlhood. Some guessed that what was happening was special and they have always celebrated the gift of ejaculation. While others didn't care what it was, it just felt good.

Women not experiencing this ejaculating is not unusual because of the repressive conditions of an "anti-ecstatic culture we live in, but it is unfortunate for her. To be very clear, this is not one more thing for a woman to feel shamed and pressured about. Rather, it is something to realize as a natural part of the female experience, so you can welcome the *Amrita* when "she" comes to you and not be afraid or embarrassed.

The good news is almost every woman has probably ejaculated at some point in her lifetime. The bad news for those who don't experience it currently, is that it probably was shut down as fast as it started up when you or a lover thought you urinated in the bed and shamed you. It could have happened riding a horse at fourteen, singing passionately in choir, or during high arousal in the back seat of a Chevy, and you thought, "My God, I have peed my pants, I have lost control. Well, I am never gonna let *that* happen again." And it doesn't! The trauma was too great and misunderstood so, BANG— the muscles tighten up, and control is put in place to keep you free of "embarrassing" wetness.

For some women, it may only take knowing ejaculation is possible and natural. For others, it will take a safe place to heal the emotional trauma that is stored in her psyche. The *Amrita* will flow very naturally at some point. Your attention must first focus on the need to control and then on letting go. Relax your Yoni. Relax your whole pelvis area. Breathe. She should not be pushed, criticized, or compared to other women. She will have her own timing and it will be perfect.

A woman can sense a feeling of fullness— almost like a pressure, maybe even like she wants to pee— and if she can just give the slightest push and a bit of bearing down, this may help her release the *Amrita*. Do not demand it to come. Court it, seduce, romance it, embrace it, and most of all, honor the timing. Let the gift come to you.

## Continuing experience

You may already be experiencing some of the energy phenomenon discussed in this book. If you are not yet having these experiences, it doesn't mean that you can't or won't— it simply means that you haven't yet. You can learn the new ways of becoming beloveds and you can unlearn what may be in the way.

If you are already having some of these experiences, terrific! But don't settle there. Sexual loving is one of the great mysteries meant to explore, not achieve. Whether you are a beginner or more advanced, exploring and practicing will take you deeper into the mystery.

## Life long touch

People do not outgrow their need to be touched. Infants need it to thrive. Babies can die without it or fail to develop properly if they aren't lovingly touched. When do you think that touch stopped being important to people as they grew up?

It hasn't! Loving touch is essential to well-being and no one should be ashamed of their need for touch. Hearty hugs are critical for all ages of people. Non-sexual caresses and massage are appropriate for the children, elderly and platonic friends. And between sexual beloveds, both sexual *and* non-sexual massage are called for.

How many hugs or how much significant touching did you share today so far? How do you *feel? Open? Alive? Shut down? Separate?* Well, do the math. Does there seem to be a correlation between how you *feel* and *how connected you are* compared to how much touch you've shared today? So have a hug. Get a massage. Get connected to life again when you're not— through touch. Help your partner reconnect, and honor the need for touching. Keep in touch.

## Sexual magic

A part of sexual magic is the option to redesign your bodies— *energetically*— and to play as you never thought possible before. For instance, you can use your imagination to alter the size and shape of your Lingam or Yoni to accommodate your needs. In fact, you could even imagine exchanging gender roles, and make love with one another from the energy of the opposite sex, complete with genitalia, to see what that experience is like– using the same formula.

Here's how magic works. If you are a woman who's partner is very large and intercourse is painful for you, *imagine* your Yoni growing bigger and expandable to accommodate his Lingam. Men, if your Lingam is hurting your beloved, you know how guilty you feel wanting intercourse with her. You have probably tried many things, including avoiding attaining full erection, in hopes that will help. Try this. *Imagine* that your Lingam is actually smaller, *pull* your size back— but only in your imagination. You will feel terrific getting to be fully erect, but she will not feel the full size. In addition to your being gentle, and making sure she feels prepared for penetration, this imagination exercise may considerably help your Lingam/Yoni connects.

"It's not how big it is, it's how you use it. " Men have often heard this and assumed that meant that good technique in movement would compensate for size. Here's the other part of "it's how you use it." When you are both desiring his size to be larger than life, simply imagine it. Men, imagine filling her up, all the way up to her heart. Imagine your passion and the love from *your* heart being grandly funneled through your Lingam and directly into her Yoni. Ladies, prepare to have your heart embraced as seldom before. It might take a couple of tries for you both to master this, keep trying. Energetically, there is a transmission of *Shakti energy* that passes between you and the benefits will amaze you. Try it!

## Return to your senses

When your senses are dulled and your mind is over-stimulated, sex may seem like it doesn't quite hit the mark, seeming disappointing or frustrating. What are the physical senses? You see with your eyes. You smell with your nose. You hear with your ears. You touch with your body or skin. You taste with your tongue. If one of these senses is not working for some reason because of a handicap or medication perhaps, the other senses will compensate and become more sensitive.

On the other hand, when the senses are bombarded constantly with rush hour traffic, high speed life, sitting for hours at a time, fast food, poor digestion, hours of television, ringing, faxing, talking, beeping, coffee to pep you, other things to slow you, and on and on stimulations, they ultimately send your senses into hiding for self-protection.

For great lovemaking, your want you senses tuned up and turned on but not bombarded with distracting input. Without your senses turned on, your impulse for sex goes from your head to your genitals and back to your head, essentially missing all the other body parts and energy centers in between. It's like putting a napkin on your lap before dinner, at some point eating a big bite of steak, not eating the rest of the steak, potatoes or salad, and then pulling out a toothpick to clean your teeth. Then you wonder why you're not satisfied and why you're hungry again so quickly. You have missed the meal!

To coax your senses out to play again so that you may enjoy your full body sensations and awaken your energy centers alive and vibrant, make some time to awaken them. Prepare a ritual where you can stimulate all the physical senses.

### *A return to your senses ritual:*
When you walk into the ritual space you want it to *look* inviting, interesting, and out of the ordinary. How each of you dress and adorn your bodies will add to the visual awakening. The lighting will create a mood, so put your attention on what kind of lighting you would like. Are there flowers? Pretty things to see? How is the view? What colors

do you have present? Have you noticed the sparkle in your beloved's eyes?

What are you listening to as you come into the ritual space? Is there soothing, rhythmic, soulful or erotic music? Is there an ocean lapping or river rushing near by? Are there crickets or birds singing? The wind howling or a fire crackling? The whisper of your beloved's breath near you? Notice these sounds and tune and awaken your hearing.

What aromas are in the air? The wood burning? Your hot peppermint tea or warmed apple cider? The flower arrangement of Tuberose, Roses or Star Lilies? Essential Oils on your skin, in the bath or in the diffuser? The breeze coming in from the window filled with whatever is outside; pine trees, tropical weather, flowers, salty air, rainstorm air? Incense? The undeniable aroma of your beloved? *Notice*. Awaken!

What will you use to awaken your sense of touch? The silky clothes you're wearing against your skin? The soft or furry sheets you will be lying on? The caresses from your beloved? A feather for a light massage? A rabbit fur for a light massage? A slow dance embracing one another? A warm oil massage on the massage table? Washing her hair? Warm cloth shaving him? The water of the shower, hot tub or bath?

What will you have nearby to taste? Tastes that are sweet, tangy, sour, wholesome, bitter? Luscious fruit? Chocolates? Wines? Teas, juices, lemon water? Crackers, warm breads? Cheeses? Where else will your tongue explore? Tasting the nectar of your beloved's body?

Blind folds and ear plugs can be used in the ritual to awaken your senses one by one. Take turns being the sensor and the sensory awakener. Have one of you cover your eyes and plug your ears while your beloved waves different scents in front of you, placing different tastes on your tongue and touching you in different ways . . . surprising, delighting, awakening, stimulating, vibrating. One by one, introduce a new sense until you uncover and awaken each one. Change roles and explore that way too. This is an exercise that you can do over and over again with new sights, sounds, tastes, touches, and smells. Be as creative as you desire. Think of all the wonderful things that you can use the next time you do this ritual!

You are a multi-dimensional being encompassing so much more than just your mind—so awaken your sensory connectors and come alive to more of your pleasure potential. To your *j-u-i-c-y* potential.

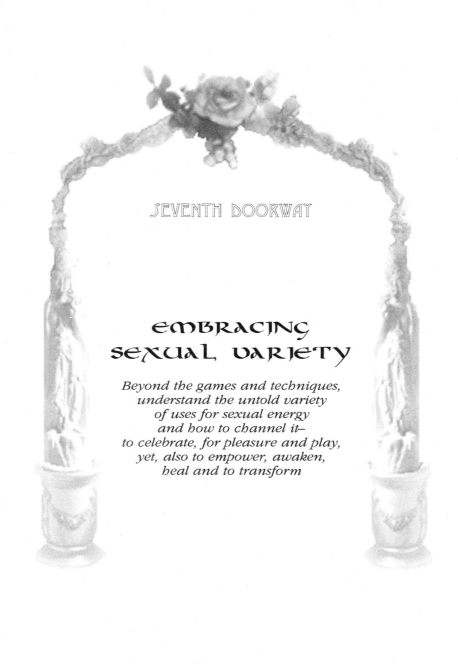

SEVENTH DOORWAY

# EMBRACING
# SEXUAL VARIETY

*Beyond the games and techniques,*
*understand the untold variety*
*of uses for sexual energy*
*and how to channel it—*
*to celebrate, for pleasure and play,*
*yet, also to empower, awaken,*
*heal and to transform*

## PART ONE

Imagine you live in a little house with a living room, dining room, and bedroom. You don't venture outside much. You're either happy with this situation, unhappy, or don't care much either way. One day, you go out in the yard and are amazed to see the length and width of your house. It's not small at all. You see for the first time it is a very *big* house. "What could be in the rest of that house?" You can't wait to enter again to explore these other rooms. This realization and curiosity can be likened to your sex life.

Most people live in only three or four rooms of their sexual potential. They romance in the dining room, make-up in the bedroom, have kinky-sex in the living room, and maybe fantasy sex in the kitchen or home office. Although there are variations of these areas which you may engage in, regrettably only a limited few additional rooms (*or potentials*) are rarely ever accessed.

No matter how many rooms you are currently living in, if you don't realize you are actually residing in a royal mansion with thousands of spectacular rooms, exalted halls leading to the other prestigious wings, ornate balconies with a view, and secret gardens, then stay tuned, because we are going on a guided tour of the palace.

When you begin to explore these hidden or forgotten rooms, you can see all of a sudden that yes, indeed, there **is more** to that house than you had known before! Most of us will admit that we *thought* there was more to sex than what we had been experiencing or *hoped* there was, but didn't know what to do next to invoke it.

When you realize that sex could be more than whatever you thought it was before you picked up this book, you have just opened the door from your little house to the *palace* hallway beyond.

Each time you come to your sexual loving sessions free from pressure to perform and free of expectations, you open a new door to one of the palace rooms. Each time you see the beloved in your partner, when you relate to them in an honoring way and allow yourself to be honored as well, a new door to the palace opens before you. When a door opens, it need not be scary nor upsetting. It *is* just the way it is. Life is unpredictable. You can't control it. The rest of the mansion will open to you as easily as your willingness to surrender to your *natural* self.

This is also the cure to boredom. Impatient and bored people go on looking for the next thrill outside of themselves. They will inevitably be let down and disappointed. When you explore the sweet, *virgin* territory of your soul's interior in the presence of your beloved's soulfulness, there is never a dull moment. Never the same experience twice. New rooms are continually available to be explored.

## Sexual energy

Sexual energy is your vitality. Suppress your sexual energy, or use it inappropriately, and you will feel a general lack of vitality or a block of creativity. Access it mindfully and naturally, and you will feel alive and vibrant. You have a choice: spend your energy foolishly by dispersing or repressing it, or, raise your sexual energy by learning how to increase and savor it.

Sex energy is simply energy. You could build a barn or run a marathon with the same energy that you use to make love. Creativity is sexual energy. Making a baby is the ultimate creative force. But that *same* force could be channeled to produce a work of art, deliver a speech, raise your children, or create a car that runs on banana peels and gets 200 miles to the gallon.

Energy is always moving. The energy system that *you* are wants to move. The human body, which runs on creative/sexual energy, must move that energy often. No living thing enjoys being stagnant. If you are depressed, or not very interested in life, ask yourself if you are moving your energy regularly. If you are not making love, expressing your personal talents, living your dreams, awakening your soul, running, dancing, playing, or moving your energy *in some way*, you are sitting on the equivalent of an atom bomb. The force of fusion untapped and unleashed is the life force awaiting release.

Your sexuality and your creativity are eternally linked. Is there a creative project you know you should be doing right now that you have been putting off? How is your sex life? If you are sitting on a creative project, your sex life may be practically non-existent also because you are *sitting* on your creativity. *Or* you might be spending your creativity having sex every waking moment of the day instead of juicing your project with that creativity. Balance is important. Understanding how to channel your creative/sexual energy is an important skill. *Moooving*, not stifling, your sexual/creative energy will bring you rich experiences.

You can channel your sexual/creative energy anywhere you want or need it to be. Channel it into your career, artistic abilities, health and well-being, and education, as well as to your relationship, ecstasy, love, awakening latent talents, conceiving children and more.

This chapter discusses how sexual energy can be consciously cultivated and channeled in various ways.

## Exploring

When you are ready to explore sexual intimacy as more than a physical phenomenon, don a new pair of eyes so that you can see the expanded territory with a fresh perspective, just as you did when you discovered that your "little" house was really a large house with unexplored rooms. Now, pretend that you have just arrived on an unknown tropical island. Explore the territory. Get curious. Become interested in how this island is laid out. Where is the drinking water, food, shelter?

We can get so accustomed to things the way they are that we forget to be in the moment with life. If you, too, have forgotten how to look at things with fresh new eyes, you may be inspired by the following entertainment movies. Each movie has characters who have been put into dramatically new situations and, as viewers, we get a peak into the extra-ordinariness of ordinary life.

*The Blue Lagoon*   . . . with Brooke Shields & Christopher Atkins
*Splash* . . . . . . . . . with Tom Hanks & Daryl Hannah
*Dad* . . . . . . . . . . . with Jack Lemmon, Olympia Dukakis, Ted Danson
*Regarding Henry* . . . . with Harrison Ford & Annette Benning
*Big* . . . . . . . . . . . . with Tom Hanks
*Being There* . . . . . . .with Peter Sellers
*Earth Girls Are Easy* . . with Geena Davis & Jim Carrey
*Junior* . . . . . . . . . with Arnold Schwarzenegger, Danny DiVito, Emma Thompson

Explore each other's bodies like they are new in every moment. Do your own experiential research in these areas. Explore like kids. Have fun. *Brreeathe*. And enjoy.

## Deepening intimacy

Some believe that sex leads to deeper intimacy. If that were the case, lots more people would be experiencing tremendously satisfying intimacy. In actuality, what brings deeper intimacy into one's life is practicing being intimate. Instant sex is not necessarily instant intimacy. Intimacy grows over time— building on mutual trust and honest communication. It requires being present and being conscious lovers in all ways. You must be willing, allowing, present, relaxed, connected to your source of love, communicative and, juicy. *Also,* it helps to have some knowledge about how sexual energy works as well as its range. This is what this chapter will introduce. In some order and balance, all these things are necessary. What would happen if you tried to drive to South America in a car with two rear view mirrors but without a fuel tank? Or you tried to get there without *you*, the driver at the wheel? Each car part from ignition to brake lights, and each operation of the equipment is required to get there. If you have two of one part, no matter how relevant, it won't make up for missing another part or step. You could have enough gasoline credit cards to pay for the trip, but if you don't have a fuel tank, you're stranded. *Each step* is important. Each skill is worth developing.
- Trust is key to obtaining intimacy.
- Trust that love is there for you.
- Trust in your ability to experience balance in your love life and lean your attention toward it.
- Trust in your ability to connect with an appropriate partner and to not engage with someone dangerous, unavailable, or unaligned with your spiritual soul.
- Trust the processes described so far and apply yourself to them.
- Trust that your body will not let you down (even in illness or with physical

limitation because intimacy can still be transmitted).

- Trust that as your armor drops away, you will feel comfortable and more able to flow through life because of the new skills you have been practicing.
- Trust that you deserve all the love that comes your way.
- Trust that you will recognize love and care that is shown to you.
- Trust your body to transmit and receive love with another person.
- Trust your feelings enough to listen to them.

Deepening intimacy requires more than hope. It requires more than infatuation and hot attraction. And deepening intimacy doesn't automatically respect the extended number of years a couple has been together— for you can be glued together without being intimate. To enjoy intimacy that will continue to deepen over time requires *living* your relationship, not merely "having" a relationship. Each of you needs to be an active participant.

Consider not taking for granted that your partner will be there forever, regardless of a devitalized connection between you. Acknowledge, appreciate and love that your partner is in your life *now*, because he is fulfilled sharing his life with you and you with him. You are both growing and learning. This is the intimacy of partnership. Partnership is built on trusting in the commitment of living your intimacy fully, rather than to a forever commitment which, because of fear, tends to promote stagnation and too often can limit full expression and potential. Rather than striving to stay together forever at all costs (as if surviving a life chained together is a true test!), the commitment of beloveds tends toward living life being *forever connected* to the mystery of life, spirit, love, and connection to self and beloved.

Trust that intimacy which is deep, rich and full may be supportive to you, rather than like experiences from your past which may have had little to do with authentic intimacy. Those painful, suffocating experiences happened to you perhaps to teach you what intimacy **is** by revealing what it *is not*.

You may have pain in your history from when someone you were close to left. You felt abandoned. People *do* leave because of unforeseen and sometimes, unreasonable circumstances. But also, people leave when they are not up to the challenge of revealing themselves. Try hard to not take this personally. When this happens, *it is not you*. It is her process. If you think she is leaving because you didn't do it right, you may be taking on more than your share of responsibility and will miss the opportunity to allow someone else *her* process of discovery and healing. You will grieve the loss, but you don't need to punish yourself, because you did nothing wrong. Each person will commit to deep intimacy only as they are interested, willing, and able. Period.

Instead of feeling responsible for the actions that another takes, when you are reviewing what there is to learn from a past experience, ask yourself what aspect of *you* disappointed you, betrayed you, or has been left behind. Without blame, judgment or incrimination, review and become aware of the deeper meanings of your past experiences and how each one will teach you about the inner mystery of you— when you are available.

## Loving to love again

If your heart has broken with grief, betrayal, and other wounding, bring this tender or armored heart to bed with you and let it be healed. Let your heartbreak be felt. Your heart didn't break in two to *break you*. Your heart has simply been broken *open*. Wide opened. Resist the temptation to patch it. In fact, remove the patches you have placed on the many wounds of your heart. Melt them because those patches are covering your joy, also. *F-e-e-l* your heart. Let yourself *know* what you are feeling. Let your heart give you the fullest experience of living. Don't miss one delicious drop of life by boxing yourself into safe little walls.

However, if you have had your eyes closed to the last drop of juicy-ness, open them now to the next one. You can begin this at anytime. You can forget to do this and then remember again. And then re-remember as many times as you need.

Allow your sexual expression to be healing for your traumatized heart. Purposefully orchestrate some of your sessions for nurturing and tenderness. Arrange them specifically to rebuild trust where you need it and honesty where it counts. Some say that life doesn't really begin until the first time your heart breaks, because there is *more room to love* in a heart that has been stretched to find meaning in the "unfairness and injustice" of the gut-wrenching pain of a heartache. Is there some relief for you in that?

Bless your heart. Bless your heart with the sweetness of the connection you have with your beloved. Bless your heart with the passion of your body dancing with the passion of your beloved's. With every wave of ecstasy and with every orgasm, let your heart be healed. Send the healing energy of each tender touch and every soulful glance directly into the center of those wounds to unburden your heart.

## The Inner Flute

Just as your throat is an open channel between your mouth to your lungs for the passage of air, so is there a channel that connects various centers of your body for the passage of vital energy. This energy channel can be explained as an "inner flute." If something gets caught in the throat and air cannot pass through it, a person may choke or even suffocate for lack of air.

When the inner flute is clogged, the result can be this serious also. However, there are also other unfortunate consequences. Emotional and spiritual disconnection, insensitivity, boredom, never-ending cravings for a "sexual fix," lack of or unsatisfactory orgasms, and disappointment are just a few examples of what you can experience when your inner flute is clogged.

A man with a clogged inner flute will have more trouble resisting ejaculation before he's ready. A woman may think she is not orgasming and may not feel orgasmic when, in reality, she is. An open channel is what allows you to experience the love part of making love and to feel connected to one another. So when there is an inner flute obstruction, you may feel *absolutely and painfully alone* even while you're making love with your most beloved partner. An open flute is what allows you to feel connected to yourself, your beloved, and to life itself. It is what allows you to have whole-body orgasms and multiple orgasms. An open *inner flute* helps you feel supported, embraced, safe, loved, expressive, tuned in and united with Divine presence.

*The inner flute* connects all the energy centers, or *chakras,* as they are also called. If you open up the body you won't find them; however, the electrical *current* they transmit *can* be registered by medical technology. You may not see them on the outside of the body either, although it's possible, but you can feel them. Each center is associated with different resources and different bodily functions.

The first energy center is located near the base of the spine, between genitals and anus. It has to do with matters of safety and survival, as well as the link to the physical world. The functions influenced are elimination, intestines, sex drive, and creativity. You intuitively guess when people are clogged in this energy center by what phrases you use to describe them: "control freaks," "tight-assed," "stick up their butt," "constipated." A person like this is run by his need for perfection and control. (An example would be Felix Unger from the "Odd Couple.") When this center is open, there is a deep connection to nature; you are trusting and feeling secure in the flow of life. The sense is smell.

The second energy center (most commonly referred to as the sex center) is located inside the pelvis at, or just above the genitals. This center has to do with creative energy–sexual, artistic, reproductive. The masculine sex-drive meets the feminine sexual-response. The bodily functions are reproductive organs, endocrine system, immune system-cleansing and purification. A person who is stuck here may be called a "sex maniac," "workaholic," or "greedy." An example of this is the person who never gets enough of whatever the addiction is. As soon as sex is over or a project is completed, there is immediately the need to do it again, usually accompanied by a *deep lack* of long-lasting satisfaction. When this center is open, your vital energy can be connected and channeled to any other energy center in a synergistic way to carry out your dreams, visions, goals, and commitments. The sense is taste.

The third energy center is located at the navel area. It is associated with gut feelings and power. The bodily functions are stomach, liver, gall bladder, sympathetic nervous system and adrenal glands. When someone is stuck or blocked in this center, we say they can't control themselves, that they have no discipline, and little follow-through. This energy center has to do with both extremes of power. An individual will at one end, give away power to other people or situations, *or*, at the other end, may overcompensate for his lack of personal power by becoming a tyrannical dictator or "wife-beater," political ogre or "power-hungry" financial mogul. The way to heal this *chakra* is by reconnecting to your personal will by listening to and honoring your emotions— all of them, even the sad, *seemingly* "weak" and inconvenient ones. When this center is open, you acknowledge the power of your emotions and the part they play in your en-light-en-ment, while surrendering the need to defend. Your outward behaviors and accomplishments become aligned with your inner guidance. You feel at ease and empowered. The sense is sight.

The fourth energy center is at the breast area. It is associated with Heart presence, compassion, healing energy, harmony and peace, and unconditional love. The Heart is the harmonizer between the lower three centers and the upper three. The Heart is the center of balance. Some of the bodily functions associated are the heart, rib cage, circulatory system, and skin. When this energy center is clogged, a person offers insincere love or expects rewards in return. It can also be difficult to receive love from others. When this center is open, love is able to express itself without conditions. There is tolerance and acceptance. After the Heart center is activated and accessed, sexual sensations expand beyond the confines of the physical only. The sense is touch.

The fifth energy center is located at the throat and is the *chakra* of self expression and expansion. It is associated with the body functions of lungs, vocal cords, throat, jaw, neck, thyroid, nervous system, and voice. When the throat center is blocked you feel insecure to express yourself ("she got the words stuck in her throat"), or are fearful of silence. This center is adversely affected every time a child understands she is to be seen and not heard, be pretty but not smart, be strong but not emotional, be smart but not hip, be funny but not accountable. Although all the *chakras* are connected to each other and work together with the others in the *inner flute*, this fifth energy center is particularly connected to the sexual center. When energy is blocked at the throat it will significantly limit the experience of pleasure and the potential of overall sexual satisfaction. When this center is open, emotions become expressions such as laughter or crying. Also, a person will listen to the "inner voice of wisdom," and will easily trust intuition. The sense is sound.

The sixth center of energy is at the brow, commonly referred to as the third eye. The reason it is called third eye is because of the additional insight that comes from accessing its intuitive capabilities. The physical associations are the eyes, nose, sinus, face, and pituitary gland. When you are blocked at this center, you are limited in life to only the "physical" facts of a situation, focusing on the intellect, and perhaps unable to sense wonderment or a higher purpose in life  When this channel is open you feel psychically protected, intuitive, connected to a larger universe, and prepared for ecstasy. The sense is *all of them, plus* itself.

The seventh energy center is located at the top of the head, the crown *chakra*. It is knowledge beyond intellect. The body parts associated with this center are the brain, cerebellum, skull, and pineal gland. When this energy center is blocked, a person might "worship" false gods like intellect, money, power, or fame (relying on fear rather than a sense of universal unity). When open, you trust that you are connected to something bigger than yourself and there is no doubt of your worthiness. You feel a direct line realizing why you are here. You feel purpose in your life and a connection to Divine Presence. The seventh center senses beyond the five elemental physical senses.

The first three energy centers are the ones commonly referred to as the "lower three." They are the untidy, misunderstood energies that most people would like to sweep under the carpet and ignore. When these centers are clogged, they promote addiction, abuse of power, survival and greed that a person can be drawn to. That is why society in general, religious doctrine, and now "New Age" thought prefer to mainly focus on the "upper energy centers" of love, divine inspiration, and connection. Somehow these seem more holy.

However, all the energy centers need to be addressed and healed, unlocked and experienced. *All the energy centers are holy.* With balance, life is fulfilling, sex is great, spiritual life unfolds, love is abundant, and sexual encounters which are soulful finally make sense at last.

When the energy centers are blocked, information cannot be transmitted to the other centers and chaos rules. Consider the way the body functions when the brain sends a signal to the feet to take a step, but if the pathway to the legs has been blocked in the spinal cord, the message is disrupted and not completed. If the spinal blockage is repaired or cleared and pathway is resumed, then the message can travel to the feet to get them to walk.

The *chakras* in your body must be able to communicate with each other as well. If one shuts down, the others must work harder and less efficiently. And, as it applies to connecting with your beloved, blocked energy centers render you unable to send or receive messages from your feeling center or Heart Center— you then are limited to experience life in a diluted, wonderful, but less interesting— form of physical sensations only. To experience the immense variety available in sexual loving, you must clear the inevitable clogs that have formed in your inner flute. Only then will the following menu of possibilities come alive. Practicing the material from the previous chapters will help with this and the more you practice, the more it comes alive.

# PART TWO

## Introduction to sexual healing

What else is there in preparing for soulful lovemaking besides making certain that the inner flute is tuned and clear of blockage? Sexual Healing! You may already have an idea of something that needs to be healed in you so that you can be a full participant in your sexual relations. Or you may not be aware of what that could be. There may be ways that you *are*, ways that you defend, or ways that you behave which you don't like and thought were unchangeable. Fortunately, this is probably not accurate.

When you think you are not pretty enough or handsome enough to get love or good sex, then sexual healing can help. When you fear you are not worthy, not creative enough, or not assertive enough, sexual healing may help. Critical judgments of you or about your performance do not serve you; they hinder you, and *this* can be healed. Inhibitions, embarrassment, fear of abandonment and rejection can all be softened by the sexual healing ritual.

Sometimes the painful memories of past sexual abuse, molestation, rape, and emotional wounding can be relieved by soulful sexual healing. Perhaps it's reconciling with the shame one has received as a child for being curious about sex, or for touching one's self sensually at the dinner table, or being caught playing house or doctor. The fear or *excitement* for young boys of getting caught masturbating (possibly establishing a pattern of ejaculating too fast), has promoted certain fantasy requirements and sexual problems for men as adults.

Sometimes it's the years of unconscious sex that must be released from your body/ mind memory so that you are healed and freed-up enough to re-choose conscious sexual loving. For a woman, it's the years of having sex with a man who, without any warming up, started pounding away, but without much significant pleasure happening for her, as he rolled over and went to sleep. Or another scenario, maybe even more emotionally wounding; a woman whose lover was very interested in her having orgasms, but only for his satisfaction, to make sure he did a good job, not to find out if she is happy. If she didn't orgasm, he would blame *her*, perhaps ever so subtly, or she's called frigid or "she's not very sexual." Perhaps his action started out as a caring one on his part, but she didn't feel included, she felt only blamed and pressured, and it was hurtful to her. She would feel completely disregarded and, in the first scenario she may feel abandoned. But in both cases, the woman can be left feeling used and insignificant.

For a man, years of hearing rejection after rejection from the women in his life takes a toll on him. When he hears how her other lover did it better, or how if he doesn't start getting interested she'll find someone who will, or that he should be this or that, he becomes wounded. It can also be things like: "It's too big." "It's too small." "How come you always have to do it?" "How come you never want to do it?" "You're *done* already?" "Aren't you done yet?" "Not now, honey!" Emotional rejections of all kinds can be stored detrimentally inside a man's psyche.

Any violation, shock, or embarrassment regarding a woman's femininity or a man's masculinity can be cause for emotional or physical armoring. *It could range from*:

- Poor dating or mate selection experiences,
- Cold speculums and sleazy gynecologists for women,
- Circumcisions and undescending testicles for men,
- Affairs, lies, divorce, separations,
- Deaths,

- Breast, cervix, uterine or prostate cancer,
- Surgeries, illness, abortions and miscarriages,
- Threats to leave the relationship,
- Critical judgments,
- Lack of commitment,
- Indifference,
- Push-pull on-off romances,
- Betrayal,

and so much more trauma has touched each life. Everyone has experienced wounding in some way, and have dealt with it as best as they could or stuffed it away as well as they could. If it hasn't occurred to you that some of these situations may have left their mark or wound on you, would you take a moment to consider this now?

Any of these scenarios that have been swept or stuffed away under a rug *are still in you somewhere* and it's up to you to move the energy into resolution which will free you for deeper intimacy. Or, you can take the chance that what you stuffed will never return to haunt you which, of course, is unlikely. It's important to understand when you acknowledge these wounds, it's not about wallowing in them and generating more pain. It's realizing how these things are controlling you without your conscious permission. Then, it's making active steps toward releasing them so you can reclaim the energy that is being wasted by covering the hurt places and defending against them.

A person who hides from his pain can never heal from it. Emotional haunting, because of years of "stuffing" could look, smell or act like guilt, rage, avoidance, lack of commitment, picking fights when things are good, leaving when things get hot, being overly nice, overly caring and accommodating, being overly controlling and rule-bound, insensitive or overly sensitive, domineering or macho, fragile or whining, overweight or underweight, a man-hater or women-hater, fearful of sex, untrusting of intimacy, untrusting of emotions, impotent, non orgasmic, and many, many more. If you feel you've experienced any of these situations or more than a couple of random people in your life have pegged you with these, that could actually be good news for you. Own for yourself what you have been hiding away, because this is a big step toward healing.

Sexual healing is about reclaiming your natural self from the patchwork of fragments you may have become while getting *here*. It's about accepting the lovable and, supposedly, not so lovable parts of yourself also. It's about becoming whole. Be willing to make yourself whole and joyful.

Your willingness to bring your pain, wounds, and unfinished business to a soulful sexual healing is the next step. The process will be described in this chapter. You need not be a doctor of medicine or psychiatry to perform the healing rituals (*however, professional services should not be replaced where needed*). You will need your compassionate, healing Heart. Ultimately *you will touch these wounded places with your love.* Attention, mindfulness and *Love* will be your medicines.

As you explore the various rooms in your palace, be on the lookout for the locked doors and the ones with armed guards standing sentry. Don't go barging into these rooms, or into your beloved's rooms until you or they feel ready to begin, or until you have created a safe, conscious environment to do so. To move ahead prematurely would be just another violation. Timing and patience *are* everything. However, court the opportunity to do so gently and consciously, and integrate what you are learning in becoming beloveds to assist you in creating what you will need to clear the blocks. There will be other exciting and wonderful rooms to explore in your palace which you may not be able to enter until these initial rooms of unfinished business have been explored and attended to.

You may be surprised to find how easily these blockages can move even after all these years being stuck with them, *just* by tending to them. Tears and raw feelings may surface and it's important to let them be expressed. Instead of judging the expression of this energy, know that it wants to move out of you, if you will let it go. Letting go is a process of not being attached. This means that when you begin to experience feelings which are surfacing, you will feel them, but not assign any particular meaning to them other than "this is the feeling that is here now" and you will allow them. "Now I feel scared, now I feel sad," or, "I feel really alone and vulnerable." You won't need to fix the feelings because the feelings are not broken. It's like letting the pus out of a wound or cleaning out the dirt. Do you need to fix the pus? Of course not. As the pus clears, you begin to heal.

It will be empowering to you and your relationship to learn you can be unburdened from the blockages. It is not unusual for blocks to reveal themselves during the periods of deepest connection, when things are going well. This is not a punishment but an opportunity, even a reward for the amount of love that you are sharing. When blockages happen, it may mean that you are mature enough, connected enough to each other, and safe enough to explore the muck and release it. Too often though, this is when people give up and complain about the "problems," referring to the muck that is surfacing. Understandably, it looks like *ongoing* trouble, rather than resolution, but *only if* you do not have a context for healing in your mind.

It's also empowering to understand this aspect of clearing as a way of spiritual development so you can distinguish between what is muck and what is love. Learn the difference between what is your unresolved baggage and what is *You.* You are not your hang-ups. You are not your shame and guilt. You are not your pain and suffering. You are not fear. You may experience hang-ups. You may experience shame, suffering or fear, but you are not made of these things, nor is your beloved. You are not a human being trying to have a spiritual experience, *you are a spiritual being trying to make it as a human being.* Plan for grace, but easily forgive the clumsiness.

## Loving the whole woman

Share your emotions of everyday life when you relate to a woman. This is vitally important—I can't emphasize this point enough. Begin to share and express emotions so naturally that it becomes a very easy part of your everyday interactions.

Love everything about her. Love her creativity. Love her mothering skills. Love her career mastery. Love how she loves *you*. Appreciate how she dances and moves her body. Appreciate her wisdom. Appreciate her ability to heal and to comfort. Appreciate her special gifts and talents. Love her sexuality. Appreciate her intuitive hunches and her outrageous courage. Love her stillness. Love her clarity. Appreciate her rage and willingness to fight for relationship. Love her patience. Love her body. Love how she is aging and maturing. Love and appreciate all of her. You do not need to agree with her, *but do love all of her.*

Your love of her and her love of herself will together *heal* her whole. Be part of manifesting a world in which all women are *inspired, allowed and expected* to be whole. Allowed to be all things: wise and spirited, spatial and complicated, sensual and erotic, sexy and strong, nurturing and simple, teachers and peacemakers, visionary and artistic, intellectual and athletic, beauties and crones, whimsical and angelic, bold and determined, irrational and emotional, from tender to torrential.

When a woman is living wholly as her complete, natural self, not having to apologize for her powerful presence, she is a most charismatic influence, a tremendously nurturing and potent resource. You just want to *be* a woman like this, or stand near one, or be healed by one, or be loved by one, or work with one, or apprentice with one. *Being* a *whole woman,* or living with one, is simply an experience not to be missed.

## Pleasuring a woman to bliss

To be in good rapport with a woman's body, it's necessary to harmonize to her rhythm rather than to your own. You certainly must be aware of your own body and rhythm, however, you must not try to arouse her body "according to" *your* drive. To pleasure a woman into *bliss*, caress her at *her* pace or just a little less. This awakens her. As she awakens, she will crave more and will let you know she is ready for a quicker or harder pace by her faster breathing, verbal requests, or by extending toward you the body part that you are touching. But until then, relax and go at this slower pace. Breathe in harmony with her. Touch her lovingly. Look softly into her eyes. Tell her what you love about her and what you love about her body. Let her know how much pleasure it brings you to bring her pleasure.

## Yoni massage

There is an entire art form of massaging your beloved's sacred space, her Yoni, with your hands. Always remember the basics. Be present. Open the space for healing. Let these be your only goals. You can hope for blissful outcome, but don't be driven toward it— there's a big difference. Clean off any distractions from your day so you can be present and relaxed by moving your energy, breathing, meditating, getting into water, or walking in nature. Breathe into your Heart and access the resources of compassion, healing, harmony and peace, and unconditional love. Channel this love and caring from your Heart through your hands and into your beloved's body. Touch her over her entire body from head to toe. Have your eyes open to her at least eighty percent of the time so she has a wondrous place to look into. Sometimes this whole body caress will take an hour or so, but sometimes it may be only a few minutes. It will depend on her needs and how much time you both have allotted to this loving session.

Use massage oil on her body and have a personal lubricant available for inside her Yoni. After a period of massaging, ask her gently if she would like her Yoni massaged.

Only after she says yes, begin to massage the outer lips at first, softly but firmly, rolling each plushy lip gently between your fingers. After some time of this, explore the other folds of her outer-Yoni using the lubricant. Be very slow and sensual. Nonchalantly, graze over her *clitoria* from time to time to let her begin to feel *that* sensation, but don't linger there or increase the stimulation— yet. You are still in the awakening phase.

The slower you go, the more relaxed she can learn to be even during increased arousal, which is extremely important to heighten states of bliss. Learn to play her body like a finely tuned musical instrument.

Ladies, the same preparation applies to you. You must clear the distractions of your day and become relaxed. Move your energy, breath, meditate, soak in a tub like a priestess, or take a walk in nature. Let the goals of orgasm and any other goals drop away. Offer your body to be cared for by your beloved. Breathe fully and feel every stroke of his hands. Relax and let go into the pleasure.

As her energy rises, you may want to transition from a massage touch to a more stimulating one. Spend more gentle attention at her *clitoria*, stimulating her just the way you know she loves it or experiment a little and find out what else she likes. If orgasm happens that's fine, if it doesn't, that is fine also. Don't worry. At some point, ask permission of her if you could enter her sacred space. It's a very considerate gesture to make, one that is extremely healing to the little girl inside her who wonders if her Yoni even belongs to her.

When she says yes, you may enter her with your ring finger and copious lubricant. Enter, point your finger up toward her belly and then park. You may feel a magnetic pull. Gently, shift to that spot and then park. Without moving your hand, begin to channel your caring thoughts from your Heart, through your hands, to her Yoni. Look softly into one another's eyes. You will begin to feel a pulsing sensation coming from her Yoni, and that will be your signal that you can begin to stimulate her here. The pulsing means she has brought her conscious attention to her Yoni. You may want to add another finger now. Use your middle finger and/or your ring finger and begin to move inside of her the way you have discovered she enjoys. Alternate among raising the energy and calming down the energy, becoming very still, barely moving.

Ladies, become very aware of the energy that is awakening in you. Let go into it. Move with it. There is no need to control now. Let go. Breathe fully now through your mouth. Don't hold your breathe because that will limit the orgasmic flow. Teach him what you like. Trust that he wants to know. Keep in mind, the healthy, mature masculine energy desires to *serve* the feminine . . . to offer the world to her. If at any time you feel uncomfortable with something, it's okay to stop for awhile to center yourself.

Both men and women have been wounded by previous sexual experiences when the "action" was interrupted for some reason, and if they didn't get the arousal going again, they were both left disappointed or frustrated. Unfortunately, there had not been a context for how *beloveds* make love. As beloveds, the miracle of stopping for a break in the lovemaking movement is that when you continue once again, the loving can usually venture even deeper. This can only be possible when there is more to the loving session than foreplay, intercourse, then ejaculation, and the constant steady drive towards the promised land of the orgasmic. Beloved's lovemaking is an ever-moving state of flow.

Ladies can, and may be active, moving on his hand while he offers it to her. Her erotic spot, the area just inside her Yoni on the upper floor under her pelvis, will appreciate stimulation. As you massage, it engorges. Get into a rhythm and go at a speed *she* enjoys, which will sometimes mean driving her into wild bliss with your stroking. However, never underestimate the erotic power of going s-l-o-w. You may kiss her. Touch other parts of her body with your other hand. Suckle her breasts. Your hands can move in her in ways that your Lingam just can't, so go for it and explore.

She may want you to enter her with your Lingam. Let her dance on your "Wand of Light" for awhile. Let the energy rise and then during a time when the energy is periodically waning (which is natural), remove your Lingam and again offer your fingers to her in an increasingly stimulating way. This can give you quite a workout for the love muscles in your arm and hand, so over time, you will be building the strength of endurance. A man is truly empowered by the passion that is raised in his beloved when he offers this kind of lovemaking.

This can continue for some time: raising energy, then waning, then Lingam, fingers, then stillness, *bliss*. When it's time to end the session, tell her you will be coming out and then cradle her Yoni gently and hold her body close to yours. Breathe together in rapport and share sweet somethings with one another. You can whisper "I-love-you," say how your body is feeling, and you can share how you're feeling emotionally. Many times there are no words— *just silence*. Except for the sound of your breath and the rhythm of your beating hearts.

Massaging the Yoni in this way is extremely pleasurable and great for her well-being. It helps her move emotional energy that may have gotten blocked during the day (over the past week, or lifetime!). When this kind of energy is flowing and not getting clogged down, it can help her with her PMS symptoms. Not surprisingly, it's also *the men* who report tremendous results from regular Yoni massage and what it does for *their* well-being. Daily massage is wonderful, even for a few minutes, but even every couple of days is beneficial for both giver and receiver. Experience the unique benefits of Yoni massage often, just for itself. And guys, offer it generously. This massage can also easily be included into daily lovemaking after you both become familiar with it as a ritual. Integrated into your daily loving practice is where you are headed.

## Women's sexual and emotional healing

In variation, Yoni massage can be offered as a soulful sexual healing for her. This can help her express herself more consciously and freely in her sexuality, heal an armored heart, and initiate her into a more conscious way of knowing her own body and feminine expression. A soulful healing received in this way can bring a woman more fully into her power as a whole person connected to the magnificent woman that she is. Indeed, a woman can begin to feel the Goddess that lives in her blood and in her soul. She begins to feel her body as sacred, her erotic expression as divine and herself as worthy. She is more able to honor the cycles and rhythms she goes through from girl to woman to wise woman crone. A woman who is connected to her personal power consciously offers herself in her intimate relations as a beloved partner capable of balance and unity.

When her *Goddess spot* (G-spot, sacred spot, or erotic spot, as it has many names), is massaged, it can be tremendously orgasmic for her. Sometimes the initial contact, though, can feel irritating or even painful as past armor is embraced. She can feel like she has to pee, which tells you that you are in the right area because it does also press against the bladder. This area can also feel numb. Backed up feelings and years of unconscious, penile pounding can generate this. Remember, numb is a feeling too, so don't be discouraged. Regular massage will awaken the area. People tend to stay clear from an activity where there is discomfort or a numb response. This is a natural reaction without a proper reason to continue. However, with the possibility of healing past trauma and awakening new sensual territory, try lovingly massaging the Goddess Spot regularly, with the coaching you find in this section.

In a soulful sexual healing, beloveds are using the signals they get to teach them about their bodies and to find out what and how they need to heal. Have you ever been in a sexual situation when the woman just begins to *cry*, just right out of the blue? More than likely, the Goddess spot was being activated. When that happened, a *sensitive* guy would usually stop what he's doing and hold her, bringing the sexual loving to an end for the time being. *In a soulful, sexual healing ritual*, both partners are expecting feelings to arise and, although action may slow down or stop momentarily, the healing energy is still moving and the movement will most likely resume again shortly.

When feelings surface, let them express and pass through. You do not have to assign meaning to them. It would not be unusual for her to have a big cry followed by a huge belly laugh, followed by orgasmic waves, followed by more tears and laughter, all within a couple of minutes. When you don't expect one feeling to last longer or another feeling to end sooner, it will all simply flow nicely.

## Preparing for her soulful sexual ritual

The ritual of a soulful sexual healing for the woman is similar to the Yoni massage. However, for this experience you will need two-and-a-half to three hours set aside.

Ladies, in some ways you will have the harder of the two jobs. You will be the receiver. You will not need to give back in any way because you will be receiving. Prepare for being the receiver by getting into your body and relaxing. You can dance, do Yoga, swim, read, do breathing exercises, hot tub, etc. in preparation for the ritual.

Men, you will be the ritual facilitator and healer for your beloved. You will be responsible for the atmosphere, food, drinks, her bath, and most of all, bringing your full attention and loving care to her soulful sexual healing. To be most successful, however, all these aspects you will do with flow and grace, rather than in a "doing," "get the job done" mode. In other words, you need to be relaxed also.

After having some opportunity to move your own energy by running, dancing, or doing something aerobic, have a shower. Then draw a bath for your beloved. You can arrange candles around the room, and put rose petals in the bath on top of the bubbles. Make sure the room is tidy, of course, and feel free to decorate it in a new way if you like. For instance you could move in some of the big plants from another room and create a tropical garden while she bathes. Make sure the water and room temperature are good for her, and when you've created the atmosphere, you can lead her into the bath and ease her into the tub. Your sensitive and responsive caring for her invites her to relax. Now tell her in words to be prepared to be completely pampered by you for the rest of the evening.

While she is in the bath, if you haven't already, transform your bedroom or whatever room where the ritual will take place. You want the room to be surprising to her when she enters it. You want her to feel she's entering a very safe, womb-like, sacred place where anything is possible, even miracles! Perhaps it will take place in different rooms each time. You will want lots of pillows, lit candles or lamps covered with pretty scarves. Scent the room with Rose, Ylang ylang, Lavender or some other scent you both love. You can have the room filled with flowers from your yard or from the florist, and you can bring in plants from the other rooms. You will want to have a lubricant near by (Silk, Astro Glide, PrePair, ForPlay, etc.) and a sweet smelling massage oil (you'll find a nice variety at your local health food co-op or store).

Have available nearby your ritual, a plate of luscious fruit, some chocolate if she likes that, little crackers or pastries. Have tea or wine and some water also. And let's see, what will you wear? *Hmmmm?* How about a piece of silk fabric, tied at your waist and nothing on top? Or a sensual feeling robe? Perhaps you would wear the hat or your leather jacket which are her favorites on you, with your boxer shorts? Or whatever you will feel comfortable in.

## Emotional preparation

When the ritual space is the way you want it, but before you bring your beloved in, sit down for a minute and center yourself. Put your hands on your heart and meditate. Begin to let go of the business of preparing the space. Now that the room is set, you need to prepare *yourself.* Your role for this ritual is to be your beloved's healer. This means that although you will be conscious of your own body and comfort, your primary attention will be on her. You want her to feel as trusting as if she is in a safe womb.

To create this place of safety, you do not have to know everything that would have her feel this trusting, but you need to be open to her comments and requests on how to create it. Some "requests" ("I wish we were at the beach cabin right now") are really just feelings that she is sharing; they are meant to be acknowledged, but not fulfilled— right this second. Remember, it's her *feelings* about the requests for which you are attempting to create a supportive space. (If you are unsure, you can ask her if she'd like you to do something about that particular thing.) So listen to her. Listen for the feelings. Let her know you care about what she is expressing.

You might want to elicit her idea of what a safe place would be, by asking her what a *Garden of Eden* would look like to her? What would it *feeel* like? Smell like? Taste like?

Prepare yourself for the emotions that may surface. No matter what she expresses verbally, you must be present for her and verbally let her know that you are there for her. Be there for her even if the stuff is about you— even if it's not true, or even if it seems unfair, unkind, whatever! It's a tall order, I understand. But, you can actually do it if you stay present in your heart, keep your breath moving, and understand how valuable it is to both of you. It's *because* she feels safe that this emotion will surface; the purpose is not to punish you with it, but to clear it. If you move with the feelings, no matter how irrational they seem to be, they *will* move! They will no longer be lurking under the facade of congeniality, from which they could explode at any moment.

Staying centered and being present to your beloved's emotions will become easier with practice. In the beginning, or during particularly trying times, it may help to count your breath so that you can stay present without getting defensive, running away, or checking out emotionally. Count one for the breath in, and two for the breath out, then three for the next breath in and four for the next breath out. Continue until you get to ten and then count backward to one, then back up to ten, and so on. Use the counting to help stay present without becoming attached *to* or detached *from* your beloved.

Sometimes it helps to consider that her outbursts are like that of a great actor and you are the director.* As the director, you have been trying to elicit a certain emotion from your star actor. And now in front of your eyes you have it: the profound demonstration of that emotion. *Voila*! You feel jubilant. Your star actor is going for it!

Even though she may be very interested in receiving this wonderful healing from you, there could still be some apprehension on her part. She may respond the way many people do when they're scared, by picking a fight with you. Stay relaxed. Anticipate such a reaction and just love her even more. Ask her to tell you how she is feeling; not what she is thinking, but what she is feeling. She may say that "*something* is too this" or "you are too that" and you can simply let her know that *you understand* . . . and then, ask her how she *feels* about *that*. Gently keep coming back to what she is feeling. Eventually she may say what she is afraid of or concerned about, which may include aborting today's ritual. This healing process is about your beloved being authentic and being in her own power so she always has a choice in matters that concern her. Take her feedback as gracefully as you can, because if the ritual does not happen now, with your supportive encouragement, it may happen someday.

When she has the power to say "No" and is truly able to use that power, only *then* is her "Yes" fully able to express itself authentically. So, if it looks like she is leaning toward *"No,"* just let her know that you are still there for her, that you would love to give to her, you love her, and want to be her healer. Offer to simply hold her and cuddle. Most likely she will love that. At some point, she will feel safe enough to say "YES." The timing will be her own.

Ladies, what should you wear? Wear something simple like a tunic or a light robe that opens in the front. Wear something that helps you feel like a goddess, princess, or queen. You won't need lingerie or anything overtly sexy tonight because you are raising the healing energies, not the erotic. You may enjoy wearing a flower in your hair or pearls around your neck. You can prepare yourself as if this is your very *first* intimate experience.

---

* Thank you to Jeru for this example.

## The healing ritual

She has been soaking in warm water and you have prepared yourself and the ritual space. Now, invite your beloved out of the bath. You can gently towel her dry very slowly. Have your soft eyes open to her. Lead her slowly to your relationship altar where you can light a candle for the healing that will take place there tonight. Perhaps you will say a prayer together or dedicate the energy that will be raised to your love blossoming.

For this ritual, the woman will lay down upon a throne of pillows raised slightly enough so that she can easily make eye contact without crooking her neck and stopping the energy flow. The man will sit between her legs, probably with a firm pillow under his tushy. Face one another, bring your soft eyes into contact, and place your hands in prayer position in front of your heart. This is a salute to the Divine Presence in each of you. Begin and end every ritual with this honoring. The respect goes very deep into the psyche.

With both of your hands resting on her belly in order to help calm and center her, say out loud what your intention for this session is. You might consider something like, "Beloved, I offer myself as your humble healer. I will be *here* for you. I will listen to you with my heart. Whatever you are feeling is okay with me. I will offer you my hands for this healing and my sensitivity for whatever comes up. You don't have to give back to me at all. It is my honor to give to you for all that you are, and all that you give to me. *You* receiving this ritual from me is *my* gift. If you need anything, just ask. I love that you trust me enough to let me honor you in this way. I bless the goddess in you. *You are* beauty to me. You are my teacher in matters of love and relationship. Let me give to you for all the love you share with me." Whatever you say, make sure you include that she is free to express herself— that she can ask for what she wants and get her needs met.

Women, you can respond to his declaration by acknowledging your own willingness to be an active part of the ritual by receiving from him. Let him know that you are honored by his offering and are grateful for his attention. *Your* declaration of gratefulness and willingness begins to soften *your* heart and brings you more into your body. A satisfying, soulful sexual healing is not only what he is able to give, but what you are consciously able to receive. So thank him for his efforts. Be grateful for his loving. Forgive him any clumsiness or nervousness in trying something new and appreciate his willingness to be a conscious sexual lover with you.

Men, make sure your eyes are open to her at all times; then, whenever she opens her eyes you are right there for her. This, in itself, is tremendously healing for the wounded psyche. Sometimes your beloved may want to close her eyes to focus on feeling something, but within a couple of minutes if she hasn't opened them on her own, you could invite her to come back with her eyes.

Take a full breath deep into your belly and exhale with sound. Coach your beloved to do the same. Take more deep breaths and then go into your breathing pattern of connected breathing. Take some warm massage oil and begin to massage her belly, very slowly. Firm but not hard. Deep, but not so that she is squirming. Channel the love in your heart through your hands into whatever part of her body you are touching. Massage with the whole of your hands and when you find bumps and knots, send your loving energy into those places to melt the blocked material. Most everyone has some knots. Spend no more than about ten seconds on each knot and then move to other places. You can come back to the knotted areas again for the short melting sessions, but then move on.

After you have worked on the belly for a while, gather up the emotional muck you've been unclogging in there as if you are sweeping a pile of dirt up off the kitchen floor. Move your hands (with the gathered muck) up her body to her shoulders and then down her arms, then *whoosh...* pull your hands off of her hands, then her fingers. Move up to the shoulders

149

on her inhale and you whoosh down her arms on her exhale. Do this two to three times.

Both of you will probably feel much better after you do this. You will probably feel your breath deepen, your face soften and experience a general feeling of relaxation and peace. But you are just getting started. Go back to the belly and massage some more. *Knead.* Use lots of oil. Then move it all up to her shoulders on an inhale and down her arms on an exhale. You should work on her belly anywhere from five to twenty minutes.

Make the sweeping motion one last time and then move your massage up to her breast area. Massage the whole chest firmly but not too hard. These strokes aren't for stimulation; it's to remove emotional residue. The massage is also to help her to be more in her body and less in her head. After you have massaged her chest for a while, sweep the muck up to her shoulders on an inhale and down her arms, off her hands on an exhale.

Massage this area between five and twenty minutes. The slower your strokes (but firm), the slower her mind becomes. You are massaging up the *inner flute,* cleansing out the residue so that when she raises her sexual energy it has some place to travel. She will be more likely to whole-body orgasm when that time comes (*later, during this session or, . . . someday).*

Your beloved may start to get fidgety somewhere between five to thirty minutes, and wonder if you are becoming bored; she may say she wants to stop, or wonder if she should do something for *you.* This rarely means she is not having a good time. On the contrary, it means that it is *too good* and she wonders if she deserves it. Does your beloved deserve to be pampered like a queen? Let her know she does. She needs to hear from you verbally what you are getting out of this session as well. It may not even occur to her that *you are in heaven,* so let her know. In fact, about every five minutes whether she *seems* to need it or not, tell her how beautiful she is and what you are feeling as you care for her. Tending to her in this way demonstrates to her that she is worth it and *deserves* to be treated with such care and attention.

Now it's time to work on her inner thighs. This area may be very tender indeed. You must work very, *very* slowly with full palms only. Massage the whole upper leg, especially the inner thigh, firmly but not hard, from the knee to her groin. There is a lot of tension wrapped up in those thighs in the average woman. When it's time to sweep off the emotional residue, you'll pull it off of her legs this time. Gather up the muck and now pull towards her feet on her exhale, and at the tip of her toes flick it off. Massage her thighs a little more *for ten to thirty minutes* and, periodically, make the sweep. And then, *ever so slowly,* begin to massage her groin with as much of your full palm as possible. Massage on top of her pelvic bone rubbing firmly. You may take another cleansing sweep before you continue.

You can ask her now if you can begin to massage her Yoni. If she says *yes,* begin gently and slowly to massage the outer lips and the perineum area (between her Yoni opening and her anus). Lubricant is helpful here. Send her your love. Be gentle. Go slow. You are here to heal, *but it's certainly okay if it feels good to her!* Say hello to her *clitoria* without trying for arousal.

Ladies, become in touch with how you are feeling. Stay connected to this experience. Let yourself have what you need. This is for you, not for him (although he is having a *fabulous* time). You will miss the value for yourself if you are just going through the motions for him. *This is for you.* Together you are awakening even more of your consciousness and sensuality. Allow it. Go for it. You really do deserve it.

At any time during this ritual the woman could begin to express emotions. Men, be a safe space for her feelings. When she is emotionally expressing, you may wonder if you should continue massaging or not. Depending on how dramatic the emotions are, you may want to keep your hands on her, but without moving, and simply listen to her attentively. Or, you may continue moving your hands very slowly and listen.

When you sense the time is right, let her know that you will be asking her three times* if you can enter her internal sacred space as part of the ritual. When she has responded yes for the third time, you may now enter her. Something such as, "May I enter your sacred space? May I enter your Temple of Love? Beloved, may I honor you in your secret garden? " She may never have had the experience of a man asking permission before. This simple ritual question, alone, has the potential of intense healing for her wounded psyche. She may easily get teary when she is asked permission and feel a host of complex feelings. This is wonderful and common!

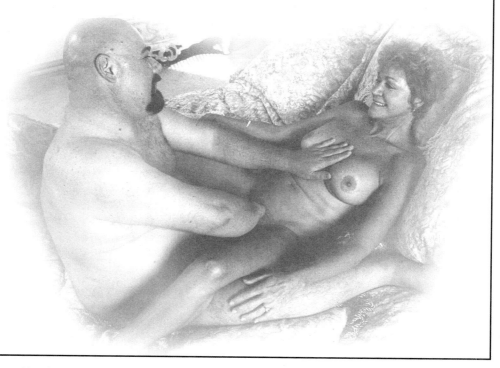

*This ritual tool is inspired by the work of Charles & Caroline Muir.

151

With plenty of lubricant, enter her with your ring finger. That finger is energetically like water and more like her own energy, so it has the most affinity and is the least threatening. Come in, up, and park. Simply breathe connectedly and wait for a pulsing to begin. At this time you can begin to wiggle your finger slowly from side to side. Your intention is to bring as much consciousness to the area as possible. You might say in your thoughts, "Beloved awaken your heart, connect your Yoni sensations to your heart."

Draw circles with your finger. Tap and Pulse. Explore the whole Yoni. Let your beloved feel herself inside her own Yoni by your touch. She may have never touched a Yoni herself. Tell her what's happening in there. Tell her when her Yoni secretes more nectar, tightens in on your finger, or spasms. This will help her relate to her Yoni in a deeper way. Pull your finger towards yourself in a 'come here' motion, stroking her in this way for some time. Next, go ahead and stimulate her in ways that she would like, fast or slow and varied. Add your middle finger. Energetically that finger brings the quality of fire, so it will add some intensity. You can ride the waves into orgasmic intensity and then back into the lapping waves of peacefulness and quiet joy. You can raise the energy up and then slow it down. Alternate between the high intensity and the lapping waves. The quiet waves between the high intensity ones are equally as relevant. Without the quiet ones, you might miss the undulating rhythms that lead you into ecstasy.

Remember, it's okay to: laugh; tell each other how you are feeling; giggle; compliment; appreciate; bless; eat fruit; and worship. Laugh some more. Drink water. Be filled with gratefulness.

Soon enough, you may be wondering where all the time has gone. You have discovered present time. Two to three hours can pass very quickly when you are in present time. And sometimes when you have only a few minutes to connect, it may feel like eternity. Time passing can seem magical. Present time is the ultimate answer to time management.

When the sexual healing is for her, there will be no intercourse that night. Lingam/Yoni is excluded from the ritual to give the psyche of the woman the experience that you are coming to her just to care and honor her, and not solely to *get off* in her. This is not to accuse you of such behavior, but most likely she has had experiences somewhere in her past which have left behind a negative impact on how she makes love today. So, even if she pleads for Lingam/Yoni, tell her— *that* yummy gift is waiting for her in the morning and if she can't wait, she can wake you in the middle of the night after you both have had a little sleep to seal in the experience.

Another reason she may seem urgent wanting Lingam/Yoni is because the intimacy is so lovely and nurturing that it inspires a woman's passion. And finally, she may unconsciously desire a Lingam/Yoni finish because she fears her partner is unsatisfied. She doesn't quite trust that he has experienced joy by simply giving to her.

Let her know you would like to give her a healing session again, very soon. Try to offer her a ritual like this once a week or once every two weeks.

Ladies, as much as you love having your beloved deep inside of you with his Lingam, on your special night, please be willing to be satisfied with his hands and lips. This is not a punishment, I assure you. You may think this suggestion odd, but try it for at least five of these rituals over an eight week period and then *you* decide. After those five sessions where the healing is just for you, you may continue to pass on the Lingam/Yoni connect, *or go for it*, based on your needs.

To come into closure for this session, tell her you will be coming out soon and then slowly remove your fingers. Place one hand over her Yoni and the other over her heart. Share what you enjoyed about being her healer and what you have learned about her and about yourself. Ask that these two centers— heart and sex— always be connected, never separated again. Together in harmony, an ultimate union. Tell her you would love to serve her again in this role very soon. Tell her what you love about her. You might say something like, "We have just spent our evening tending to the deepening of our relationship. We have focused our minds on love, and we have opened our hearts to our Divine nature. We have healed another layer of human wounding with the compassion of our attention. We have practiced kindness with one another and we have practiced conscious loving. Thank you. Thank us. Thank God." Place your hands in prayer position before your heart and slightly bow, saying *Namaste.'* As you do this say in your thoughts, "I honor the Divine Presence in you and the Divine Presence in me." The ritual for this evening is complete.

Cuddle up and sleep. Be aware of your dreams. You have just participated in some very deep work. And congratulations. Each time you share in a ritual like this, the energies will move in various ways. One time there may be enormous emotional releases, while another ritual may be so gentle there's barely any movement. The purpose of a healing ritual is to move whatever energy there is to move, and to share love.

## After shocks

Don't be surprised if a woman feels sensitive and vulnerable the next day. This is not unusual. Men, be prepared for outbursts from her and be emotionally available to offer her affection. Just love her and have compassion. If you will simply let her have her feelings in your presence, you will not need to fix anything.

Ladies, after a such an intimate experience you are bound to feel a little off-guard. You are in new territory because there isn't as much to *guard* anymore. Try and resist the impulse to pull all your old pieces together again. You may have become so accustomed to the way you were that you feel strange at first. Allow in the vulnerability from this much trust and intimacy, and just notice who you are *now,* after releasing another layer of emotional armor. It is melting.

Sometimes you may fear that his being so extra amazing was for one night only and that sexual loving will return to the way it was before (even if it was okay). Practice the soulful sexual loving exercise so often that it spills out into your everyday lovemaking. You can both declare your interest and intent toward this.

## Appreciating the whole man

Appreciating the whole man . . . and *appreciating the man whole*. The most healing thing you can do for a man *is* to appreciate him. Appreciate what he does for you, how he loves you, cares for you, and desires good things for you. You do not have to agree with him in order to appreciate him *nor* for him to feel your appreciation. Appreciate his body, his look, his style, and most of all appreciate his Lingam and how much pleasure it brings you. His Lingam is very important to him and most men have not been filled to capacity by having their Lingams loved and appreciated.

Most men have experienced as boys the ridicule of being uncircumcised (or circumcised), getting untimely erections, or the common competition for who has the biggest one. Competition, fear, and rude remarks have haunted men for entirely too long. In addition, men have been concerned about their abilities to perform, and have continued to believe that "size matters."

More than anything else, this concern about performance, (including *worrying* that his penis size is inadequate), affects a man's ability to perform. We are emerging from a phase in which our culture promotes boosting a man's ego at any cost, including approving a man's exclusion of his partner's pleasure and well-being. Boosting a man's ego may have been a step in the right direction toward his being appreciated, but it has missed the mark entirely for what is necessary for *soulful* beloveds. Soulfully relating beloveds, more than anything else, enhance the esteem of the other, and would not consider diminishing the other to be a viable option of personal ego stroking. *Beloveds* are into *real* relating where balance on all levels is important. Both partners need to be individually recognized and loved fully.

Appreciating the whole man means honoring what is good and true about him, as well as what you both are calling forward in his nature as a conscious lover. It means honesty and vulnerability. The woman does not give up anything to make this appreciation available to him, nor must he have to beg her for appreciation.

And, yes, this is indeed possible!

Men, allow your beloved to love you with her appreciation. Remember the importance of actively receiving her appreciation and care. Realize how much you need and deserve this, especially if it is difficult for you. If you take her appreciation for granted, get in touch with why you would block being loved. The most important ongoing appreciation you can count on, though, is from yourself. When you can say that *you* love yourself and mean it, *this* is what's most valuable.

Culturally, men have been celebrated for their abilities to raise fortunes and conquer everything from nature to nations. Unfortunately, men have been given entirely too much credit to conquer their own feelings as well. Companies operating on this masculine principle have been built on facts and financial gain, rarely on the humanity that comes from emotional and honest relationships. This is changing now in the boardroom but an indelible impression has already made its mark on the men in our lives. Men are having to *unlearn* the unfortunate messages that have blocked their permission to be emotional and whole beings. This is a *process* which will take some time, will respond with one's individual permission to do so, and will require ongoing compassion.

Appreciating the whole man means understanding how he has been trained, which in some cases, has been to be robotic. Always know that *good men* live under those robot suits or macho images. Soulful beloveds will work together to give space and opportunity for his emerging emotional nature to express itself. It must emerge and express itself for his soul to be recovered so that he can play his part in becoming beloveds.

Men, please understand that you do not have to always be right and never wrong. You will survive and be fine. Only the armored, inauthentic, superficial ego will crumble. Your *essential self* will thrive. Understand that you do not have to be 110 percent responsible for the sexual response of your partner. It is okay if your Lingam is not hard all the time. It is okay if it is. It is okay if you cry or get teary at the movies, during emotional situations while having sex, or any time. It just is! It is natural that you would have deep feelings for your beloved, your family, your community and your career. *And . . .* it is okay to show it.

Look at small children and see how free they are to be themselves. Infants will wail when hungry or uncomfortable, and when the need is handled, they forget it. They have successfully moved the emotional energy associated with their discomfort. A toddler is always on the go. Moving energy. Exploring. Learning. If either of you feels that you have lost touch with your authentic self, then become apprentices to children who are between birth to three years old. Study their spontaneity. Their spunk. There is a difference between childish and child-like. *Childish* refers to how people are when they are wounded such as: "You can't make me," or "I'll show you," whereas, child-like says: "Let's play!" or "Let's learn!"— all from a sense of wonderment and big eyes.

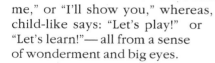

Men, allow yourselves to be appreciated for more than simply your role as provider and protector, even though those contributions are truly appreciated also. Providing for your physical well-being is indeed important, but so is balance. Let your whole self out to play. Check in with your emotions and take your inner magical child out for a spin. See what opening to your inner little boy and to your feelings can do for your love life.

## Men's sexual and emotional healing

Few men actually feel the freedom to express themselves in as natural or balanced a way as they would like, both sexually and sensually. Unfortunately, what men do to achieve this in our culture is to try to have "more, better, and different" as much as possible in their sexual scenarios, as if the solution to freedom is outside themselves. When a man allows his natural sensual sensitivity to emerge, *he* becomes the "more, better, different" that he seeks. Sexual / emotional healing for a man is tapping into his soulful passion connected to his Heart, and releasing any barriers that would prevent this connection.

Men often report how frustrated they are by their own needy emotional hunger*, the yanking around to fill the neediness, and all the ongoing chase and frequent disappointment they experience to get even a "bone" thrown to them. They want to be free to enjoy abundant lovemaking without all the hit-or-miss chase for sex and the subtle rejections (even the self rejection). Men want to feel that they are accepted for who they are and want their masculinity honored.

This is not too much to ask. And much can be done toward this with mindful attention from both beloveds as they bring healing energy to his body and to his heart.

## Releasing his performance anxiety

The last thing a man needs is *more* arousal if he is impotent or ejaculating prematurely, whether this is a temporary situation or has been long-term. More arousal is also the last thing needed by a man who seems not very sexual and is avoiding sexual contact. Additional arousal is likely to be felt by his psyche as increased pressure to perform. These men have been traumatized. The Lingam does not go limp because *it* is having a problem, it stays limp because the *man* is having a problem. He is most likely having personal concerns that he is unable to resolve (except in cases of medication side effects), and it is simply unrealistic to expect his libido to respond on the outside when he is emotionally wounded on the inside. If he insists on fixing one of these *"problems"* without researching his emotional interior, he is now one more step removed from the actual problem and off base from resolving it.

Holding the Jewels is very helpful for the above situation. The soothing, relaxing environment it creates helps release in an emotional way, the over-stimulating charge that is being held in the genital area. It is as if men's energies are being short-circuited,

---

* In Robert Johnson's book, *Lying with the Heavenly Woman,* he exquisitely details the inner psyche (anima) experience of man's own unresolved "needy" tendencies. This is worthy reading for every man *and* woman involved in consciousness.

sometimes over-amped, by over-stimulation. This can be caused by several conditions. Over-stimulation can consist of continued arousal without heart connection. It can be a result of history, from having to "hurry up and ejaculate before mom finds you masturbating in a locked bathroom." It can be from a steady diet of thirty-minute-or-less sexual experiences. And, over-stimulation also comes from limiting the touch to a man's body only to his Lingam, while seldomly touching any other body part during sexual encounters— as if the Lingam were the *only* erogenous zone. *Every single spot on the human body is an erogenous zone* if embraced with sensitivity and awareness. To get you started on other areas, check out his ears, underarms, forearm skin, thighs and nipples, and then try others.

Holding the Jewels is also helpful for "Type-A" personality men living in the fast lane. Having sex *as* or *with* an A-type is like the difference between eating fast food or savoring a nine-course French meal. Holding the Jewels can help relax his speediness and "doing-ness."

As with the Yoni massage for women, make time for this essential practice of holding the Jewels for men. It's the equivalent of an apple a day for your sexual health. Holding his Jewels centers him. It helps him get into his body, and to feel his body completely.

This practice is very empowering for women as well. In times past, many women have refrained from actively making a difference in their own sexual situations because they felt powerless to do anything about the hungry-needy pull from their partners. A *powerless* woman feels her only choice is to either leave the relationship, or to stay. But if she doesn't find value when she stays, she responds only half-heartedly leaving her body emotionally unattended while *it* has sex and *she* thinks about something else. You can imagine how unrewarding this is to both sexual partners.

A woman can suggest a Jewel caress and can sense what a difference is made with her healing presence. At any time she feels his emotional attention has become distracted from the intimate connection, she can shift her participation to holding his Jewels to help bring him back into his body. By doing this, she takes a positive step to help him be present, which in turn makes it easier for her to feel comfortable, and be present.

## Preparing for his soulful sexual ritual

Ladies, you will be the ritual facilitator and healer for your beloved. Men, you will be the receiver. Set aside two to two-and-a-half hours for his healing ritual. Begin your time together by moving some energy: dancing, running, doing yoga, etc. Get your breath *moooving* for at least ten to twenty minutes.

Draw him a bath that he can melt into and never ask him if he wants one in advance because he will probably say "No," he'll "just jump into the shower." Unless he has declared that he hates baths, put him in one. Unless he is a bath lover, he has probably forgotten how delicious soaking can be. When I hear men share about their healing experiences with their beloveds, they often mention how moved they were to be put into a bath. A man will often say that no one has drawn him a bath since his childhood. And many will make this report with teary eyes. (*It is so precious.*)

It is your turn to transform the room into the healing temple for your beloved. Consider some of the suggestions offered for your ritual (from the section on Preparing for her Soulful Sexual Healing). Make an altar or add to an existing one. Include some very personal items to him. Hang his baseball cap on the bedpost. Adorn the room with his prized awards or trophies, symbols of projects that he is working on like rebuilding cars or other hobbies. Place photos of important people *to him*; of you, children, parents, mentors, etc. Have drinking water available, as well as food, lighting, pillows, lubricant, oil, and a warm wash cloth for later (it can be wrapped up in plastic wrap or foil and kept in a heating pad).

Wear something simple like a tunic, a fabric wrap or light robe or nothing at all. Wear something that does not arouse his mental fantasy, but which inspires his respect of you as the High Priestess.

## Emotional preparation

There was a time very long ago, when wise and respected women were the Temple keepers and men would visit these High Priestesses in order to be purged and healed from the ravage of war experience before returning home to join their families. This visit was accepted as holy and men went to be healed, renewed, and to receive power. This was a very different opportunity and experience than the pit stop that some men make today at a topless bar or with a prostitute.

Men, imagine the high priestess image in the sacred temple as you prepare for your session this evening. Your beloved will invoke the knowledge and wisdom of the temple healer for you. Put your trust in her and let go into her care. You will not be in charge tonight, but you will be safe. Relax and open to your own heart's vulnerability. Tune into the subtle energies running through your body. Be available to the feelings in your belly and really *feel* them courageously tonight as if the quality of your love life depends on this (practically speaking, it does!). When your arousal gets awakened, mindfully open your heart energy and make the connection to your sex energy. (Turn that old *slow moving freeway* into a super highway of inter- chakra million dollar commerce.) Trust yourself to be loved and lovable.

Ladies, when the ritual space is the way you want it, but before you bring your beloved in, sit down for a minute and center yourself. Now that the room is set, you need to prepare *yourself.* Put your hands on your heart and meditate. Begin to let go of the business of preparing the space. Your role for this ritual is to be your beloved's healer, and your main healer tool is *your love* for him. This means that although you will be conscious of your own body and comfort, your primary attention will be on *his* feelings and on loving him. You want him to feel as trusting as if he is in a safe womb.

You do not have to know everything that would have him feel this trusting, but do be open to his comments and requests. Most importantly for him to let go and relax, he must understand who is in charge — *you.* If he is unclear about who is running the show in any way, his attention in part, will be on controlling the situation should you become nervous, unsure, or needy yourself — and he won't be able to completely relax.

Make it clear to him that you've got it all covered, you're in charge so that he can relax. Don't sweat it if you fear that you don't have it all together, because if you ask for guidance from *inside* yourself, you may feel magically inspired in your role as the healing priestess of the temple during his session, and will likely be pleasantly surprised at how capable you can be.

Prepare yourself for the emotions that may surface. No matter what he expresses verbally, be present for him and verbally let him know that you are there for him. Be there for him even if the "stuff" is about you— even if it's not true, if it seems unfair, unkind, whatever! It's a tall order, granted. But, you can actually do it if you stay present in your heart, keep your breath full, connected, and moving, and, understand how valuable his venting (if any) is to *both* of you. He is able to express emotions because he is feeling safe; the purpose is not to punish you with it, but to clear. If you move with the feelings no matter how irrational they seem to be, and send your love into those painful and dark places, they *will* move! These murky, uncomfortable feelings will no longer be lurking under a facade of congeniality while threatening to explode at any moment.

*In general, men will simply be blissed out during a soulful sexual healing.* But when emotional outbursts do surface, don't be surprised if it manifests in torrents of rage. This may be because of the limited range of cultural permission allotted to men for the expression of their emotions (they are generally allowed only despair or "non-feeling," at one end of the spectrum, or rage and fists through the wall at the other) . Be prepared to offer him pillows at his sides so that he has something there to put his fists on. The intensity that comes from him may be a bit scary, but keep breathing, stay centered, and intend healing. It may help you to use the counting breath meditation (mentioned earlier in this chapter) when you are trying to stay present to emotional expressions which *seem* difficult to bear.

For the purpose of this ritual, you both must understand that you are not there to fix the rage (or any other feeling) or find the reason for it; only to *mooove* it, send love into him and let it go. Allow the presence of Love to illuminate the shadowy places. If a man chooses to express himself with a little pounding of his fists into those pillows at his sides, he does it only to assist him in moving his feelings, not to see how demonstrative he can get, and it is certainly not to hurt his partner in any way. Let Love be your guide.

Even though he may be excited about receiving this sexual healing from you, there could still be some apprehension on his part— particularly the part of him letting go of control. He may respond the way many people do when they're scared, by picking a fight with you even before you begin the ritual. Stay relaxed. Anticipate such a reaction and just love him even more. Reassure him that his feelings are okay with you, suggest that it is good for him to share what he is feeling— *not what he is thinking*— although he may often mistake the two at first. ("I think this ritual business will limit my spontaneity" is the thinking mind trying to prejudge the experience. A more honest sharing of what's really going on is "I feel scared trying something new.")

He may be urgent for you to get on to the "good" stuff— the *seemingly* more sexual components of the ritual. Whenever he becomes impatient or distracted in some other way, you can always reach down and hold his Jewels and this should help him relax. Gently keep allowing space for whatever he is *feeling*.

Ladies, what should you wear? Wear something that helps you feel like a goddess, princess, or queen. You won't need lingerie or anything overtly sexy tonight because you are raising the healing energies, not the erotic. You may enjoy wearing a flower in your hair, pearls around your neck, or perhaps a jeweled head-band— anything that inspires the priestess of love in you. You will be the *Dakini* (sexual healer*)* tonight. The wisdom of the *Dakini* is an archetypal part of every woman and you will access that wisdom by inviting her and being open to it.

Ladies, be present. Be attentive. And hold the space for him. If at anytime he begins to assert himself, look to see if *you* have dropped the ball, through doubting yourself or deferring to him. Obviously, you are tending to him in a loving way, but you are also holding the space for all this to happen— from watching the time, if that is a concern, to managing your own emotional process so that the ritual continues to be *his*.

## The healing ritual for him

Hopefully he has been soaking in his king's bath or equivalent. You might even want to get in behind him at the end to wash his back and whisper in his ear that the evening tonight is just for him. That he doesn't have to give back in anyway, and that you just want to love him up. Bring him out of the bath with a towel to dry him. And from this point forward, have your soft eyes open to him. You might want to lead him slowly to your relationship altar where you can dedicate the energy from the healing that will take place there tonight.

Before you get into the lying down position, the woman may want to massage his neck and head. Massage the face, and really get into the scalp and neck knots. Then as you begin the ritual, the man will lie down upon a throne of pillows raised slightly enough so that he can easily make eye contact without crooking his neck and stopping his energy flow. The woman will sit between his legs, probably with a firm pillow under her tushy. Face one another, bring your soft eyes into contact, and place your hands in prayer position in front of your hearts. This is an acknowledgment of the Divine presence in each of you. Begin and end every ritual with this honoring. This respect will ripple deep through you.

Hold his Jewels to help relax and center him, as you say out loud what your hope for this session is. You might consider something like, "Beloved, I offer myself as your sacred healer. I will be *here* for you. I will listen to you with all my heart and attention. Whatever you are feeling is okay with me. I offer to you my hands for this healing and my sensitivity for whatever comes up. You don't have to give back to me at all. It is my honor to give to you for all that you are in your world, and all that you are to me. *You* receiving this ritual from me is *my* gift. If you need anything, just ask. I love that you trust me enough to let me honor you in this way. I bless you. *You are* strength to me. That you are offering me your vulnerability is even more proof of that. You are my teacher in matters of love and partnership. Allow me to give to you for all the love you share with me." Whatever you say, make sure you include that he is free to express himself and that his needs will be taken care of.

There are some other things you want to say as you begin the ritual as you hold his Jewels. Speak about anything that you think he might worry about. Since you want him to be in his body, and any worry takes him away to work it out in his head, let him know that it's okay with you if his Lingam is hard or soft, that you know that it has a life of its own. (The reason this needs to be said is because if he is being aroused but his Lingam doesn't respond accordingly, or, if he is being massaged but not stimulated, but he still stands up all perky, he could feel like he is *not doing it right* in either case.) Just reassure him that he can relax about it. What could your beloved be concerned about? Find a way to reassure him about that.

Men, you can respond with a declaration of your own by acknowledging your own willingness to be an active part of the ritual by receiving this soulful healing. Let your beloved know that you are honored by her offering and are grateful for her attention. As you proclaim *your* gratefulness and willingness, *your* heart begins to soften and you become more mindful of this moment. A satisfying, soulful sexual healing is not only what she is able to give to you, but what you are consciously able to receive. Appreciate her efforts in advance and be grateful for her loving. Forgive her any clumsiness or nervousness in trying something new and notice her willingness to be a *conscious* sexual lover with you.

Ladies, if you keep your soft eyes open to him during the complete session, even when he closes his, then, whenever he opens his eyes, you are just right there for him. This is tremendous healing for the wounded "little boy" inside of him. Sometimes your beloved may want to close his eyes to focus on feeling something, but within a couple of minutes if he hasn't opened them, you could invite him to come back with his eyes.

Take a full breath deep into your belly and exhale with sound. Coach your beloved to do the same. Take more deep breaths and then go into your breathing pattern of connected breathing. Take some warm massage oil and begin to massage his belly, *very* slowly. Firm but not hard. Deep, but not so hard that he starts squirming. Channel the love in your heart through your hands into whatever part of his body you are touching. Massage with the whole of your hands and when you find bumps and knots, send your loving energy into those places to melt the blocked areas. Most everyone has some knots. Spend no more than about ten seconds on each knot and then move to other places.

Follow the massage of awakening his body and clearing the inner flute area using the instructions offered previously in the woman's healing section. The exception to his massage is that you can touch his Lingam from time to time as you tend to the rest of his body. You don't stick around there long enough to get him aroused, but simply graze over his Lingam and Jewels as you pass by in your "sweeping," communicating wordlessly— "I'll be back, relax, I'll be back soon." (A man will often perceive that when "it" gets touched, it's time to get up and get to work. This kind of automated behavior can lead to performance and anxiety problems on his side, and feelings of avoidance on hers. Over time, a woman learns she can't just fondle and play with him without "going all the way," so instead of taking the chance that he will feel teased, she just doesn't touch him unless she knows she wants more.)

Part of what needs healing in the man's body/mind memory is an urgency to have to "get up and then not go down before he wants to." With your steady, loving touch, he begins to heal that image so many men have— that sex will be taken away from him before he's done with it, that she will get a headache or suddenly just want to stop. So you are helping him to heal the unconscious worrying he is plagued with surrounding the whole sex-act itself.

Work your massage up his torso, from his belly, up to his chest and neck if you can reach that far, and then remember to regularly sweep off the gathered-up muck.

Allow the connected breathing and the massage to help you become more present than you have been for awhile, and to soften and relax both of you.

Another purpose of sexual healing for a man is to help him discover very powerfully that he is a lot more than his genitals when it comes to arousal and orgasm. Through his willingness to open up his *inner flute* channel, he increases the likelihood of whole-body orgasms, multi-orgasm and orgasm without the energetic loss of his ejaculate. When this channel is opened, the *urgency* to "come" is not as all-encompassing, and he is able to feel those orgasmic waves throughout his body from his toes to his crown. This may or may not happen the first time you try it so don't press for it, just be open to it. With practice, it's just a matter of time.

Your beloved may start to get fidgety somewhere between five to thirty minutes, and wonder if you are becoming bored; he may reach out to touch you and want to pleasure *you*— both for you and for himself. This rarely means he is not having a good time with what you are doing. On the contrary, it likely means that it is *too good* and he simply wants to reciprocate. Thank him for his concern or desire to please you, but assure him that you are very happy to just be giving to *him*, and then take your hand and physically press him back down onto his throne. Remind him how honored you are that he is allowing you the pleasure of serving him. Even though he would probably *love* to fondle your breasts, and may even say he needs to or wants to *just for him*, lovingly suggest that you will offer him your bosom a little later. Because it can be extremely arousing to you, and possibly distracting when you are preferring that your attention be directed toward him— but the other reason is to encourage *his* attention focusing on *his* own body and not on yours when the ritual is for him. A common habit for men is to lose contact with their own bodily experience when making love to a woman. This can limit his experience so that it becomes a mental-genital one *only* — leaving out the vital, juicy synergy of his own heart and emotional connection.

He may also begin to fidget if his bladder is full, so be aware of the need to take breaks to relieve that concern. And he may wonder if he deserves so much attention and love. Well, does your beloved deserve to be pampered like a king? Let him know— and often! He needs to hear from you verbally every five to ten minutes what you are getting out of this session as well, even if he doesn't seem to need the reassurance (especially during his first five to ten healing rituals). It may not even occur to him that *you are in heaven,* so let him know that also. Tell him how handsome he is, and how precious and how courageous he is to you.

After you have worked on his inner thighs with lots of oil, begin to massage into his entire groin area— slowly, deeply, but not so that he tightens up. Massage the whole pelvic bone area with massage oil down into the muscled perineum area (*between his testicles and his anus*).

Emotions can surface at any point along the way, and you want to encourage his freedom to express and your willingness to listen with big, non-judging ears. When his emotions well up, only you know as his friend if he needs verbal encouragement from you to let it flow or, if anything verbal from you would actually hinder his attempts to express. *Feel* it out if you don't know. The other thing you may want to offer if emotions surface is to hold his Jewels. Especially when he is overcome with his own feelings, by holding him, you offer a base of safety as he explores his emotional territory, moves the emotions and lets them go. Send your love into him with your hands and your thoughts. There may be times when the whole session will be holding his Jewels while he expresses feelings. This is natural and encouraged when he is emotional.

Men, become aware of how you are feeling. Stay connected to this experience through your eyes as you look into this beautiful goddess loving you. This is for you, not to please her (*although she is having a fabulous time*). You will miss the value for yourself if you are just going through the motions for her, waiting around for the "good stuff." Together you are gathering home more of who you are as sensual–spiritual beings. Allow it. Go for it. You really do deserve this much attention and care, but, if you must require another "practical, good reason" to submit yourself to such a long session just for you, then understand that you are becoming a better lover by subjecting your body to this level of relaxation and re-patterning.

After you have massaged up his inner flute and down his thighs, all the while sweeping off the muck, you can ask him if he would like to raise some energy. You will arouse him clear up to the point of no return, but not quite, while he breathes through all the intensity and sweeps the arousal to other parts of his body using his focus, and his hands to move the aroused energy around.

Begin to arouse his Lingam with your hands just the way you know he loves it. Your eyes are still lovingly gazing into him and you can use lubricant or oil on your hands. Stimulate him until you think he can't quite hold it anymore and then immediately stop stroking his Lingam, and sweep your hands up his torso to help him move the intensity from that one location. It can help to use sounds with your hands sweeping up his body that simulates *swooshing* sounds. You can help him recover some composure from his intense ride up the inner flute by taking his Jewels into your hands.

Hold him this way for ten to fifteen minutes or so. And while you are both relaxing, remember that it's okay to laugh and tell each other how you are feeling. You may be inclined to giggle; compliment; appreciate; bless; eat fruit; and worship. Laugh some more. Drink water. Be filled with gratefulness.

Then you can raise him

up to that high arousal place again; and again stop stimulating him before he goes over the edge. Together, sweep the intensity up his body while he breathes fully, spreading the energy to other body parts. Then, cup his Jewels and rest. Breathe fully! For this soulful ritual, you are going to raise him up a third time. But there is one possible exception.

This "exception" is not a requisite of every man's soulful healing— he will certainly benefit greatly from all that he has experienced so far, but it is indeed very helpful to him for many reasons. Both partners must be comfortable and not feel pressured to perform it. If there is any hesitation on either side, perhaps you can discuss openly the possibility at another, less, vulnerable time. However, do bring it up at some point.

During the third and final "raising up" to this ritual, and after he becomes erect, you can also massage him inside his base center (at his anus, and into his rectum). This is an area of many mixed reactions from embarrassment, to perceived as *immoral*, to thrilling anticipation. Realize you may be affected by the extremely uptight culture we live in, and so you or your partner may be sensitive to this subject. With great compassion and wonderment, ask your beloved if he would enjoy being entered at his base. If he declines, simply move into raising his arousal without stimulation to his inner sacred spot area and continue the final part of the ritual.

Continuing on *without* the sacred spot stimulation will be discussed first. Before you begin to raise him up for the final time, ask your beloved if he would like to retain his ejaculate or release it. Remember that this may seem like a ridiculous question to the man on the street who *lives* for his ejaculations, but this is a perfectly appropriate question put to a man who has been pampered and introduced to his energy system the way your man has been during this ritual to this point. So, in the resting period between phase two and three, while you are cupping his Jewels, go ahead and ask him what his preference is. He may choose one way one time, and another at the next session. You both could be pleasantly surprised (*maybe even shocked at*) how *absolutely* and *perfectly* satisfied he is without "coming." Rest with that understanding— don't let your mind nag either of you into making something else happen. Ladies, please remember that your role with your beloved is to love him, not get him off, so if he chooses to try the new way, please support him in that.

As you raise him up for the third time, juicing him, loving him, telling him how much you love him, how appreciative you are that he wants to be as conscious as possible loving with you, just keep your soft eyes available to him. Remind him to breathe if he forgets and move the energy around a bit. Pleasure him slowly, or intensely, or alternate to keep him guessing (that will keep him alert). And then after five, ten or twenty minutes of arousing him, help him sweep the energy up his torso, hold his Jewels and come in to closure.

If big emotions surface for him at any time, they should take precedence. Stop the arousing touch for a moment, cup his Jewels and listen. *This,* and sharing intimately, may be all you do now for the rest of the hour or two. However, no matter how nurturing this will be to him, he may still feel like he missed out on the *other* ("more important stuff"), and so assure him that the "other stuff" will happen next time, *promise.*

If, in all of the excitement, he happens to ejaculate early, or at any time before the end of the third raise up, celebrate *that.* That's fine. Again, he may be disappointed that he missed out on something, so assure him that you're looking forward to doing other rituals with him. Hold his Jewels and help him release the disappointment and become present to the love that he is sharing with you. If you have your warmed wash cloth near by, place it over his genitals with the cupping of your hands.

Sometimes a man will not become erect enough to actually do the three raise-up parts. That's okay too. Simply fondle him for his pleasure without trying for erection, but just for the sensual fun of it. It's important for the man to release any pressure that he must be "hard" for this ritual to work. All that is needed for this ritual to work, is that he let go and have a good time (erection or not!) Then, every fifteen or twenty minutes, simply move into holding his Jewels for a time. It will be the nurturing of this experience without the pressure that will heal him and clear the space for his potency to return. Judgment, urgency, and expectation for it to be any other way will simply prolong the unwanted situation. Men are asked to relax, and let go.

Now, back to the final raising *with* sacred spot arousal. When the sexual healing is for him, on the third rising, he gets to have the choice of ejaculating or retaining his ejaculate. He may choose one way one time, and another at the next session. You both could be pleasantly surprised (*maybe even shocked at*) how *absolutely* and *perfectly* satisfied he is without "coming." Rest with that understanding— don't let your mind nag either of you into making something else happen. If he would like to "come" in the common way, you could offer him a choice of continuing with your loving hands or perhaps you would enjoy, and therefore offer to him a Lingam/Yoni connect. Your question to him then is, would you like to come now in the raise up, or save it for me until later when we make love?

Your beloved may be someone who is well aware of the added pleasure he receives when his base is massaged. If so, or if your partner is encouraging you to explore, then begin by applying a lot of lubricant to the base area. (You might prefer to use a doctor's glove on the entering hand. This is not to avoid touching him personally so much as thinking ahead to later, when your finger emerges and you want to caress him in other places without jumping up to wash.) Massage *exxxtra slowww* so that you give him the best chance at relaxing in an area that might tend toward tensing with unfamiliar touch.

One of the many benefits of massaging inside his base, just like massaging his perineum— is that it's the home of *his* sacred spot— an area in great need of *un*armoring, as well as a trigger point for heightened arousal when awakened. Realize that there is an enormous gathering of nerve endings right at the base (in fact, I've heard physicians discuss how they knew to stimulate the area as a medical procedure during triage to bring back an unconscious soldier). This illustrates the point perfectly. You become *very* alert and present when this area is touched or stimulated.

After he has agreed to your entry, and you have begun to stimulate his Lingam to at least semi-erection (it may not be as enjoyable for him without being somewhat erect), and with plenty of lubricant, bring your (ring) finger to rest right at the base (*anus*) opening. Be still, and breathe. You may feel the muscles open and contract under your finger. When you feel him relax, and on *his* inhale (*his receiving breath*), you can begin to enter him. Come in very slowly and tenderly. After you have two-thirds of your finger inside, point your finger up and park. Relax, and together breathe fully and feel the energy that's raising and settling. The non-movement can be just as healing as movement, so there is no hurry to get beyond this point.

Another purpose for accessing the base chakra is for the caring massage and mindfulness that can be brought to a man's prostate health. The seriousness in our culture of our men's prostate health inspires us to bring as much love and illumination possible to an area so vulnerable to disease. Imagine the love that a woman can deliver through her touch into her beloved's prostate. Perhaps with touch like this, it will be just that much more difficult for disease to get a hold of (or grow) in an area that is conscious and so loved.

Continue to stimulate his Lingam just enough to keep him fifty to sixty percent erect. Send him love from your heart into your finger, into his internal space. You may then wish to stretch out your finger and reach straight back and up. The tip of your finger is now making close contact through the rectum wall to his prostate gland. You can massage very slowly. Fast movements can make him feel like he needs to go to the bathroom, so easy does it. Some men (even perfectly healthy hetero-sexual men) will arch themselves right into your hand and crave to be filled up. For them, add another finger, one at a time, and with them, you can probably offer more of a movement, even an in and out stroke would probably be arousing. Men who are familiar with this kind of stimulation and like it, report that the orgasms they experience with this are the most intense ones they have. Never stay in too long if your beloved is just too nervous and tense. Go ahead and come out and try again another time.

When it's time to take your finger out, let him know ahead of time. Then on *his* exhale (he's pushing something out), slowly, even *slower*, bring your finger out. Grab the rubber glove at the wrist, pull it off inside out and toss it to the ground. Reach down to cup his Jewels.

Soon enough, you may again be wondering where all the time has gone or that you have been in an altered state of *no-time*.

Men, if she is offering a choice to you, only choose to have a Lingam/Yoni connect based on if *you* would like it. You may sense that *she* would like it, but remember that this is *your* night, so choose your preference with out any pressure to perform whatsoever.

Before you change your position for Lingam/Yoni, come into closure for this ritual. Place one hand over his genitals and the other over his heart. Share what you've enjoyed about being his healer and what you have learned about him and about yourself in the process. Ask that these two centers— heart and sex— always be connected with an open flow of communication and separated no more. Together in harmony, an ultimate union. Tell him you would love to serve him again in this role very soon.

Men, this would also be a time to put into words how you are feeling. Share your gratefulness, and mention things you've learned about yourself and your beloved.

Ladies, you might say something like, "We have just spent our evening tending and deepening our relationship. We have focused our minds on love, and we have opened our hearts to our divine nature. We have healed another layer of human wounding with the compassion of our attention. We have practiced kindness with one another and we have practiced conscious loving. We are beloveds together in love and partners in liberation. Thank you. Thank us. Thank God." Place your hands in prayer position before your heart and slightly bow, saying, *Namaste.'* As you do this, say in your thoughts, "I honor the Divine presence in you and the Divine presence in me." The ritual for this evening is complete.

Drink a lot of water, cuddle up, and sleep. You have just participated in some very deep work. Congratulations. Be aware of your dreams. Each time you share in a ritual like this, the energies will move in various ways. One time there may be enormous emotional releases, others might be big mental or spiritual *"ah-ha's,"* while another ritual may be so gentle and tender that there's barely any movement. The primary purpose of a healing ritual is to share love with one another and to move *whatever* energy is present for you to move— spiritual, emotional, physical, or mental— and to simply surrender to the process.

## But will you still respect me in the morning

A man may be extra sensitive the following day. He may be moody. If he was weepy or shared any of his more vulnerable emotions, he may even feel embarrassment, regret, or even shame that he let so much show. He needs to verbally hear, and demonstrably experience from you, that he is still your hero— and even *more* so now; that you have been extremely touched by his *courage* to share his emotions so intimately, and that you continue to feel honored by his including you in his process. He may also need to hear from you an overview of what is happening to him so he can maintain perspective.

If the man was penetrated during his session, he may have additional insights. He may also begin to realize for the first time or, more fully realize what a *woman* actually experiences when she opens her legs and her body to a man to penetrate her. Many people (men and women) often mistakenly think that sex is the same for men and women, and even criticize women, thinking her weaker for not being able to enjoy superficial sex, or, even difficult, that she requests or *expects* that sex come with love. When in fact, sex is experienced completely different between the genders. A woman's body is not built for superficial sex; sex for *her* is bringing inside her body and psychic space someone *other* than herself and his energy is then *merged* into hers. He will often even leave behind a dollop of his DNA in the form of sperm to complete the energetic transmission. Women being the emotionally-based creatures they are, can empathically take on the man's energy who is inside of her because she can intuitively know his problems, read his thoughts, feel his pain, connect to his dreams. Of course a woman wants the energy that is merging into her very being to *love* her and to love with her! Wouldn't you?

Ladies remind him, and guys, understand, that the armored stuff that has kept him unhappy, or unworthy of higher paying jobs, or whatever it has been for *him*, is melting. That, what has separated him from his passion and dreams is being exfoliated and washed down the drain. He needs to understand that he doesn't have a *new* problem, say, *sadness all the time,* he simply just has the opportunity to finally feel sadness from an earlier time in his life when his reaction *then* was to deny the feeling. Feel the emotions, whatever they are, and breathe, let it go, and it's . . . gone. Not stuffed down somewhere or lurking around. These inconvenient feelings are no longer left behind as something to be ashamed of, be defensive about, or guard. They are simply gone! Give yourself this peace.

He might want to be alone or he may want you to hold him. Both are normal. Many shadowed places may have been uncovered during your ritual together, and it may take a few days or longer to integrate. You both are encouraged to be compassionate, understanding, and most of all, *non-judging.* The more vulnerable a man can be, and can illuminate for himself the shadowed places in his psyche, the more glorious he becomes.

As mentioned earlier, there may be outbursts from him that seem to come from nowhere and you both need to prepare yourselves consciously for how to move that energy. Resist the need to fix it or figure out how to stuff it back into place; instead, simply understand that the healing is still working on him. Ladies, just love him and be affectionate if he seems open to it, but understand that he may instead need to go out and move some energy, move some muscle, pound some nails, or hit some baseballs. That's terrific also. He may feel more tender again later, and letting you hold his Jewels will be very comforting to him. Trust your instincts. And don't take the "stuff" personal— either one of you. Be truthful to your Hearts and keep the lines of communication open; you're in a process.

Practice this soulful sexual loving exercise often for additional insurance on the well-being of your relationship. You can both declare your interest and intent toward this.

## PART THREE

## Spiritual awakening

For many people, a highly erotic sexual experience can lead to a spiritual awakening. The heart explodes open. The ordinary and mundane become profoundly meaningful. Two beings become as one. The complicated becomes unmistakably simple. The fragmented becomes united. The separated become whole again. The mystery is momentarily unveiled. Many people have experienced this kind of transcendence during sex and then long to repeat it. *But, how?*

Bring your undivided attention to your life in general, and to your love life specifically, and you will increase the opportunity to witness spiritual awakening for yourself through sexual arousal. *Attend* the lovemaking with your awareness. Bring all of your consciousness to bare. Meditate together *and* separately. Prepare for the loving in as many ways as you know; relax, breathe, and become authentically *yourself.* Simply *showing up* is a spiritual act. Spiritual awakening has to do with awakening your *be-ing*.

## Ecstatic loving

Has this ever happened to you? You are making love with your mortal husband or wife, when all of a sudden your partner begins to look translucent, *beyond* beautiful or handsome— more like a living god or goddess? Your bodies merge into one and you are *in heaven*. You may have used a different description at the time, but the memory is not questionable. You have met the Deity *archetype* in your beloved.

Does this help you to explain an experience that you have had, or does this sound preposterous? It could sound odd, particularly if you can not recall such an occasion. To bring this into perspective, think of a time when your partner was really, *really* upset. You may not want to admit it, but did your beloved look like a monster then, like her face was almost unrecognizable as your sweetheart? And when your partner is happy, doesn't she look *more beautiful?* How you feel on the inside sincerely affects how you will appear on the outside. And, how you feel on the inside affects how you perceive others.

When you are present to yourself as a Divine aspect of creation and you witness this Divine aspect in your beloved, you are transported beyond time and space into the enchanted world of *Shiva* and *Shakti*, the eternal archetypes of Divine Love and union. You needn't be alarmed. It means you have let go of the mundane *for a moment*, and you have stepped into grace. Enjoy.

Your role in this experience is to allow the Deity to visit you. You prepare for this ecstasy through the things you are learning and practicing in becoming beloveds. You relax, become present, breathe, drop your goal-oriented pressures and *feel* your feelings. In this process you are being cleansed of blockages in your system and made available to experience the most delightful, sensual, and connected loving.

When the mystery of *bliss* visits you, it is a gift to you both. It is not meant to be torture to you if you are not *blissfully* visited every time. Do not make a goal out of this. The secret is in gratefulness. Put your attention on *preparing* your heart for a "visitation." Move your energy often. Love your body. Bless your humanness. Honor your sacredness. *Allow the gift to come to you.*

## Increasing vitality

The core of sexual energy is vital and energizing. Depend on the merging of sexual loving to give you that special glow. It is the glow of being renewed. Your energy has moved, awakened, and you are made into a new, enlivened person.

Yet, for some people, just the *thought* of initiating an act of sex is exhausting; the act itself is seen as demoralizing and depleting. *Why?* How could an act, that in reality is energizing, be experienced as depleting?

For some, it could be the burden of high expectations and pressures to perform and satisfy. The pressure just wears you down. For others, it's the lack of a heart connection. If this has been your experience or that of your partner's, you are now learning how to transform the experience through the thoughts and practices you are discovering.

Let sexual energy "enliven" you. Let it vibrate in your bones. Allow it to renew you. If there is ever any resistance to letting this happen, don't apply pressure, apply the loving practices of relaxing, breathing and *be-ing*. This energy will supply you with more vitality to live your life in all ways. Be energized. Let sexual loving *juice* you. Become more alive!

## Conceiving consciously

Raising children is sacred work and it begins before conception. Conceiving consciously is preparing your heart and your mind to become a conscious parent, or become parents once again. It is an opportunity to enter into a relationship with the child even before the child stirs in the womb. You can do this as simply or as elaborately as you wish.

Very simply, while you prepare for lovemaking, you can light a special candle for the overflowing of love and commitment to be parents that you have between you. In this step, you are honoring yourselves and your willingness to raise a family.

Light another candle for this little being whom you are inviting into your family. You can talk to this child as if he or she is in the room with you, acknowledging the possibility of the child's spirit presence. Introduce yourselves. Talk about your home and the environment you are offering. Let the child know what your commitments will be, that you will provide safety, nutritious food, education, preparation for life, listening ears, reasonable boundaries, respect. Promise you'll always do the best you can as parents, and that *you'll* be learning too.

If you have other children, you may want to include them. The other children can speak about why they want a little brother or sister and what they enjoy about living in your family.

Ask that your request for a child be granted. Ask for good health, a welcoming womb, and a healthy baby. Ask that you'll always be guided as loving and good parents. If you listen, you may hear responses.

This kind of ritual can open your heart, and begin a healing process for you, also. Emotions may surface. You may begin to clear emotional wounds you received while growing up, inflicted by hurtful things you felt your parents did or said to you— the kinds of incidents that kids swear they will never do to their own kids.

This ritual can prepare your mind for what you will need to do to really parent. You can begin to stretch beyond your normal limits of comfort and routine as a couple, and begin to think about living life with children who have needs specific to their personalities and individual life missions.

While making love, honor the Lingam and Yoni as sacred vessels of conception. Prepare them through massage, sacred touch, and blessing. Let your eyes connect. Know and connect with whom you are making this baby. Celebrate conception with your breath, receiving love with each inhale, giving of your love with each exhale. Fill your bodies with your love. Fill the entire room with your love. Call this baby forward into the garden of your conscious relationship.

These rituals can be done regularly and with variations. The point is to presence yourselves into a *child-welcoming* state of mind. You can add other rituals. You can prepare the body for conception by detoxifying your body of junk food, drugs, and alcohol during the year before conception. You can *ceremoniously* do away with your contraception.

How glorious to raise a beloved child in the home of you two beloveds! Raising children is sacred work which begins before conception. Sacred lovemaking is an integral part in an immaculate conception.

## Major illness, surgery, aging, and sexual loving

We are so fortunate to have good health, but when major illness threatens our way of life or our partner's, too often, our reaction is to cease relations. Sometimes you are simply too ill to do anything and, at these times, your energy is best used to become well again.

However, there are too many people with conditions resulting from breast cancer and prostate problems (and many other conditions) who virtually just abstain from relations because of appearance sake or because "it" doesn't get hard any more. This reaction is just as unfortunate as the illness and its corrective consequences. As beloveds, please understand that you are more than your erections and more than your breast tissue. You are not your illness– whatever it is. There will be real feelings of loss to grapple with– emotional and physical. But share these feelings together. Bring your pain, loss and fears to the sacred space between you, and let the intimacy and wisdom of your *beloved-ness* release the emotional armor you may be tempted to erect.

You are still you. Your body may change dramatically, but you are still you. It may not be easy to accept the changes, but accept them together. One way to think about severe illness is that it is another test of whether you will separate yourself from love or embrace love. Will you be tempted to think yourself not lovable or beautiful? Will you be focused on the scar of your beloved as a repulsion, *or* as a medal of survival and will to live?

Recognize all the feelings of outrage that you may have, that something so devastating has happened to you, and continue to move them through you by any means you know of– talking about it, crying, working out, being held, praying for understanding and acceptance, cursing, or all of it. Don't be tricked into being ashamed of your feelings; they are *real* — move them. Everyone is still lovable even when ill, or incapacitated or scarred by surgery. Even you. Even your beloved. Keep this present.

C.S. Lewis is quoted as saying, "I never expected to have, in my sixties, the happiness that passed me by in my twenties." Seventy, eighty or ninety— whenever, or if ever, your testosterone level fades away, yes *that* part of your sex life may lapse, but, so lapses the distraction to make love without love. As you age, don't give up sex. Just give up the outdated ideals about how sex is supposed to be.

A Lingam can run electric energy whether it is hard or soft. Don't let a soft Lingam put a stop to your lovemaking. Simply arrange your bodies so that the Lingam can be placed inside the Yoni and then energetically and mentally, send the energy up to her heart. Use your breath to open yourself and sense the movement of the energy. Until you actually feel this movement, just imagine it in color. You can both have orgasms this way. Very sweet orgasms that you might want to call *Yin-gasms* because they are so sweet.

As beloveds, remember that there is more to lovemaking than intercourse. Use your hands to pleasure each other and use your mouths. Kiss. Hold hands. Look into each other's eyes. Breathe in harmony while you lie spooning. Bathe together. Exchange massages. Stay connected. No matter how sick someone is, there is a very real and appropriate way to stay connected and bring as much joy as possible into the situation.

## For romance

Romance is juicy. A long-term relationship can exist without it, but romance is color-ful and brings vibrancy into the mundane. The romance of *beloveds* reminds us to be present to special occasions, and to make rituals and special moments out of ordinary routine. Romance can be a Caribbean cruise or a thoughtful deed done. When you notice how much your beloved is affected by a memory or dream— find some way to bring it alive. Use your imagination. Romance is acting on and expressing your thoughts and feelings.

## Physical pleasure

Yes, of course you can (and do) use sexual energy for physical pleasure. But, as has been discussed all along, cultivate the experience of physical pleasure which is more than the pleasure of "tension release." Pleasure is felt as a completely different experi-ence when it is the relief of something which is almost painful (like the build up of sexual tension or emotions), than when the pleasure is an opening to something that you are tracking (following the flow of energy), and easily flowing effortlessly. True physical pleasure is a natural outcome when the pressure is off. Breathe and follow the flow.

## The sport of it

Go ahead and be wild and adventuresome. Explore your sexual energy as a source of recreation and entertainment. Have your sex be an athletic work-out sometimes; why not? Play your games, act out your fantasies, express your dominance and submission rites of passage for balance, engage the *inner teenager* in you who has all kinds of ideas and desires. If you go by what brings you authentic joy rather than what you think you "should" do to be a sexy lover, then you will have a healthier gauge to go by. It is defi-nitely okay to have fun in sex. Fun is soul food. So let your jesters come out and play and your joy will be food for your soul and for your relationship.

## Creative expression

When Michelangelo was asked how he was able to make his sculptures, he replied that all he did was chip away that which was not part of the statue. There is no need to be envious of people who seem to be more creative or have more fun than you, because *your* joy and *your* creation are still within you, waiting. All you have to do to access it is let go of that which is *not* your joy. We are all sexual artists and magicians. Let go and remember to leave your ego-mind, the judging mind, at the door. Nothing suppresses your creativity faster than criticism. So, Play. Perform. Mimic. Romp. Toy. Dally. Fantasize. Amuse. Frolic. Be sprightly. Create your relationship with more love. Create yourselves as willing artists of love.

## Erotic expression

What is erotic has much wider influence than our culture would have us believe. Model shaped images and macho brawn as the ultimate in sexual ecstasy are such insults to the erotic nature of who we really are. Realize that your erotic nature is in the sensitivity of your senses. Having an erotic look, for instance, is only one of the senses. Awaken your senses as well as delight your senses and experience the world beyond the ordinary-mind consciousness. Erotic is not something you *do*. Erotic is you *being who you are*. Be *e-r-o-t-i-c*.

## To relax

Bring your bodies together often just to relax. Lie down together in a quiet room or hang out in your bathtub in warm bubbles. Experience lovemaking sometimes as a relaxation meditation. You can come together in a peaceful, non-goal oriented way, and place his Lingam (erect or soft, with some sexual lubricant) inside her Yoni, and simply breathe together. Without going anywhere, *orgasmically speaking,* you just enjoy lying together, and maybe share some feelings about your day.

## To bless

Use your sexual energy to bless your body, your beloved's body, your relationship, your bedroom, home, careers, finances, children, and health. Simply acknowledge that you bless these aspects of your lives. The blessing is in your mannerisms and in your attention, and in your heart. Bless your sex energy and be blessed by it.

## Making-up

When you desire to have as much abundant love as possible, your shadow or dark side is bound to surface as well. Spats, arguments, disagreements, misunderstandings, ego problems, childish stand-offs, bizarre circumstances, and life's tragedies are par for the course. However, they need not leave you permanently wounded or separated.

Acknowledge each other by doling out big, exquisite praise for the one who has held the space for you both to enter into harmony once again. Take turns. Practice. *Develop this as a life and relationship skill.*

Sex is certainly capable of repairing a broken connection. Sexual energy is a very powerful force. But it can be used consciously as well as unconsciously. Used unconsciously, sex can hide a problem. This, however, does not help you when the conflicting "issue" surfaces next time. Instead of using sex to forget the problem, use it to let go of the problem, let go of the actual "hard feelings" that you have. Use the sexual energy to release the pain, the bitterness and mistrust, or hurtful words that play endlessly in your mind.

Use the pleasure in sexual loving to remind you that life is more than your suffering. Use the fire of the arousal to cleanse apathy and depression. Let the sweetness of sex remind you that you are loved, lovable, and loving. Give this feeling to one another. *Make-up*, imagine, that the separation between you is temporary, and that you will make a step towards reconnecting. *Make-up*, (imagine, rediscover, re-choose), that sex is sacred, and when engaged in soulfully, is a divine tool to presence you into a loving space with one another again.

## Making love for well-being

You know how after you make love, and you look ten years younger? Your face is softer. Your body is relaxed and you can float through the room. Your ego has stepped aside for at least a moment in time to include your beloved intimately into your personal space. Your heart and playfulness can emerge temporarily out of the barrage of daily living. Lovemaking is a gift from life to unburden you and bring you joy! Allow the gift. You deserve it.

## Making love for good health

Remember that energy wants to move and the sexual energy that moves through you in lovemaking is no different. Illness results from blocked or misguided energy. When you are freely allowing your sexual energy to move like waves through all your bones, muscles, skin cells, circulating blood, and energy centers, you lay out a pathway for good health to follow.

## Celebration

Celebrate what your bodies can do! If you have legs that move, celebrate getting up to dance to your favorite band. Celebrate what your arms are capable of doing when they reach out to hold your children and your beloved. Celebrate the mystery of how your genitals heroically expand to accommodate each other and let *this amazing miracle* of life be a model of flexibility and inspiration for you in your relationship. Celebrate the heartbeat of your beloved when you lie on his chest, and celebrate the lubricating juices of arousal, the perky nipples, and goose flesh. Celebrate your relationship— the good times, and the challenging ones, as well as the mundane. Celebrate silky skin and freckles, furry chests, and laugh lines around the eyes, legs that wrap around you, and soft bellies. There is something to celebrate at every minute of your day. *What is it in this moment?*

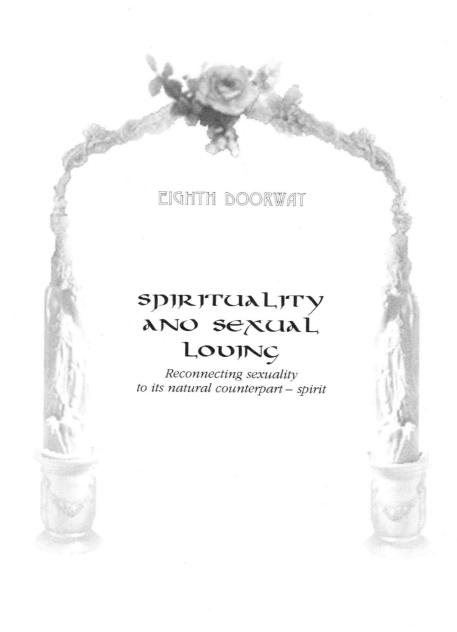

EIGHTH DOORWAY

# SPIRITUALITY
# AND SEXUAL
# LOVING

*Reconnecting sexuality
to its natural counterpart – spirit*

## Reconnecting sexuality to its natural counterpart— spirit

Sex and spirituality are not contradictory terms. In western culture there has been a tendency to deem above-the-waist activities "spiritual" and below-the-waist activities "sinful." Sex is not the culprit, however, only the scapegoat. It is the lack of sacredness and soulfulness in sexual relations that causes sex to *seem* sinful and divisive.

The *whole body* is a temple, not just parts of it. Your *whole being* is spiritual, not just parts of your being. When the body is denied and said to be sinful, *that* is the shame. Lovemaking is a gift to be shared and cherished. Through true lovemaking, beloveds can generate more depth in the relationship. But when sex is perpetually used instead to build separating walls between you, to degrade, punish or shame one another, or to *compete* for glory or for attention with one another— then it is time to reevaluate your spiritual values.

What if, instead of asking the question, "How do you make your lovemaking more spiritual?" you ask, "How have you blocked your sexuality with past baggage and limiting perceptions, thus separating an important part of you from the spiritual aspect of yourself?" With so much negative conditioning concerning sexuality as it relates to spiritual practice, the pathway to a union between these aspects may not seem so well lit. However, if we keep it very simple, and begin to recognize that there is a connection— a strong one, a *direct* link— the pathway unfolds gracefully before us.

## Living in spiritual grace

What does "spiritual" mean? What kind of behavior denotes spirituality? There is a wonderful parable in which one monk says to the other, "My spiritual master is so enlightened, he can materialize rare jewels and he can levitate his body." The other monk replied, "Ah, that is very clever indeed. But my master eats only when he is hungry, and lays down to sleep when he is tired."

A *spirited* or spiritual life is walking in harmony with one's basic needs, a *walking meditation of awareness.* Where is your attention right this moment? What are your bodily needs, right now? What are you feeling? What is nagging at you to do, that if you just did it, you could relax? What do you always put off until later? How many feats of brute strength and stamina will we expect our bodies to perform even if we don't tend to its own needs for rest, nourishment, and movement?

When you are in your last few moments of life, how do you want to remember how you lived? Did you put off quality time with your partner until the kids were grown or until the career got off the ground, or until you found yourself starting over again with spouse number two or three?

Did you "show up" in your life or did you play it safe, and follow all of the "rules?" Or did you hide your emotions, never being vulnerable to the truth of your heart. Did you think yourself wrong to cry or show feelings, so you "toughed" things out rather than be open or flexible, and then expected others around you to do the same?

Did you live in agony trying to be someone that you are not, or trying to live up to someone else's idea of who you should be? Were you authentic to you? Did you express your gifts and did you develop your talents? Did you just get good at channel surfing and never really get off the sofa and out to live your life?

Did you dull your consciousness through indifference and fear?

### Did You Love?

Did you say "*NO*" to the love in your heart and let it go to seed when the love of your life did not meet your mental picture of standards? Not wealthy enough . . . not slim enough. Had kids? Couldn't have kids? Wasn't attractive enough. He was the "wrong" race, age, or occupation. Did you partner up with someone you cerebrally saw as the "right" person but on a spiritual level regretted the choice?

Did you love, like, and appreciate *yourself?* Did you *receive* love and appreciation from those around you? Did you express your love and thoughtfulness to those nearest you: your beloved, your children, *their* spouses or partners, to everyone you met at work, in your community, and wherever you were?

Did you forgive and did you accept forgiveness? Did you play and relax and create? Did you *really* make love? Did you surrender to the mystery of sexual loving so completely that you were awakened out of a sleepy life and set free like a bird?

Did you allow the sweetness of loving to remind you that you are beautiful, and that you count? Did you allow lovemaking to heal your wounds of "not enough" and "not worthy"? Did you allow lovemaking to teach you about trust, and joy, and union with God?

*Walk your talk. Love yourself and love your people.* Be authentically *you* and who you came here to be. This is living life soulfully, spiritually, and fully. A rare, yet possible form of spiritual grace.

## Heaven on earth

Beloveds are in *heaven* when their love is abundantly expressed and free to grow deeper. Beloveds experience heaven each time they allow their appreciation and love for each other to flow through them. Beloveds are in heaven each time they embrace the challenge between them while residing inside the compassion of their hearts and minds. When beloveds' hearts and minds are open to living life fully, not denying certain "uncontrollable" feelings but instead allowing the full expression of feeling to emerge and pass, they are in *heaven*. Love's only goal is to experience itself, to return to love when love has been forsaken— to love for *Love's* sake.

When beloveds are afraid to love or to let love in, yet fear losing something, it's like they are in hell. Your partner can seem like an enemy. At the point where you begin to judge yourself or your beloved as *something* less than worthy— human or divine, you have just entered the *hell* zone. Your *perception* of union has changed. Your love perspective has flipped into fear. This fear is the opposite of love and compassion.

When you become other than loving (critical, jealous, suspicious, blaming, defending, sarcastic, etc.), and would like to return to love, try this: meditate on your feeling of love, or meditate on your feeling of fear. Go to a quiet place, sit without distractions and become aware of what you fear. Are you afraid you will be abandoned? Are you afraid you will not get what you want? What are the fears? At times like these you are feeling afraid of something, so it is a matter of realizing and accepting the fear, not bulldozing over it in a futile attempt to protect yourself.

Your fear is not your enemy or the thing that brings you heartache— protecting yourself from *feeling* fear is. Fear is only a signal. Perhaps there is a reaction to the new territory you are adventuring in, or a new cycle is occurring in your relationship, yourself, or your partner. Maybe there is an opening of an old, yet forgotten wound. The fear you feel will teach you about yourself if you listen. Meditate on fear when it visits you. Don't be so quick to disregard it or to avoid the discomfort of it. Acknowledging the fear in you is a very courageous stand to take. It may not be easy at times because your mind will habitually tell you to defend or attack or separate from it. But when you deflect, attack or separate from fear or any emotion, you're actually lashing out at your beloved by feeling separate from *him or her,* as well as from yourself. With each time you practice stepping away from the habit of separating from a loving perspective, love becomes the easier behavior to take. Though it can be difficult, the reward you will ultimately feel is liberating and indescribable. *This* is Heaven on Earth.

## Devotional surrender

Beloveds merge into one. Described another way, beloveds become an energy that is bigger than who they are separately. This merging is only possible when your heart is liberated— freely able to love deeply and naturally, free of your mind's habitual reaction to disconnect.

Surrender to the process itself of *Loving.* This means being mindful of compassion and expressions of *Love* that will naturally flow through you, and then surrendering the habit of protecting yourself because of fear. Surrender to *Loving,* rather than to the lover. Listen for the Divine essence. You must not surrender to the dominance of the other nor become a slave. To do that distracts lovers and takes them into non-partnership, or even distrust. Rather, listen for the devotional quality of the relationship's essence of heart space. Listen for tenderness and peace.

Listen for how Love expresses itself even during fear, anger and sorrow, not only because these are times when we need the blessing of Love the most, but because often we have been made so dearly vulnerable. These are times where our exterior facade has been cracked and we may come nearer to our inner true self. Experiences such as sorrow become like windows through which to view love because they tend to give us new eyes to see our inner nature, *if we will look.* We are brought into the moment through our vulnerability.

Devotional surrender to Loving is beyond traditional contracts and rules, and although you may still engage contracts and agreements, there is likely to be a different flavor of livability in them. You may get the sense that participating in a *soulful beloved* way of life will allow you to be and express all that you are as a *spiritual/sexual* human being.

## Listen to your heart

Your mind will try to understand how to achieve bliss and soulful intimacy and, clearly, understanding is valuable; but it is *in your heart* where becoming beloveds will actually make sense to you.

Listen to your heart. Every morning ask your heart to teach you about *Love*. Your heart has the answers to the questions that you have. Ask. Then Listen. Then obey. Honor your heart's wisdom.

## The dance of the Divine

"Space. The final frontier." There continues to be so much fascination with the unknown of "outer-space." And now there is more and more attraction to the "inner space" of one's own being. Meditation is the great doorway into that inner space.

Meditation is focus. Meditation is letting go into being. When sex is a meditation, it is your doorway to the Divine. The Divine Deity dances through you. *You become* the Love of God. You become the spirit of life itself. Your bodies are the bodies of the creator. Your passion is the bliss of existence.

Has your beloved ever looked like the most beautiful man or woman you've ever seen in your whole life? Remember in the early days of the relationship, when your lover could do no wrong and the love you felt between you was unbelievable, unstoppable, undeniable? Do you remember feeling it would last forever, that *this* love affair was *different?* This was the divine Deity expressing through you, teaching you that it is *Love* which is forever. *Love* which is unstoppable. That *Love* is unbelievable . . . to *the human mind.* The face of God *is* the most beautiful face. You were seeing the Divine Presence of *Love* in your lover's face.

Then "real life" sets in, right? The honeymoon is over. Little annoying habits become apparent, and differences in values and priorities are defined. So . . . yes, real life does set in, but the Divine is also ever present. Both are accurate. You'll find it valuable to discern the presence of "real life" and "Divine" in the evaluations of your experiences. When you become disillusioned by the "real life" person who is before you, the invitation from the Divine will always be to wake up to Love, not become disheartened because you think that a love affair has tricked you once again.

You have tricked yourself by assuming that the love you feel is dependent on the person with whom you are feeling it. The purpose of these Divine visits is not to reward you by introducing you to the person who will *finally* give you all the attention that you deserve, nor to punish you for your misdeeds. These Divine visits are to teach you about *Love* — the love that's in *you*.

Consider this: Just because the Divine Deity has expressed itself to you through a lover and you experienced extreme and ultimate *Love*, it does not mean that this person is your forever beloved. It simply means that extreme and ultimate love has been expressed to you in the presence of this lover, *in this experience*. *Love* is your beloved. The beloved you seek in another is actually *Love* itself. What will make you *feel* like beloveds with another person is actually your *desire* to express love with that person, and your *willingness* to not take the human conditions so personally. Some people are lucky enough to be with the person they love the most, or whom they get along with the best. This may or may not teach you about *Love* itself. But you could count yourselves very lucky indeed to be with the person with whom you enjoy remembering and learning about *Love* the most, challenges and all. You can choose a beloved based on how many mental standards of yours they meet, or, you can choose based on the opportunities you have with them to explore *Love* and compassion.

What we call "real life" is another way of talking about humanity. Being human means having very real, but somewhat messy ideas and experiences about what love, life and sex are all about. Since there is no master plan, everyone must discover what humanity is for her, but not without a lifetime of research and discovery. We must deal with our personal sense of purpose, value, satisfaction, and destiny. We must accommodate our needs for safety, shelter, warmth, and nutriment. We must deal with the ever-flowing, inevitable emotions we feel— from serenity to hate, from passion to indifference, and from embarrassment to greed— emotions which pass through us over a lifetime. This vast array includes the emotions we prefer to have— the ones that make us feel *good*, as well as embracing the undeniable emotions that seem distasteful, uncomfortable, inappropriate, uncontrollable, inconvenient, or too loud.

"Humanity" will always include *being* human. However, Divinity will also be present always. But . . . Will you notice the presence of the Divine? Will you look for it? Will you allow it to express itself through you? The Divine will express itself through you whenever there is an open space within you. You can cultivate an open space through your spiritual practice. You can stumble across it, such as when you first meet someone and you have a fresh attitude about him, no preconceived ideas of who he is or who he is supposed to be, and so consequently, he seems perfectly marvelous and wonderful to you . . . until when? Until you or he then stumble into some human condition and the human-ness is judged as less than your suitable expectations for relational bliss.

Be compassionate with all of the resources of your being, from the human being to the Divine. Expect to be challenged by human conditions, but not undone by them. Expect to learn, unfold, and grow from dealing with your own humanity. Expect to remember. Learn how to trust your heart. Remember how to listen to your feelings just as a child does. Become aware of how your mental focus discerns each of your resources— how they operate and can benefit you. Be available for the dance of the Deity. Be the dance. Give yourself to *Love*. Be *Love*. And dance through that doorway to the Divine!

## Sex as a spiritual doorway

Sex is also a doorway to our divine nature. You can't easily get around it. Every person is a sexual being whether or not we actually choose to engage sexually. Erections and menstruating are sexual actions. Everything we do from eating to sleeping is a sensual experience. Anything that touches the skin is sensual because the senses are engaged. Anything we smell from baking bread to fresh-cut grass is sensual. Whenever you open your eyes to look or your ears to hear, you are being a sensual creature.

Your body is a temple. Let everything you do in it become a celebration of devotion and awakening. When you smell the baking bread, celebrate the food and bless your nose for the blessing of smell. When your body vibrates with the excitement of orgasms, celebrate that ecstasy and bless your body for the gift of aliveness. When you arrive tired from a busy life-filled day and your spirits are lifted by the togetherness you share with your beloved as you merge your bodies into one, give thanks for the upliftment and bless your heart's ability to refresh you.

Sexual energy is abundant. It's what life is made of. Embracing your sexual energy is a doorway to those inner resources of life energy. When your sexual passion is consciously connected to your heart energy, the inner journey you will explore is as vast as outer space seems to be— only you won't need an expensive spaceship or space suit. You do not need to wait for the rules or the directions on how to proceed. Everything you need for this journey is already within you, including the permission and courage to ask for help when you need it. You will also need your willingness, your heart-fullness, your consciousness, and your connected breath. And you'll need a commitment to mooove your physical energy regularly.

Most of us were taught that sex was sinful under certain circumstances and not quite as bad under others. Either way, sex has rarely been celebrated as the physically vital, spiritually empowering energy that it truly is. Why? Has the world been put to sleep by suppressing the sexual energy of its people? Could it be that when the masses wake up to the potential that our sexual energy has to restore our health and our well-being, and to retrieve our soul's vibrancy, that the world will be a better place to live? *Hmmmmm!* Go ahead and open the door.

## Sex as a spiritual teacher

What kind of sensual/sexual being are you? What kind do you want to be? What kind are you trying to be? When you feel expectations placed on you, how are you tempted to respond? When your passion is rising, do you ride it in a flowing way, welcoming the "shakti" (pure energy), and appreciating the gift? Do you shut down your connected breathing and stop your orgasmic potential? Do you project blame onto your sexual partner for "not doing" you the right way?

What have you realized about yourself from how you love, or hate your body? How much permission have you allowed yourself to be fully orgasmic? Has your sexual passion been compartmentalized from the rest of your life?

What can your sex life teach you about *you?* How is your persona in your sex life just like your persona in the rest of your life?

Are there parts of you that you have *dis-owned* in your public life, that you can only allow in your bedroom activities? Are you a big, strong, authority figure in your job, for instance, who prefers seeking balance by becoming sexually passive and submissive with your mate? Are you as quiet as a church mouse in the world during the day and behind closed doors, you are as vocal as Tarzan?

By becoming aware of the different aspects of yourself and where you express them, you are able to glean a tremendous amount about yourself for your own self development and well-being.

## What does God have to do with sex?

What does God have to do with your sex life? Well, nothing, if you haven't invited or included God into your sexual practice. However, God's Presence can have a lot to do with it, depending on your very personal choice. Soulful lovemaking is not *dependent* on a spiritual connection with God, but some couples who want God's presence guiding their sexual connection, and don't feel it, wonder why they have been abandoned. This is a case of "Ask and you shall receive." Open the door to your hearts and make the invitation for God to influence your sexual loving.

Actively and regularly, invite God, or Divine Presence, into your relationship. Let that inspiration direct and nurture you during the inevitable difficult phases of life.

When your heart is heavy with doubt or confusion, or your head is spinning out of control with fear, upset and chaos, ask God to talk to you. You can listen to God's wisdom through that still, quiet voice in your heart. You usually can't hear the message if you are not quiet enough to listen. So, slow down, and sit still or walk in nature. Then, to best *understand* the wisdom coming to you, be clear with what your requests are for help. If you are asking why your husband is such an "insensitive clod," you will not likely get the kind of answer that will help you very much. Instead, ask that God teach you how to understand your partner's behavior in a way that serves you both. Or ask what there is for you to learn about yourself in regard to his behavior.

If you have not invited a higher power into your relationship, One more knowing than ordinary human understanding, you have unnecessarily limited the depth of connection that you can reach. And you have left out a very important source of spiritual support also. What most couples will experience if they leave out this spiritual connection is being uncomfortably stuck in mundane human separation. You may tend to squabble endlessly over turf, right and wrong, worst and best, my way, mine!

Having your relationship guided by your higher values, does not guarantee immunity against having squabbles; it's just that you have a structure set in place, other than your ego mind, which guides you to make decisions from a place of heart and spiritual purpose. You can admit your vulnerabilities and needs, and be made stronger by them. "We are lost." "We have different answers from one another, and we're learning what each other knows and contributes." "We are looking for our common ground."

In relationship, there are often so many childhood incompletions that we are working out, and sex is one of the playing fields where these incompletions come into play. Few of us come to the bedroom as a whole, emotionally healthy adult ready to engage with another whole, emotionally healthy adult. Instead, we look to our partner to be the mother who will be able to predict, and then fulfill, our every desire, or the mother who will love us no matter how wretched our behavior, and the daddy who will always protect us from ourselves.

Beloveds in a spiritual-connection request help to be compassionate with themselves and with their partner when a childhood incompletion is surfacing. Spiritual beloveds understand that when they become aware of each other's childhood traumas and projections, this is not grounds for divorce. Rather, it signals the beginning of the spiritual journey into wholeness together. Since these incompletions can be so tremendously powerful, vastly overwhelming to our ego minds, it can only serve us to be closely related to God to help us understand and help us heal.

## Nurturing the soulful couple

Allow your friends to help you care for your spiritual union with your beloved. Your friends are no help to you if you do not include them in your struggles. Your friends are no help to you if they take sides when you bring them a problem. You need compassionate listening when you are challenged in your relationship, not someone who says they always knew your partner was no good.

Asking for help may be the hardest thing you'll ever do, but please ask for it. Asking for help does not indicate that you are failing; it means you are bringing to bare the most consciousness possible so that you can heal and get through something. Your spiritual partnership will require wise input from your chosen circle of friends, your "relationship midwives." When the success of our relationship is based on our mutual desire for spiritual awakening, and our relationship becomes a tool in this awakening, our "relational midwives" become priceless to us. There is so much adversity challenging committed relationships that you must sometimes seek support just to balance the negative, simply to stay afloat. No couple is expected to do it alone.

It can be so tempting to go to a friend who will pity your situation and who tells you how right you are, and how wrong your partner is. But you never win with that kind of counsel. You become one more step removed from getting the spiritual re-connection that will bring your relationship back into harmony.

As much as you might like to discuss *anything* with your beloved, sometimes you just can't. This can be a time to have a compassionate friend *just listen*. A compassionate friend becomes a "relationship midwife" when they ask you questions that bring you back to your own open heart. These are focused questions that bring you back to your center, the part of you that can appreciate the struggle that you're in, and access your own wisdom. Your friends or relational professionals can help you remember love when love seems to have abandoned you. Some couples will notice that they don't have any friends able to assist in this way, and will have to find new friends committed to these principles. They are out there— look for them.

Please be this kind of "relational midwife" friend to your couple friends in return. Beloveds in spiritual partnership can be the strongest bond on earth, but without support from your community of friends, you could discover how fragile strength can be.

## Learning from the feminine wisdom

In matters of relationship, particularly sexual–emotional relationships, women are the teachers. A woman's body and psyche are doorways for each of you to pass through to attain complete wholeness. In order for a woman to "think" that she is clear enough to do this, she must *feel* safe. For a man to be clear enough to surrender to her wisdom and psychic barometer, he must also *feel* safe.

As a culture, we intuitively live by this concept in part already. The wisest of men will defer to the wisdom of their wives and both of them benefit from the power of this understanding. The man who follows this way is actually empowered by it. There is another, bigger group of men who also defer to their partners, but do so with an edge. They may do the task, but without surrendering in their heart which is where they can realize the *power* of learning from women.

The other way our culture condones sabotaging the benefits of learning from women is how we will defer to women in private, but on the surface, we say, act or *mean* something different. "She gets to do such and such, but I'm still the man (king, boss, master) of *my* house." Or, he may say "Yes dear, whatever you say dear," but, then do whatever he likes anyway. Women have often supported this by agreeing with it. Yet every time a woman allows a man to take credit for the wisdom that comes through her, she supports the notion that men *are* weak and have fragile little egos. She may even think it compassionate on her part to let him *think* that he is the boss. Also part of her fantasy is that a man has an ego fragile enough to break if she does not protect it. It could be her way of feeling superior. Spiritually what he needs more than coddling is his own open heart directly connected to a source that will liberate him from the pain he suffers from keeping his heart closed and his ego-mind intact. Connecting to her heart and psyche is his liberation. This also applies to surrendering to her sexually. For a couple to meet in union, they must both realize and embrace the feminine flow that unites them and moves them through the realm of Love.

In reality, it is the "feminine quality" who is our teacher in the realm of relationship, and so this wisdom will come through sensitive men as well. The request is to pay attention, listen and heed the direction of the wisdom, *whoever* is the messenger.

There is other wisdom and spiritual opportunity that will only come through women. Remember, men are spirit–based and that women are earth–based. Because of this earth connection, women know things. They feel it in their bodies. Because often they can not explain the reason of how they know, their wisdom has too often been discounted. The success of a relationship *requires* her "knowing"— much more than it needs to know "why" her knowing works. It simply does. Woman, Love— it's all a mystery.

*How* to learn from a woman is as important of a skill as knowing that it is a good idea. Because so much of a woman's wisdom is perceptive and bodily–felt, it can all be very subtle to actually understand— for both woman and man. This grand wisdom will arrive sometimes as brilliant, stop-the-presses, high wisdom, but often, *she* won't even know what it means until she has had a chance to bring it out into the open and *be* with it. This is why it is so valuable to have an environment established between you that is condusive for a woman to "just have her feelings" without assessment, fixing, or fear of incrimination. When her hunches, fears, aches, sleepiness, crankiness, rage, jealousy, and *all* emotions, reactions (including excuses), and ailments are accepted and deciphered as "CIA (Central Intelligence) information" rather than something negative, you then have established a spiritual environment for discovery.

Her psyche is like a walking barometer system. An inner, cryptic barometer. Learn to read her. Just like you would recall a dream and interpret the many levels of meaning, so can you access wisdom for your relationship and family when you interpret the female's "CIA information." As beloved partners, you honor her rhythm, cycles, feelings, and other "CIA information." When this "data" is out on the table, so to speak, the wise spirit of the masculine is profound at helping observe, interpret, and protect.

An example of allowing her "CIA information" to be accessible is often just an observation and sometimes a question. Let's say she is trying on outfit after outfit after outfit. He observes, "Looks like you're trying on different costumes to see which one will suit you today." A simple observation like this without judgment can be *so* empowering to the feminine that from out of the oddest, or most ordinary of moments, her wisest high-wisdom can come through. A man's part in a woman's ability to express her wisdom shared for the benefit of them both can not be underestimated. He holds the power to embrace her and make it safe for her to be expressive, and the more expressive she is, the more data you have to work with. With your acceptance, encouragement and participation, your beloved partner's insight becomes ever more heightened and clear.

A woman's nature can be so emotional and changeable that she may feel embarrassed or off track by just running the energy through herself, or by comparing the chaos running through her, to the coolness of the male nature. And for this reason also, it is extremely important that a man remind his partner of her special role as *their* spiritual relationship barometer.

Men, the part you play in offering your beloved an environment of emotional safety will return to you tenfold when your beloved becomes an "inspirational buddha" living right there in your house, as well as a goddess of love sleeping in your bed— the doorway to your spiritual enlightenment.

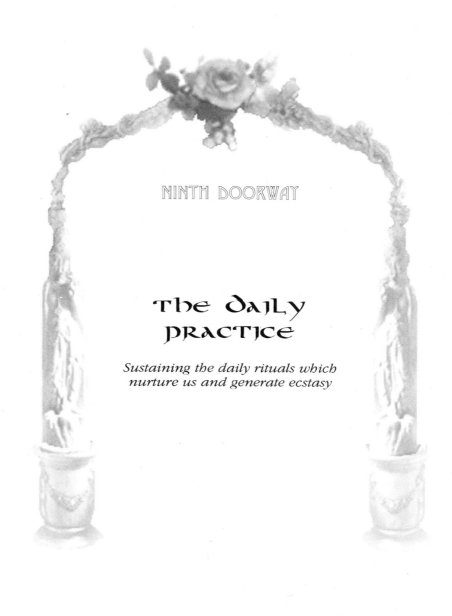

NINTH DOORWAY

# THE DAILY
# PRACTICE

*Sustaining the daily rituals which
nurture us and generate ecstasy*

## Sustaining the daily rituals which nurture us and generate ecstasy

A daily practice of becoming beloveds is sustaining you over a lifetime. Being beloveds will at times require effort, but more importantly, it takes your conscious attention. The reward for this kind of attention will always generate healing— usually emotional, ultimately spiritual, and sometimes even physical. You need to show up, and express the truth in your heart. This means to be present to what your truth is in each moment and in every detail, from bodily sensations to future dreams.

Your relationship is not something to line up for a rainy day. It is not something to establish, ride until it runs out of gas and then divorce. *Being apart* may be your truth; if so, it is worthy to acknowledge that truth and separate. This is very different, however, than simply **not** juicing a *good* and appropriate relationship. The success of your relationship needs you to be committed to *being* present, *being* relaxed, *being* communicative, *being* truthful, *being* flexible, *being* available, and holding the space for this essence of partnership to deepen you.

Being beloveds is opening to *Love* in an ongoing process. It includes comfort, safety, intrigue, stretching, forgiving, accepting, apologizing, connection, disconnection, disappointment, growth, laughter, truth, emotions, tenderness, unconditional love, compassion, greed, lust, frustration, unwillingness, willingness, sweetness, tears, confusion, learning, testing, awkwardness, awakening, trusting, and so much more. Bless each experience, they are your teachers. Being beloveds does not mean you will never have another "bad" day together or an inharmonious one. Being beloveds invites you to meet at the next level of connection and depth. Whatever comes up, beloveds deal with it together as a team and as loving partners. Even when one partner takes some solo steps of discovery, she or he will bring back the benefits into the relationship.

Practice healing together as well. You each have a past. Help each other heal the areas where the past has become limiting to your present life together. Allow the healing process to unfold inside of you. Respect the timing of healing experiences or how deeply you each can go, moment to moment. Listen for what you each need in the area. Sometimes you may need professional counsel. Go ahead and get it. You are worth it.

Consider some of the areas you have explored so far. Where in your love life can the various applications of the *doorways* and *secrets* benefit you? What's the next step for *you individually*, and as a beloved? What is the next step as beloveds together?

- Do you need experience, for instance, letting go of distractions so you can have your attention available for good lovemaking? Practice that.

- How's your communication? What do you need in order to open up communication with your beloved? Do you need to make more time to talk intimately? Do you need to listen to each other more closely and more compassionately?

Take any issue that feels challenging to you and check it through the first eight *doorways* of becoming *Beloveds in Bed*. Which of the secrets through that *doorway* can help you with your particular challenge? Remember to practice often, even the simple things.

## Investing in your health

Your body is most capable of achieving pleasure and bliss when it is treated well. To maximize your capacity for erotic, orgasmic, blissful sex, prepare your body by taking care of it. A positive attitude, physical exercise, a whole-foods diet, clean drinking water, fresh air, expanded breathing, and *being* loving are your best *sex-ercises*.

Keep all your muscles toned and flexible. Stretch them. Walk. Play. Breathe fully. Eat nutritiously. Notice how you feel after taking a walk together compared to watching television all evening. Being sedentary deadens your interest and ability to have good sex. So does being dehydrated. So drink some water and get up and *m-o-o-o-v-e-!*

If you want to have an alive, vital, multi-orgasmic body, then do your sex-cercises. Every body, at every age, is capable of becoming more fit and healthy. However, *it is a choice*. Give your body the attention and care it needs. As beloveds, inspire each other to care for your bodies without judgment or criticism.

## Food has sexual energy

Food has energy. You really are what you eat. It's true! Understand then how important your diet is in contributing to an ecstatic sex life. Eating heavy, fattening, dead foods will make your body feel dense, fat and dead. When you are dense, you are less likely to experience the other rooms in your palace. Eating foods that are alive and whole will help you "lighten up," relax and have the best sexual loving and intimacy possible. Do your own experiment and you be the judge.

After a week of fast food cheeseburgers and pizza, then try a week of fresh veggies, whole grain breads, cereals, and pasta, tree ripened fruit, foods that are alive with potency. Drink half your body weight in ounces of purified water per day (if you weigh 150 pounds, drink 75 ounces of water).

Specifically notice how your moods and your thoughts are. Notice your ability to change sexual positions, your intimate desires and hungers, your capacity for intimacy, and of course, your ability to orgasm energetically and whole-bodily.

Make eating well a priority. Don't criticize your beloved for having a second helping or a decadent dessert, but rather, encourage your beloved to honor his or her body's temple with conscious, alive food. Find the time to cook together or to cook for each other. Prepare meals that nurture you and delight your senses. If your schedule demands too much of your time, perhaps you can find a chef who will prepare meals for you. It's important that your food preparation be made consciously, lovingly, and gratefully.

## Yoga for lovers

If you want to be a better lover, or be able to receive love more easily or enter into the mystery of sexual love with deeper vulnerability, then the practice of yoga will be a worthy guide. Taking a one-hour yoga class once a week is enough to get you started, but take caution; it will wet your whistle for more because you will feel *s-o-o-o* wonderful. Ultimately, two or three classes a week will enhance your vitality so profoundly that sex as you know it today will be transformed into a more vital, conscious, energetic, physical, and possibly healing experience.

Yoga has been deceptively associated with contortioning positions. Yoga practiced by conscious lovers for flexibility and youthening is much, *much* more than contortioning.

Yoga helps you gently stretch your body so that you have a bigger spatial territory to live in. With yoga, you will gently dismantle armor stored in the body memory. Your mind becomes more flexible. Your breathing will become easier because your lungs are being exercised. Yoga even offers you a *fountain of youth*.

There are different styles of yoga, and each have unique benefits. Try different forms of yoga until you find the one(s) you like the best. *Hatha. Kundalini. Iyengar. Birkam. Partner Yoga. Kripalu. Ashtanga.*

If you have tried yoga and have not enjoyed it, consider that the conditions or the teacher were not quite right for you then. Try another class. There are some quality yoga videos to practice with at home, but as yoga beginners, attending classes regularly or occasionally will give a teacher the opportunity to correct your postures and breathing, but also to encourage your efforts. Look for teachers who make you feel good and comfortable to be in their class. You'll feel most comfortable with teachers who are inspiring to students at all levels of competency and flexibility.

Practicing *Kundalini Yoga* is particularly helpful because of its focus on the breath, which is so important to good lovemaking. *Partner Yoga,* practicing the postures in tandem, is nurturing. You will learn how to help stretch and support one another in harmonious ways.

You can practice Yoga together either as a purely spiritual practice or as an athletic one (Athletic? *Yes!* Have you ever seen a yoga teacher's firm, beautiful body? Truly inspiring!) Or, as an emotional and physical preparation to lovemaking. The most soulful sex happens when you are in your body, not your head. And practicing yoga helps you get into your body, connected to your spirit— one of yoga's wondrous gifts.


## Silence

Make time for silence so that it can permeate you. This is not "the silent treatment" which is a cold shoulder. We all need to be bathed in stillness on a regular basis. No talking. No radio. No television. No reading. Your well-being needs a rest from stimulus overload. You are alone with your being. You can be alone together, in this silence, or apart. Each will have its time and place. When you become silent, you are more available to your heart's wisdom.

If one or both of you tend to give each other the silent treatment, consider making your behavior more loving and conscious. Let your partner know that you need some quiet time. Allow one another the space to have this. Do not demand that your partner join you— you can ask, but don't insist. When you honor your own need for silence, you may be less inclined to overstep your personal boundaries, or pick a fight, and achieve your "space," through discord.

Try silence together in various ways. For instance, while maintaining soft-eye contact, enjoy lovemaking, or meals, or walks, in silence.

## Body image

What we think about our bodies and how we judge them can seriously affect our sexual lives and satisfaction. If you love your body, *care* for it, and *express* your love through it. When you love your partner's body, and you express your love for it *often*, your lovemaking experience *will* be divine.

The most common challenging areas of body image for the judgmental mind are fat, aging, scars, cellulite, balding, wrinkles, sagging, undefined muscles, and small breasts. When someone says, "I'm not attracted to you because you are bald" or "because you have small breasts," they are actually saying more about themselves and their personal perspectives than about the person whom they are judging. They are saying that their sexuality is in their head, in their thoughts. They are unaware of the complexities of energetic attraction and electrical body transmission. They have missed the *being* inside of the body, and the energy that vibrates within that body. Some of the most sensual and sexy people happen to be notably overweight, for instance.

Also, some of the most beautiful people by our cultural standards are completely disconnected from their sexual energy, only objectified statues of beauty rather than individuals with abundant vitality.

Chemistry consists of more than physical attraction and beauty. Chemistry can be cultivated by two lovers in their own bedroom laboratory with little more than their willingness to experience the multi-dimensionality of life, along with a heart committed to compassion and truthfulness.

## The diamond in the judgment

If you always seem to be BLOCKED from getting turned on, or are unable to be present because you are thinking your body isn't perfect enough, or that your partner's body isn't perfect enough, consider this: *How does this thought or judgment keep me from experiencing the love connection I long for?*

Here's a clue:

- "I would be turned on by you if you were . . . taller, darker, blonder, skinnier, younger, wealthier, better dressed, more muscular, less bulgy, etc., etc.," or,

- "I would totally let go and be more sexual, *be* myself, dance the 'dance of a thousand veils' for my beloved, *if only* I had a body like a super model" . . . etc.

Human beings often cover up their own fear with judgments, sarcasm and anger. There's no need to make it a problem; fear is simply a signal, that's all, a *cryptic* message. So get curious. The judgment you have of yourself or of another person is your golden opportunity to see how you actually separate yourself from living life joyously, and from experiencing love or intimate lovemaking. So when these kinds of judgments are surfacing, take a full breath into your belly and let go, begin to relax, keep breathing fully, and remind yourself that you deserve love in your life. You do! You may begin to notice underlying fear(s) as you relax. *These fears* are the issues to explore rather than focusing on your judgments of physical "flaws."

Begin to ask questions like a Sherlock Holmes. "I wonder what I'm afraid of ?" and then *b-r-r-e-e-a-t-h-e*. You can help a partner who is complaining, by asking them gently, "Honey, you've been very critical of me (or of yourself) tonight, are you afraid of something?" and then, breathe. And let it alone. There may not even be an answer right away. Let it flow.

*You* are not your judgments . . . unless you *believe* that your are.

*Breeeathe*, let go. Relax. Breathe fully, let go. Relax. *Breeeathe*. Let go. Relax.

## Sacred space on the road

Now that you have a beautiful and inviting *love nest* at home, hotel rooms will never be the same again. With a few accessories, though, stale rooms can be enchantingly transformed. Call it your travel bag or love nest survival kit. I think of it as creating sacred temple where ever I am.

Drape two large silk scarves over the lamp shades to soften the lighting. When packing your travel bags, you can make room for *love nest* items and tuck in some incense sticks and a smudge stick (an indigenous ritual cleansing tool you light like incense for clearing the space energetically); two candles and matches, massage oil (pack it well, it has a tendency to slip out during compression changes in airplane travel), your favorite lubricant, a set of miniature speakers, and a walkman or CD player with some favorite music.

When you arrive at the hotel, ask housekeeping for extra pillows, towels, and sheets (for massages, and for warmth outside the bed sheets). Your requests may intrigue the clerk or housekeeping staff: tip them, chuckle,  and say you're on your honeymoon, second honeymoon, twenty-fifth honeymoon . . .

Bring your *love* energy and presence into this space, along with your attention to details. The mood of the room will respond by saying that something conscious is happening. You may want to take turns creating sacred space or prepare together. You can also add things to your sacred space that you will find from the location you are visiting like wildflowers, artwork, shells, rocks, and leaves. Have plenty of drinking water available either from water bottles you've brought or pitchers ordered from room service. When you are dehydrated, your interest in sexual activity and your desire for intimacy declines rapidly.

How do you feel when you are in your hotel room and you begin to hear lovemaking sounds? Participants in my women's circles reveal that it makes them happy or inspired. So, if it's a reasonable hour (earlier than midnight), please feel free to express your lovemaking sounds even if you know the neighbors will hear you. Since vocalizing your sounds is so important, even if the hour is late or the neighbors are near, do so into the pillows.

Don't feel pressured to perform when hearing neighboring lovemaking sounds. Hopefully, even on the road, you can be successful making room for sexual loving without making it into a job or goal-oriented activity (review chapter two). Just be together, become centered and welcome whatever sacred, sensual or mystical energies want to dance with you. Let go of trying. Be relaxed and love will enter.

## Loving long distance

Sometimes you are away from your beloved and the question of how to stay connected and satisfied arises. The phone may be your best link. Phone sex is certainly not out of the question, but the old way of doing it; talking nasty or having only a mental arousal by fantasizing, may no longer serve your needs for soulfulness.

Close your eyes, imagine your partner's eyes or gaze at a picture of your partner, and breathe together on the phone just as you would if you were physically together. As you harmonize in this way, you can begin to feel as if you were actually holding each other. Don't be discouraged if it doesn't seem too realistic the first time, it may take some practice. It helps to be able to have rapport breathing, so make sure you can *hear* each other breathing across those long distance lines.

If the energy rises in you, you can begin to touch yourself, massaging all over your body, sensually waking up your passion while your partner does the same. Breathe fully and connectedly. Speak, if you like, about how and what you are doing. Imagine a circle of energy moving through each of you, uniting you. Make sounds, purr, feel. Allow your energy to vibrate.

Even while you are away from each other physically, be sure to stay current by sharing feelings. As you talk, you can bring your partner closer by including details about your day, and enrich the experience by expressing how you feel about what you did today or what you learned about yourself. Share your feelings, and listen from a feeling-oriented position.

## Television sex

Believe it or not, sex can happen without the television on in the background. I invite you to try it. Some people use the TV to drown out their lovemaking sounds so that their kids or neighbors don't hear them. Some use the glow of the TV instead of a lamp. Others just use the TV to drown real life out altogether. They eat in front of it, relax with it, talk on the phone and read the paper in front of it. It becomes company to a lot of people. Simply out of habit, many people make love in front of the TV.

Is sex more like a habitual itch to scratch or are you trying to have an experience of soulful loving? Turn off the distractions to your love life, say good night to Jay Leno. Tune into each other. Turn on the switch to your *inner* entertainment: your breath, your heart and the great mystery of *Love* itself. You'll find a greater menu of possibility than a satellite dish can offer, if you'll only learn to master your tuning dials.

## In the mood

"I'm not in the mood" is an often over-used, probably inaccurate excuse to avoid sex. More likely, when someone is not feeling in the mood, he or she is simply feeling *pressured* to do something. Another way for both of you to assess "not in the mood" is that it probably means I'm not in the mood *to perform*. Since the sex and the performance of it are so often linked, one will get rejected with the other. Are you in the mood for cuddling, breathing together, spooning, kissing, honoring orally, or massaging? Do that. Any of these activities could satisfy you or, in a very non-intrusive way, lead to more active lovemaking.

Sometimes, sex is moving along just fine, but then there is a phone call distraction, or a mental one, and "you're *just* not in the mood anymore." If this kind of reaction is often happening where the passion disappears totally— if you're unable to clear your mind or move back into lovemaking in a graceful way— then this may be an area where sexual healing could be helpful. Realize together— "We're going to heal that!" Healthy sex isn't so fragile that you have to walk on eggshells to keep it going. Together, decide to help each other learn, heal, and let go of the pattern that triggers sex-stopping moodiness.

## I want conscious loving but my partner does not

When your partner says he does not need or want conscious lovemaking, more than likely, he is communicating fear, a lack of understanding or concern about failure. Your best bet when wanting to entice a partner to join you is to make it attractive. How do you do that? You do it by figuring out what your partner seems to want and then pointing out how this material can get him more of *that*.

Naturally, you will not beg, or nag, or control your partner's choices. If you continue to get a negative response, respect where he is, at this time. Timing is everything. Invite him again at another time.

Meanwhile, practice conscious loving for yourself. Become very familiar with the *doorways* and *secrets*. Perhaps your partner will join you in becoming beloveds later. You can also create the sacred space, light the candles, run a bath for your beloved, uncork the champagne, set the music and ask him where he wants his sensual massage to begin . . . and end? "Beloved, allow me to gift you . . . "

Let your beloved experience for himself what you mean by conscious, soulful loving.

It can be difficult to comprehend a *concept*, no matter how noble, until you actually experience it personally. Have compassion for another's assimilation time, and have mercy for your own urgency.

## Birth control

When birth control devises are needed to prevent unwanted pregnancy, the process of preparing the condom, diaphram or cervical cap will be easier when both people are involved and participating. Clearly, birth control (BC) is not only the woman's responsibility. Putting the condom on is not just the man's responsibility, nor is applying the diaphram only the woman's. And, it's only an interruption to your lovemaking if you *think* of it that way. If you are making love in a flow, versus being goal-oriented about

sex, getting your *BC "act"* together simply becomes part of the loving, even when it has already become very hot and passionate.

Here's an example. You have started to make love in a room other than where you keep the diaphram/jelly/condoms, and things are getting hot. Instead of one of you running off for the stuff, and then one of you waiting around till it's applied, how about this?: You both go get it, ever so slowly crawling on floor, side by side, shoulder's touching, prowling like big panthers. Be slow and sensual, *accccentuuuating* your long strides and arching your backs, or striding powerfully, like hot, erotic cats, licking and biting each other all the way there. Once you arrive, make the application of the BC part of the loving session. Be creative. Be juicy. It *is* part of the lovemaking session, so just go with it.

Any day now, there could be *an event addition* to the Olympics for "Most Sensual Application Of A Diaphram Or Condom." Begin practicing now. Your love life will win the gold every time.

## Yoni health

Some women are constantly plagued by *yeast* infections and *urinary tract* infections, which can range from annoying to painful and sometimes excruciating. Sexual expression usually diminishes when there is a flare-up. In the case of yeast infections, it is recommended to discontinue intercourse until the yeast is under control because the male partner can also get the yeast infection. While it is usually without symptom to him, he can return the infection to the female partner when intercourse resumes. He should also be checked out by a physician to assure he's free of the yeast imbalance.

Yeast is normal in the Yoni, however, when excessive sugars are consumed, the yeast has a party, feasting on the cakes, ice cream, frozen yogurt, candies, and sodas, and then they multiply, take over and make the woman very unhappy with the *yeast infection*. Do infections breakout shortly after a binge on sweets or a big stress situation? Are you over-consuming sweets in your diet? Stress and other factors contribute to the condition also. Explore with your health care provider what could be causing your frequent episodes.

Are you drinking enough water each day? Drinking pure water flushes the bladder and urinary tract, so it can be a vitally important deterrent to infections. Water consumption is essential for full body optimal health and well-being.

Yeast and urinary tract infections may also be the body's way of armoring, and a signal to you that something is not being honored in the sexual arena. An infection may be the body's way of giving a woman a break to consider what is working and not working about her sexual expression and giving her a second chance to change something she's doing, or change some way she's being. An infection can be a timely distraction for a woman whose body is telling her to establish a clearer boundary, identify her needs and get them met.

Ask yourself:

- Do I feel *comfortable* with this sex partner?
- Do I love my partner, does he love me?
- Is the sex act itself satisfying and enjoyable for *me?*
- Do I feel pressured . . . to perform for *him,* to orgasm for *him,* to generate arousal faster than is natural for *me,* or any other kind of pressure?
- Am I concerned about pregnancy or sexually transmitted disease?
- Is there an old belief about guilt or "good girls don't" or some other history that I haven't re-evaluated recently?
- Is the sex act *loving* enough for me? Is it spiritual, intimate, or cuddly enough for me?
- Do I look forward to having sex, or is there some resistance or concern?
- Am I happy?

Consider what might be emotionally, mentally or psychologically depleting you. Please consider how very important it is for *each* partner to be happy, *including you.* Then give yourself the space and opportunity to be both happy and satisfied by examining your wants and needs. You deserve it.

As you create harmony and security for your body, and peace of mind for your standards and boundaries, you may find your body becomes naturally strong and happy again.

## Ordinary or extraordinary romance

Everyone can be more romantically successful if they watch out for the things that make romance only ordinary— or worse.
- Being goal-driven
- Being distracted
- Not making priority for couple time
- Trying to deny emotions

For extraordinary romance, be in the moment— don't push, and go with the flow; make time for one another and share your genuine feelings.

## Love slumps

Everyone knows what a *love slump* is. It's when the spark is absent. There's a colorless quality to your interactions. The timing is off. Things seems routine. Sexual interactions may even be nonexistent. You start to ask yourself questions and then analyze your answers in an attempt to figure out where the love has gone. You may wonder why you are with this person. Maybe your mother was right? What if you are not attracted to your partner anymore? How did you get in this situation? Maybe you made a mistake choosing this partner? Then you might begin fantasizing about having other partners. "If only she did it that way." "If I could only get him to come home earlier from work." "What if we had a new baby?" or "If only we could get the romance back again." Maybe a previous partner begins to look pretty good again or perhaps there's a new flirtation at the office?

In a love slump, things can spiral out of control pretty fast. If you let things get too out of hand, you'll have a drama to clean up instead of only a love slump. Asking questions is a good place to start. However, the key is in asking the *right* questions:

- How are you doing in your body? Are you relaxed?
- How are you emotionally? Are you fearful of something that you haven't admitted to yourself yet, or haven't yet shared with your partner?
- How are you doing mentally? Do you have so much on your mental plate that the thought of sharing intimacy with your beloved seems like a burden?
- How are you doing spiritually? Are you out of touch with the essence of quality in your life? Has it been a while since you have sat quietly and listened to the stillness of your soul or the counsel of your heart?

Too often, people take their love life for granted. We think no matter how little conscious attention we give it, the relationship should always be there for us. Your sex life may be there in a shell form during a love slump, but living a balanced life will give your sex and love life full color again. Ponder these questions and identify areas that need your attention, discussion, repair, or review:

- Are you present? Are you showing up?
- Where is your love? Is your heart so armored, you can't see any goodness?
- Have you let your beloved down in some way and now you are defending yourself by reasoning instead of apologizing to him and making amends?
- Where did your appreciation go? Do your judgments and assessments blind you from your appreciation?
- Are you exposed everyday to fresh air and sunshine?
- Are you drinking half your body weight in ounces of purified water each day?
- Is your jaw too tight? Are there knots in your belly?
- Are you running, jumping and playing in your body?
- Is your body moving, dancing, expressing? *Enough* for aerobic breathing?
- Have you been in nature this week yet? Mountains, rivers, meadows, water falls? Have you been where there are no electrical lines over head? Have your feet walked in some rural environment, or at least in the grass of a neighborhood park?
- Have you thanked your body for being such a great home for your spirit?
- Are you finding ways to appreciate parts of your body that you have usually rejected?
- Are you taking time to be in a leisurely bath for an extended soak?
- Are you loving your work? Are you appreciating your work? Is your work appreciating you?

- Have you taken the time recently to partake in the activities that make you feel creative, artistic, accomplished, fulfilled, soulful, centered, relaxed, connected, blissed out? In other words, have you been golfing, tennis-ing, fishing, reading, crafting, building, writing, theater-going, ballroom dancing. What is your thing? Have you been experiencing that?
- Are you balanced with your hobbies or do you spend all your time on the Internet and little with your family or partner?
- Have you established time apart from the kids that is just for the two of you?
- Are you rested? Have you been getting enough sleep?
- How's your diet? Have you been expecting junk food and sodas to be enough nutrition for you?
- Is your home being cared for? Is it a comforting place to be in? Are you there enough to let it comfort you? Does the environment of your home reflect to you the confusion, despair or disconnection you are feeling generally? Could your home use some attention to make it feel conscious again?
- Is there always a TV on somewhere distracting you?
- When was the last time you reminded yourself of why you are in relation ship with your partner? Recall three reasons why you love this person.
- Think of three reasons why your partner is in this relationship with you. Can you remember why he loves you?
- If you have been upset with one another, have you declared a truce long enough to lay down and hold each other?
- Have you taken the time to listen to the other? Are you able to be present to hear their point of view?
- Have you been sharing your feelings with your partner? Are you *present to* how you feel? Have you asked her to listen to you with her heart?
- Are you getting feedback that you're not available either emotionally or physically? What's that about?
- Have you forgotten the intent and commitment of your relationship?
- In lovemaking, are you always heading toward a goal of achievement rather than connection?
- Have any of your loving sessions been extended times together to melt into a blissful space? Or have your loving sessions been too many thirty-minute or less quickies?
- Does the male partner feel appreciated? Does the female partner feel like he's connecting to her?
- Are you current with what you appreciate about each other?
- Have you offered the other a soulful healing lately? *Or,* a massage?
- Are you singing? Humming? Laughing?
- Are you open, available, irresistible?
- Do you always come to a loving session tired from work or a busy situation without cleaning off your day? Are you *prepared* for soulful loving?

- Are you being honest with yourself? Honest with your partner?
- Are you communicating?
- Are you attending to that which you know keeps you balanced and feeling vibrant?
- What do you know to do to get yourself in present time, connected and available to experience more love?
- When was the last time you sat down to meditate?
- Have you taken the issue that is before you to your heart? Try a heart center meditation.

## Continuing education

Your best education will be your personal experience. Practice what you have learned from the previous *doorways* and all the *secrets*— notice what you feel in your heart. If you feel you are continuing to repeat bad habits, then of course it's time to reevaluate your practice, but not necessarily by trying some new "thing," but by embracing a new attitude. Being beloveds requires the combined commitment of both partners. Being beloveds requires creating an environment which allows your *beloved-ness* to flower.

There are classes to take, videos to watch, other books to read. You can practice many of the techniques of breath, movement, self-pleasuring, ejaculatory control and others— solo, as well. But, great techniques are not the most important skill in being a great lover. What you need most is an open heart. Practice opening to your love nature. Technical skills are indeed handy but they will naturally expand from your increased intimacy, communication, relaxation, and emotional safety that you are sharing together. The previously wasted energy used to "*do*" sex becomes the energy to "*be*" sexual, sensual, talented, alive and turned on.

Reread *Beloveds in Bed* again in six months (and then again, every so often). After a period of integration, notice what has opened for you and changed in your experience. Recognize what you missed the first time through. Read from the book aloud to each other. Allow the concept of feminine spaciousness to deepen in you. Allow the spaciousness of being beloveds to mature inside of you.

## An enchanted evening

Plan a special evening just for the two of you. Especially do this if you seldom have done it *or* if you have kids *or* if you have busy careers and conflicting schedules. Set aside work details. Turn off the phones. Turn off all distractions. As we discovered in chapter six, it's "juicy" to make a date. Then keep it!

Wouldn't you like to have one evening a week (at least!) that was set aside for an extended loving session? Well, do what you can to make this a priority. It begins with you. This is an opportunity to set aside the mundane. It is a time to worship the god or goddess nature in your beloved. It is the time to invite in the Divine Love–Presence to open your heart and shower pleasure over your entire body, to welcome healing energy to release you of a painful, or a wounded past. It is an opportunity to awaken the magnificent erotic energies that can transport you into a thousand levels of *blissfulness*.

Offer to your beloved the gift of your presence this evening, by some symbolic gesture. Begin your session looking into one another's eyes. Place your hands in prayer position in front of your heart, bow slightly, and say "*Namaste*" (a variation of its meaning is . . . "The Divine Essence of Love in me greets the Divine Love Presence in you").

Take turns being the evening orchestrater. When it's your turn, you be the giver. Plan the setting or theme for that evening. You could have a meal ready. Wine? Sparkling juice? The CDs playing on automatic. The candles lit. The hot tub warmed up, or the bath tub full of bubbles. The massage table set up with cozy sheets and warmed oil ready. Is there a poem or a passage from a book that you would like to read together tonight to set the tone?

Plan to be together for three to four hours, 7:30 to 11:30 at night, for example. There is no standard to meet and no orgasmic goal. This time is set aside *to be together*. You can plan ahead of time to have certain experiences, such as a sexual healing for him, or a one-hour breast massage for her, but, do not expect a certain mood or outcome. The only goal (if there is one) is to experience your glorious self *be-ing*, and to share this "be-ing" with your beloved.

During your evening, practice one or more things from each of the secrets. Dance, sound, pray, touch, be sensual, play, let go, sing, massage, heal, relax, hold each other, give a sexual healing, receive a sexual ritual, feed each other, laugh, share feelings, raise sexual energy, celebrate, stretch, kiss, honor, exchange gifts, meditate, communicate, listen, star gaze, howl at the moon, cradle the Yoni, hold the Jewels, lick, suckle, caress, cuddle, express, make music, tickle, bathe, breathe in unison or breathe alternately, *c-o-o-o-o, c-o-o-o-o . . .*

A little of this and a little of that and *whoosh* . . . the time flies. If you can't imagine spending more than a half hour making love, just experience each sensual part *for its own sake and pleasure*. Connecting Lingam and Yoni can lead to a kiss, for instance. A passionate kiss can lead to laying down together to embrace and look deeply into the other's eyes.

Complete your enchanted evening ritual by facing one another, placing your hands in prayer position and saying— "*Namaste'*." You have just spent a whole evening practicing conscious loving and relating. The love you feel in your heart, the peace you feel in your body, and the upliftment of your spirit are gifts. They belong to you now. You may recall them at any time, simply from your very next focused breath. Bless you for your willingness to be aware lovers. Embrace your beloved lover with your arms and heart and drift into slumber. *Sweet dreams.*

## Extra – marital – affair

This is an extra marital marriage . . . as in, *more* than an average-marriage. Be a part of an extra special one. Inspire yourselves to have an extra-ordinary relationship with each other. Plan on love growing with each experience together and sex getting better year by year rather than becoming boring. Put your heart into it. Put your soul into it. Put time aside on your schedule and then guard this time together with your life. Your love life depends upon this.

Average lovers may try to get each other to aspire to each other's "pictures" of the perfect mate, but you, as *extra marital* partners can inspire one another to *be your unique selves.* You will each be so much happier when you are free to be genuinely yourselves, and enjoying good sexual living is more likely in happy, relaxed, *real* people. Have an extra-marital-affair with your beloved. *And flaunt it!*

Your home will have more harmony in it. Our world together becomes more harmonious and less combative with each couple living as beloveds, in *all* ways.

*"There is only one place of pilgrimage for you to go — your own heart."*

Yogi Amrit Desai

Namaste

## SUGGESTED READING
## For the soulful journey of being beloveds

### Relationship

The Shared Heart: Relationship Initiations and Celebrations
Barry Vissell, MD and Joyce Vissell, RN., MS
Ramira, Aptos, California

Heart & Soul: Living the Joy, Truth & Beauty of Your Intimate Relationship
Daphne Rose Kingma
MJF Books, New York

Light in the Mirror: A New Way To Understand Relationship
Barry Vissell, MD and Joyce Vissell, RN., MS
Ramira, Aptos, California

Dancing in the Dark: The Shadow Side of Relationships
Douglas and Naomi Mosley
North Star Publications

Embracing The Beloved: Relationship as a Path of Awakening
Stephen and Ondrea Levine
Doubleday

Conscious Loving: The Journey to Co-Commitment
Gay Hendricks & Kathlyn Hendricks
Bantam Books

Lovers for Life: Creating Lasting Passion, Trust and True Partnership
Daniel Ellenberg, Ph.D. and Judith Bell, M.S., M.F.C.C.
Aslan Publishing

### Spiritual / inspiration

Lying with the Heavenly Woman
Robert Johnson
Harper

A Woman's Worth
(especially recommended on cassette)
Marianne Williamson
Random House

The Anatomy of Spirit
(especially recommended on cassette)
Caroline Myss, Ph.D.
Harmony Books

Tantric Transformation: Discourses on the Royal Song of Saraha
Osho
Osho Int'l, NY

Love: A Scientific and Living Philosophy of Love and Sex
Lao Russell
The University of Science and Philosophy, Swannanoa, Waynesboro, Virginia

The Kin of Ata Are Waiting for You
Dorothy Bryant
Moon Books/Random House

A Circle of Stones
Judith Durek
LuraMedia™

I Sit Listening to the wind
Judith Durek
LuraMedia™

The Four-Fold Way: Walking the Paths of the Warrior,
Teacher, Healer and Visionary
Angeles Arrien, Ph.D.
HarperSanFrancisco

The Man Who Tapped the Secrets of the Universe
Glenn Clark
The University of Science and Philosophy, Swannanoa, Waynesboro, Virginia

## Sexuality and Intimacy

Tantra, Spirituality & Sex
Osho
Osho Int'l, NY

The Yoni: Sacred Symbol of Female Creative Power
Rufus C. Camphausen
Inner Traditions International, Rochester Vermont

Divine Sex: The Tantric and Taoist Arts of Conscious Loving
Caroline Aldred
Harper Collins

Sacred Orgasms: Teachings from the Heart
Kenneth Ray Stubbs
Secret Garden

Ecstasy Through Tantra
John Mumford
Llewellyn Publications, St. Paul, Minnesota

Tantra: The Art of Conscious Loving
Charles and Caroline Muir
Mercury House

Soulful Sex: Opening Your Heart, Body & Spirit To Lifelong Passion
Dr. Victoria Lee
Conari Press

The Art of Sexual Ecstasy
Margo Anand
Tarcher/Putnam

The Art of Sexual Magic
Margo Anand
Tarcher/Putnam

The Perfumed Garden: The First Illustrated Edition
Translated by Sir Richard Burto
Park Street Press, Rochester, Vermont

The Encyclopedia of Erotic Wisdom
Rufus C. Camphausen
Inner Traditions International, Ltd., Rochester Vermont

Women of the Light: The New Sacred Prostitute
Edited by Kenneth Ray Stubbs, Ph. D.
Secret Garden

The Sacred Prostitute: Eternal Aspect of the Feminine
Nancy Qualls- Corbett
Inner City Books, Toronto Canada

## INSPIRATION ON CASSETTE

To Love and Be Loved
Stephen and Ondrea Levine
Sounds True, Boulder Colorado

How to Love to a Woman
Clarissa Pinkola Este´s
Sounds True, Boulder Colorado

Power and Love in Relationships
Angeles Arrien
Sounds True Recordings, Boulder Colorado

Hot Monogamy
Dr. Patricia Love
Sounds True Recordings, Boulder Colorado

## STUDY GROUPS AND BOOK CLUBS
## On the *Beloveds in Bed* concepts

I encourage study groups and book clubs to meet to discuss and explore the principles and philosophy developed in *Beloveds in Bed*. If you would like to sponsor a study group, please do. Group conversations on conscious loving are always appreciated, and it helps to bring conscious loving more into reality.

### Suggestions
Group sessions would be appropriate for:
- couples
- singles
- women
- men
- pre-married couples
- church groups

As a study or book club facilitator, inform the meeting participants that you will be sharing your personal opinions and that they do not represent the author or the publisher. As the group facilitator, you are present to provide an environment for exploration and exchange of ideas, but not instruction.